Upstaging Big Daddy

Upstaging Big Daddy

Directing Theater
as if Gender and Race Matter

Ellen Donkin and Susan Clement, Editors

Ann Arbor

THE UNIVERSITY OF MICHIGAN PRESS

Copyright © by the University of Michigan 1993
All rights reserved
Published in the United States of America by
The University of Michigan Press
Manufactured in the United States of America

1996 1995 1994 1993   4 3 2 1

Library of Congress Cataloging-in-Publication Data

Upstaging Big Daddy : directing theater as if gender and race matter /
  Ellen Donkin and Susan Clement, editors.
    p.   cm.
  Includes bibliographical references.
  ISBN 0-472-09503-X (alk. paper). — ISBN 0-472-06503-3 (pbk. :
  alk. paper)
    1. Feminist theater—United States. 2. Feminism and theater—
  United States. 3. Theater—United States—Production and
  direction. 4. Afro-American theater—United States. 5. Women in
  the theater—United States. I. Donkin, Ellen, 1949– .
  II. Clement, Susan.
  PN2270.F45U68 1993
  792'.0233'082—dc20   92-38338
                                                            CIP

A CIP catalogue record for this book is available from the British Library.

Acknowledgments

We wish to thank the following people for their inspiration, commitment, leadership, and generosity in the development of this project: Helen Krich Chinoy, Sue-Ellen Case, Bob Loper, Gordon Wickstrom, Janelle Reinelt, Len Berkman, Vicki Patraka, Wayne Kramer, Shelia Bland, Jill Lewis, Bill Sharp, Jill Dolan, Elin Diamond, Lee Ahlborn, Lynne Hanley, Sharon Mayberry and Jack Speyer, Mercedes Lawry, Dorothy Marie, and LeAnn Fields. We would also like to acknowledge the following institutions: for generous financial, intellectual, and moral support, Hampshire College, particularly Feminist Studies and Nina Payne's Faculty Writing Seminar; the Hewlett-Mellon Fund; and the Women & Theatre Program of the Association for Theatre in Higher Education. We also wish to thank the editors of *Theater Three,* published by Carnegie Mellon University, for their kind permission to reprint "Directing Stein." Lyrics from "Paper Doll" by Johnny Black are used by permission of Edward B. Marks Music Company. We would both like to pay tribute to electronic mail (through the Internet) and Faxing, without which this bicoastal editing project would not have been possible. Ellen particularly thanks Larry Winship, who was an anchor throughout this process, and her two most loyal and candid critics, Molly and Grace Winship.

Contents

Editors' Introduction

Any consideration of feminist directing must begin with a reassessment of classical drama. The canon as it now stands was not written *for* women, and clearly it was not written *by* them. The roles written for men outnumber the roles written for women about seven to one, depending on the anthology; the plays written by men outnumber those written by women about ten to one. For the most part, the roles that do exist for women have been imagined, developed, and created by men. It is not that the classics don't have (a few) major roles for (white) women. But for a feminist, directing and performing in these plays is often an out-of-body experience, like being in a room in which people are talking *about* her but not to her or with her. Even when the plays ostensibly answer questions about women's lives, the questions have been posed by men and are being answered by men. The woman, even when she speaks, features as a topic of someone else's conversation rather than as an authorizing presence in her own.

In other words, not only are women underrepresented on stage, but the female characters that do exist are more closely linked to the projections and fantasies of their male creators than to the complex, diverse, and ambiguous lives of real women in history. So two kinds of damage are perpetuated: underrepresentation and distortion. And for women of color, for lesbians, and for lesbians of color, the issue is virtual erasure. If a young person "learned the world" from reading and seeing the existing canon, her knowledge of the actual, ordinary lives of lesbians or women of color would be extraordinarily limited.

This book, however, is not about making "politically correct" theater or about paying anxious lip service to categories of race or sexual preference. These categories, although they are useful for discourse, are themselves oppressive and limiting in the way they generalize and classify. This book is about making good theater, about clearing space in the dense forest of classics so that the truths of women's lives can unfold and grow.

Because theater doesn't stop with the printed page, because plays are only a blueprint for production, the director moves into a position of enormous responsibility. How the final production "reads" to an audience is her artistic and political responsibility. It is not possible to overemphasize the importance of her position. In the process of directing a play, she can completely upend the text, encourage her actors to develop subtexts the playwright never dreamed of, enlist her designers in the creation of a destabilizing visual counterpoint, or cast performers whose very presence throws the text into question. But before she begins rehearsing, she has to negotiate her way either through or around the inherited monolith of dramatic literature. Her choice of play cannot be a reflexive one. If she chooses a classic (or is advised to choose a classic), she needs to know in advance that many classical texts carry with them an implicit if not a stated social order in which all women, but particularly women of color and lesbians, either occupy the margins of existence or else are idealized, demonized, or eroticized. Their palpable existence is muted, distorted, and thin. They are never allowed to be ordinary, in the center of their daily lives. They appear instead, if they appear at all, as representatives of issues or types, with only a narrow history and virtually no power base. The feminist director is strategically placed to resist or comply with that world picture. She is the linchpin. *Both positions, the one of compliance and the one of resistance, are highly politicized, although only the activity of resistance will get named as such.*

Directing still routinely presents itself to the world as a craft to which no particular social responsibilities accrue. No one with any degree of gender and racial consciousness can venture into directing these days without an uneasy sense of leading a double life. There is contemporary social awareness on the one hand, and on the other hand a body of dramatic literature that is now in the process of being framed and critiqued by that social awareness. What can she do? Is it possible to continue working in some different way?

This book offers ways of thinking about directing in theater as intimately connected to a growing and shifting social awareness. Its premise is that if directing choices are welded to consciousness, the resulting shows have the potential for intervening forcibly in the dreary cycle by which distorted representations lie unchallenged and, after a while, become substitutes for deeper truths. In that cycle, a short circuit develops: Not only do real human beings begin to replace what they know about their lives with what they see being represented, but they also begin to lose sight altogether of how they feel and what they know. Theater audiences and, most alarming, theater artists abandon their own truths in favor of some larger Truth, because their little truths have nowhere to settle in what the critical theorists refer to as a master narrative.

In an effort to understand how women are persuaded to abandon their truths, we, the editors, identified repeated incidences all through our work in directing, teaching, acting, and playwriting that pointed toward a powerful desire to please, to be pleasing. Please whom? we wondered. Our work in feminist theory and in theater history had instructed us about dominant ideology, about the way the gaze is male and how it controls, about the woman as object rather than as speaking subject. But in the context of theatrical production the vague dread we associated with wanting to please did not quite square with the existing models. There was a need for a term or an image that was portable and evocative, something a director could call up instantly in the middle of a busy rehearsal that would allow her to stop and rethink how she was doing something. It had to capture the way this need to please preempts every other activity and leaves women feeling like they have abandoned themselves at the very moment when they have the illusion of familiarity and safety. We instinctively felt that the need to please was connected to a presence that was complex and contradictory: at once protective, generous, jovial, and profoundly disabling. This was not Big Brother. This was Big Daddy.

Big Daddy was the image we had been looking for. Like the Big Daddy of Tennessee Williams's *Cat on a Hot Tin Roof,* he carries with him a combination of paternal protection with ambient (hetero- or homo-) sexuality. He is attractive, warm; he effortlessly commands attention no matter where he goes, automatically positioning everyone around him as adjunct. His judgments are so powerful that they will resonate in everyone's head long after he is offstage. His presence is synonymous with control and power in ways that are profoundly linked to the social structures of marginalization and erasure.

But theater is an intensely social activity, one that Big Daddy could not control if he were anything less than congenial. His laughter is contagious and disarming. He knows how to enjoy himself. Working to please him is a simultaneous act of seduction and of being seduced. *He is particularly disabling to women,* whether they are directors, actresses, or designers, because in reaching for his approval, they bypass their own experience of being female; what they know about being women stays unconscious. His pleasure authorizes the validity of their work, and substitutes for their ability to authorize their own. Directing, acting, or designing for Big Daddy means showing him what he wants to see instead of exposing the awkward contradictions and ambiguities of being female in a sexist, racist society. The show as a whole, in spite of general critical approval, will be lacking in some predictable and tiresome way; there will be the lingering sense of a commodity, of something prepackaged.

Big Daddy is a complicated character. He is to be found in individual men in the theater, but he is not synonymous with all men nor does he always appear in a pure form. He needs to be understood as a form of cultural conditioning that floats in and among real men and women and has profound implications for their artistic work and their relationships with each other. If it were simply a question of the way individual men have positioned and disempowered female directors, actors, designers, or playwrights, it would be relatively easy to identify the villain. But it isn't simple. Not only is there no obvious villain, but there is not always an external villain. The cultural formations that have created that disempowerment in the first place also have become internalized by women, and that disempowerment perpetuates itself even when the overt exclusion of women wanting professional access and identity is no longer an issue.

When Big Daddy does emerge in real men, he takes on a multitude of roles. He is the pyrotechnic, prima donna director, whose power is absolute, whose approval is the breath of life. He is that producer whose very presence, and the way he looks at women on a stage, turns feminist theater into a girlie show. After the production has opened, Big Daddy may reemerge as the Critic, the Arbiter of Quality, someone whose investment in maintaining a controlling position makes him deeply hostile to productions that venture into areas he knows nothing about. Big Daddy also can be found in actors, in playwrights, and, of course, among dramatic characters.

Finally, Big Daddy is a collective term for describing how the feminist director imagines her audiences, and what she imagines will please them. But he is not just the fat man in the front row, taking up a lot of room. He is also the fat man in her head. The cluster of expectations revolving around Big Daddy may in fact exist in real audiences (of course they do), but the audiences will not change until the director understands that those expectations also inhabit her brain, where they present themselves as immutable truths. She is in a delicate position: she cannot afford to be naive, but neither can she afford the kind of contemptuous dismissal that generalizes about all men and conflates the pockets of difference in her audience into a single convenient stereotype. If she does generalize, the very contempt and exclusion that she is fighting as a feminist are now being activated in the other direction. It is in her head that the battle with Big Daddy has to be fought and won, or else she and her audiences have no chance of evolving. No one else can upstage Big Daddy as effectively as the feminist director, but she has to know where to find him first.

This book came into being as the result of our collaboration on an essay about the direction of two plays by Gertrude Stein. It is difficult to overstate how important Stein's presence has been for the evolution of this collection. Our experience with directing her plays was a touchstone for us as we worked on this book. She brought us back continually to an intimacy and privacy and playfulness that had been for us the beginning of a new way of thinking about feminism, about rehearsing, about production, and about writing plays. Stein's outrageous liberties with language, syntax, and dramatic structure helped us to imagine what it might be like to free ourselves from other kinds of structures and expectations in directing and in writing about directing. We could finally replace defensive strategies with a full-hearted vision of what feminist directing might be. But Stein was only one of two godmothers.

The second godmother has been Glenda Dickerson, whose intellectual and artistic courage and generosity have given us permission to think past the limits of our own cultural identification as white women and to begin investigating the way Big Daddy crosses into communities of color. She is indirectly responsible for the title of this book: the reference to Big Daddy ("you can't wear your scarlet dress in Big Daddy's house") in her essay "Wearing Red" has been central to the shaping of these essays. Glenda has been central also to our growing understanding that women of color must be released from the necessity for explaining themselves and their work to the outside. She recently wrote in a letter to us: "We women of color *must take as our sole and essential audience our sisters.* We need to talk our lives to each other, to bare our souls to each other, because we are confronting a hegemonic system of thought (not black men or white men or white women, but a system of thought) *which has never seen us.* We are in the process of birth; it is a birth of ourselves. I am sounding a battle call to my sisters. I cannot turn over my shoulder to say 'Do you hear me?'"

Upstaging Big Daddy loosely follows the progression of a show from preproduction, through the choice of script or the development of a new script, through the rehearsal period, and finally to postshow and recovery. Most of the contributors have focused their essays on a single specific production, rather than on more general directing topics such as casting or rehearsal techniques. It is important for the reader to know that in any one essay, problems and solutions may crop up on a wide variety of topics, and that the section headings are by no means as tidy as they may appear. Issues relating to script development, rehearsal techniques, and using feminist theory come up over and over again, in all sections. This is a book to graze in; you may find what you need in an unexpected place.

The first essay, "Women, Woman, and the Subject of Feminism," offers a model for something crucially important and consistently ignored in director training: the way directing is a political as well as an artistic activity. If a director doesn't think through where she stands politically, she is likely to wind up serving the interests of a dominant ideology, whether she intends to or not. This essay makes a strong case for waiting before choosing a script, and first thinking through the implications of theatrical production itself, and whom it has historically served or ignored. Very often a detailed, circumspect look at the history of women in the theater will have a much more powerful and persuasive effect on a company than a personal statement of commitment to feminism from the director. This essay provides much of the theoretical and historical groundwork for educating a cast and production team to the need for feminist theater, but it also suggests the crucial importance of the dramaturg, the person responsible for research on a production.

After the director's initial pause to rethink and reposition herself *as* director, the scramble for a script begins. The obvious solution, if she has the latitude, is to choose a play by a playwright who is also operating consciously around issues of race and gender. In part 1, "Interpreting the Text," critical theory and especially feminist theory come into direct use as tools for script analysis, as means for visualizing the production onstage, and also as ways to rethink the role of the director.

Not everyone, however, has the latitude to direct a script in which gender and racial issues are foregrounded and interrogated. The requirements of an academic curriculum or of a regional repertory season often compel directors to choose plays from the existing canon, that body of literature which we have argued is so deeply and subtly oppressive to "difference." The contributors to part 2, "Subverting the Text," all believe that it is possible to take on a canonical text and subvert its intended meanings and social constructions.

But the feminist director may decide to bypass the canon entirely, especially if the prospect of bulldozing into one of these plays is too exhausting to contemplate. Or she may worry that the text will triumph after all, and her efforts to subvert meaning will play only to the initiated. A third alternative is to construct a piece of her own. The contributors to part 3, "Constructing the Text," have decided that the work of the feminist director includes creating a theater piece as well as directing it. This decision appears to have been made not simply because these directors wanted to avoid the canon, but because there was a collective power and spirit moving through their companies *for which no text yet existed.*

In part 4, "Rehearsing the Text," the book moves into the practicalities and possibilities of rethinking auditions, casting, production meetings, and rehearsals. Here it becomes apparent that unless the rethinking and repositioning of the director extends from theory and choice of script *into rehearsal practice,* old procedures run the risk of producing old results, and even in a feminist script, certain untested assumptions about gender and race are likely to linger into production. The final essay, entitled "Aftermath: Surviving the Reviews," warns that even after a show is up and running, there may be another battle ahead. When Big Daddy reemerges as the Critic, the feminist director is forced to defend not only her artistic work, but also her very identity as an artist. Her ability to regroup for the next venture hinges on careful recovery. There are very real costs to this kind of work: public censure, isolation, exhaustion, and profound self-doubt are serious occupational hazards. But there are also powerful rewards.

Feminist directors do their best work when, to use Andrea Hairston's term, they allow "life-affirming truths" to be told. There is no mystery to feminist directing, but neither are there any recipes. Feminist directing happens when the director stops glancing back over her shoulder, wondering if she is doing things right, and begins to believe in the authority of her own experience. It happens when she lets go of the voices in her head that judge her work before she has even figured out what the work is. As Split Britches puts it, you have to *tell the dog to sit*. Feminist directing is working best when the director is lost in the pleasure of rehearsal, of witnessing women make the transition *from looking at her looking at them* to simply moving into the interior and listening to what their bodies and minds tell them. In this quiet way, the privacy and pleasure of the rehearsal process gradually begin to translate into the feminist politics of the final production.

Directing theater as if gender and race matter is not different from good directing, but it begins with a certain awareness. A director has to believe that theater can change the way people think and how they see. She has to know that her position as director is a political one as well as an artistic one. And she has to be forewarned and forearmed against the jovial, generous, and disabling presence of Big Daddy, in her audience, in her script, in her cast and crew, but, most alarming, in her own head.

We are grateful to the contributors to this book. In every case, their work has given us a sense of community and affirmation that is impossible to maintain in solitary confinement. We invite you to join their vision and their pleasure and their work, not as a template, but as a touchstone. It is now your vision, your pleasure, and your work.

Ellen Donkin and Susan Clement

★   ★   ★

This book, like a good theatrical production, needed a dramaturg, someone to contextualize the work of these directors both theoretically and historically and to give a common ground for discussion. We felt that without this groundwork the working assumptions of many of the essays that follow would be unclear. What do we mean by a female subject? How is the perspective of the materialist feminist different from those of cultural or radical feminists? What about mainstream theater is counterproductive to the interests of feminists? In the essay that follows, Esther Beth Sullivan clarifies some key issues in contemporary feminist theory and offers a perspective on the history of feminists working in theater.

But why history and theory? For the director, the immediate physical pressures to find a show, find a space for the show, cast it, assemble a production team, and get it into rehearsal make this long, slow, preliminary moment of reflection a particularly precious and important one. If the director is to resist participating in the way theater produces fictional representations of women, she has to know some things first. She has to know what the damage really is when certain kinds of human experience get routinely distorted or excluded. She has to understand how those distortions and exclusions of women not only parallel similar operations around racial groups but also create an entirely new level of exclusion for women of color. Most of all, she has to understand that, if consciousness is a product of material conditioning, she almost certainly will be working with women, either in the cast or on the production team, who want nothing to do with feminism or who are operating on the assumption that feminist issues all "got resolved" somewhere in the 1980s. She may encounter powerful, even angry denial that problems for women continue. There may be efforts to compartmentalize, to separate "women's" issues from issues of race or class or sexual preference. But it may develop that theater itself, the moment of making dramatic action around "someone else's problems," will make possible certain revelations, providing the company an education through the body and heart. For some people, theory and history will have been a jangling in the ears during rehearsals, an irritating waste of time. But at the end of the rehearsal period they will perhaps, like this chapter, be something to come back to. Sometimes you have to take a journey before you can look back at where you've come from.

ESTHER BETH SULLIVAN

Women, Woman, and the Subject of Feminism: Feminist Directions

In a book devoted to the pragmatics and problematics of feminist directing this essay may seem amiss. It gives no practical directives to dramatists who are or would be "feminist" in persuasion. Neither does it detail the working process of acclaimed women directors. While leaving the discussion of "directing" to the authors of subsequent articles, here the topic is that of "direction." I would like to say "and, specifically, that of feminist direction," but the field of feminism in the age of feminism*s*, and even postfeminism, lacks the kind of discreteness that once marked the earlier "women's movement." Nevertheless, I will say that this introduction addresses the kinds of directions that feminism has taken over the past twenty years in the United States and the way in which those directions have influenced and been influenced by feminists in theater.

Of course, I like the word *direction* here because it offers an etymological link to the topic at hand, directing. While both words sometimes refer to "aiming at a certain point" or, in another sense, to "instructions," it is the word root *regere,* meaning "to guide," that draws me to this specific word at this particular time. If there is anything that feminists have found to be certain over the past twenty years, it is that the ground upon which we argue continually shifts, causing us to shift our attention and perspective. In regard to direction ours is a politics that self-consciously and constantly questions our own "aims" and "instructions." On the other hand, feminism has "guided" those of us who seek to understand the complex ways in which oppression functions and, in the case of theater studies, specifically the ways in which cultural institutions such as theater enable the forces of oppression.

Issues of direction have always been a source of heated debate among feminists, who have argued about the roots of oppression as well as effective strategies for getting at those roots. In this ongoing dialogue "theory" has been used as both a subject and strategy. Whether offered as a guide or posited as a final solution, theory—as it has come to connote poststructural impulses such as deconstruction and psychosemiotics—has made its way into a large number of scholarly articles and theatrical productions. The results have been hailed by many as a revolution of consciousness, while others have argued such theory often functions more like a brick wall than a guide through a minefield. Without declaring absolute allegiance to either of these positions, what I would suggest here is that the notion of *feminist* theory did not spring to life with poststructuralist discourse. Rather, feminists have been theorizing subjectivity by means of their work, struggle, and/or "practice" for years, and poststructural theory—with its attention to how we know what we know—has augmented the already ongoing feminist project of understanding the effects of sociopolitical and epistemological structures. Moreover, I would suggest that when the notions of theory and practice are posed as a dichotomy—as two exclusive terms that define each other by their opposite spheres of influence, their opposite acts of engagement, and their opposite effects—the interests of feminism are poorly served.

In the field of feminist studies the dichotomous definitions of theory and practice have been and are being dissolved, especially in regard to theater. While the concerns of feminist dramatists over the past twenty years have been diverse and divergent, their projects, plays, and performances attest to the influence of feminism as both theory *and* practice and evidence the way in which this influence has resisted the usual boundaries that would separate theory from practice and vice versa. Of particular interest are the many endeavors that strive to put various aspects of feminist theory into theatrical practice or that attempt to produce a theater of feminist practice that can be "read" as theory or that refuse to distinguish between practical and theoretical "action." The following discussion focuses on a number of such endeavors in order to identify directions that I believe are specific to feminists working in the realm of contemporary theater. Divided into three main sections, this introduction surveys the increasingly sophisticated feminist critique of gender oppression and places aspects of that critique in relation to dramatic works that could be interpreted as coproducers of feminist theory. While the point of this examination is to show how feminist theory has "directed" theater practice, it also seeks to show how the stage—with its potential to literally visualize bodies and the effects of gender ideology—has in turn offered a unique context within which feminist directors have theorized and foregrounded oppression.

Women's Experience of Patriarchy

In the late 1960s, after nearly forty years of relative silence, the women's movement gained momentum in the United States and abroad. As this movement began to identify its political agenda, the concept of "a women's movement" fractured into various feminisms—liberal, radical, cultural, materialist. In spite of the differing theories of female oppression that marked the philosophical bases of these factions, one phrase did come to signify feminism and its direction: "the personal is the political." Responding to the traditional exclusivity of private and public spheres, feminists juxtaposed these terms in order to address the political nature of personal experience. With this consciousness feminists set out to politically undermine the "naturalness" of concepts such as the nuclear family, female domesticity, and heterosexuality.

"The personal is the political" infused the sociopolitical milieu of the 1970s, influencing the practice of many feminists working in theater. Dramatists such as Roberta Sklar, Gillian Hanna, and Carol Grosberg found themselves questioning the lack of feminist concern in avant-garde and leftist theater companies such as the Open Theatre, 7.84, and Bread and Puppet Theatre (Leavitt 1980, 6; Hanna 1978, 11). While these organizations provided models of how theater might influence and speak to "political" purposes, they evidenced a striking indifference to the "personal" issues surrounding patriarchal oppression. Consequently, feminists often found themselves at odds with these groups when it came to earning recognition for their contributions and producing plays that would deal with women's experiences. During her tenure as the co-artistic director of the Open Theatre, Roberta Sklar began noting the contradiction of the company's disavowal of sexism at the same time that women's work within the company was undervalued. She writes: "The Open Theatre was becoming very public, but my participation in it was deliberately and continuously ignored. The company seemed outraged at first . . . at the sexism of the outside world, but internal struggles soon made it clear that there was a lot of it inside as well" (Brunner 1980, 33). Likewise, in 1978 Gillian Hanna noted the frustration she had experienced working with companies such as 7.84 and Belts and Braces in England: "Something that I think most men find very difficult to understand is that most women experience life as quite alien in many ways. It is to do with the fact that the male experience is taken to be *the experience* [my italics]. I think most men are unaware of how alienated women feel" (4). These women examined their participation in male-dominated companies and found that, even in the most progressive organizations, feminist issues were given little or no priority. Motivated by this indifference, dramatists such as Sklar and Hanna worked collectively with other women to form companies and sponsor theatrical projects that might address feminist issues in dramatic contexts.

The migration of female dramatists from avant-garde companies to ones expressly devoted to feminism coincided with a grass roots phenomenon that witnessed the formulation of many women's theater groups across the United States. According to Patti Gillespie, who documented this phenomenon for *Theatre News,* by the mid-1970s thirty feminist companies had been formed (1977, 5)—an amazing number in light of the fact that the first such group was identified only in 1969 (Brown 1979, 87). These organizations often utilized and incorporated the principles of women's consciousness-raising (CR) groups. As described by Sue-Ellen Case: "The first task of CR groups was to provide women with a voice. After centuries of silence, CR groups provided a situation in which women could begin to articulate what it felt like to be a woman. The all-woman composition of the groups provided safety from the scrutiny and criticism of men and gave women an opportunity to enter into dialogue with other women" (1988a, 65).

The creation of dramatic contexts to further this kind of dialogue, and to "publicize" the voice of women, led to the formulation of "community theaters" made "by, about, and for women" (Coss, Segal, and Sklar 1983b, 236). Growing out of the CR spirit of affirmation, these groups explored the notions of "feminist acting" and "feminist forms" and maintained the need to produce their works (at least sometimes, if not always) for women-only audiences. The affirmative impulse that characterized these organizations is exemplified in Martha Roth's article "Notes toward a Feminist Performance Aesthetic," which appeared in the first edition of *Women & Performance*. She states: "I want to see new images. I want women in performance to take off the masks of male imagination. I want to see women who are serious people, for whom other women are serious people" (1983, 12). Roth's comments reflect the intent of many feminist theater groups in the 1970s. Their purpose was to recognize the oppressive conditions of patriarchy, to envision theater as a place in which women might examine and voice their experiences of being women, and to recuperate and affirm the value of that experience.

Central to this affirmative intent was the notion that such organizations might tell women's untold and unheard stories. As expressed by the founders of Women's Experimental Theater (WET), their intent was to "mine our history," to "give testimony," and "not to forget, but to remember" (Segal and Sklar 1987, 306–7). In an effort not to forget, the CR technique of narrating "one's own story" was incorporated into both dramatic workshops and productions. Such autobiographical testimony focused on women's experiences while remedying the lack of attention paid to those experiences. To tell one's story and to have that story received in an atmosphere of support and commonality was theorized as a means by which a woman might "experience herself as a woman at the center of her own life" and capable of transforming the conditions of her existence (Coss, Segal, and Sklar 1983b, 236). In this case "telling our stories" was placed in direct relation to effecting "social change" (Sklar 1987, 327). Segal and Sklar write, "We addressed the subversive impulse in women's minds, an impulse to change, to seek expansion of being and a place in the world" (1987, 306).

At the same time that WET sought to change sociopolitical conditions it also attempted to change the conditions of dramatic representation. The desire to tell stories that originated in the experiences of women led these dramatists to question not only the content but also the form of drama. "Herstories" were championed, and the conventions of "realistic" narratives were discarded. Jill Dolan states: "These women carried away some of the basic tenets of experimental theatre—the revised relation between spectator and performer and the shift away from traditional plots into nonlinear, expressionistic narratives—and brought them into feminist theatre" (1988, 85). Dolan notes that these and other "experimental" techniques were employed to subvert "realism's relentless plotting toward the white, middle-class, male privilege the history of dramatic texts maintained" (1988, 85). The realization that realism might be inscribed with patriarchal values motivated a search for other forms—forms that might speak specifically to women and their experience of oppression in patriarchal contexts. Reflecting back on this search, Sklar states: "Our minds are so socialized in a patriarchal world that our own stream of consciousness speaks for HIM half the time. This work was all about noticing the moment when a woman's mind is speaking for herself and exploring it" (Brunner 1980, 38).

One of the most notable productions to have come out of this search was the *Daughters Cycle*.[1] WET first began producing this trilogy in 1978. Conceived as a "testimony to the uniqueness and stature" of women, the cycle set out to tap theater's ritual potential in order to revalue matrilineage and women's relationships to one another (Coss, Segal, and Sklar 1980, 193). The first play of the cycle, *Daughters,* is a series of poems, chantings, recollections, and images that reveal aspects of separation and bonding in mother-daughter relationships. Similarly, *Sister/Sister,* the second play, "portrays the complexities and ambivalences in which women are enmeshed in relationships with sisters in the family by showing images of loving intimacy and terrible betrayal" (Brunner 1980, 24). The third play, *Electra Speaks,* revolves around the myth of the House of Atreus. It begins with repeated retellings of this myth, "moving from the patriarchal tale to a feminist inquiry." Here, however, the women speak on their own behalf: Clytemnestra, who must sacrifice her daughter; Iphigenia the innocent victim; Cassandra the other woman; and Athena, who defends the patriarchy. As Electra begins to speak, other voices speak over and for her. In the second half of *Electra* a family is depicted, although contemporized elements of the classic myth are recast and reworked. In the end of this "family drama" Electra decides to leave and, at that point, is finally able to speak for herself (Brunner 1980, 24).

The overriding focus of the *Daughters Cycle* is the family and how it has functioned to institutionalize patriarchy. According to the authors: "Women are socialized to live the major part of their lives infantilized in the family of origin and in a romanticized family of the future. Our analysis of the family leads us to a clear vision that we must give up the family romance" (Coss, Segal, and Sklar 1983b, 239). Because the conventions of realism were seen to have gone hand in hand with the idealized status of the patriarchal family, techniques developed in experimental theaters were employed by WET in order to distance the plotting force of that romance. Each play abandons the linearity of realistic structure. Often episodes take the form of "direct address." One such section in *Daughters* is called "The Questioner." In this scene the performers form a straight line and literally ask the audience questions that are meant to invoke personal reflections on mother-daughter relationships. "Does your mother feel loved? Can you talk about your mother without crying? Do you have to forgive her?" (Coss, Segal, and Sklar 1980, 216). Such direct address scenes are situated next to monologues that recall the personal experiences of the performers. At one point Sondra tells about her mother, saying: "I grew into the one who mothers the mother. I held my dying mother while we were each changing. I cared for my mother until there was no mothering left, only my mother dying, leaving life, leaving me, leaving her daughters, wanting to be mothered" (Coss, Segal, and Sklar 1980, 216). These personal stories are juxtaposed with scenes that employ the concept of split visual and auditory "tracks." One such episode thematically explores the way in which daughters repeat and follow their mothers. In this scene a chorus recites: "The mother said to the daughter, the daughter said to the mother." As this line is repeated, a series of poses are struck by performers on another part of the stage. The only connection between these verbal and visual tracks is their simultaneity. The montage of direct address, personal testimony, and split representation distances this telling of women's experience from the kind of formal and ideological constraints found in traditional, realistic narratives.

Further disrupting the impositions of realism, each play of the cycle begins and ends with the naming of the participants' matrilineages. This event is characterized as a "naming/reclaiming," and it often takes place as performers and audience members stand in a circle. It begins with each performer declaring her name then naming her mother, her mother's mother, and so on. Sondra begins: "I am Sondra, daughter of Lille, daughter of Sarah Rebecca, daughter of Tzivia, daughter of a woman from Austria" (Coss, Segal, and Sklar

1980, 198–99). The naming is repeated in rounds, and with each round the performers elaborate the names of the mothers/daughters with stories of their lives. The process is also structured to allow audience members to take part in the naming of their mothers. According to WET members, "the woman in the audience is the acting partner of the woman performer on the stage," and in the matrilineage "we are all performers, all 'actors.' . . . We are all witness to one another" (Coss, Segal, and Sklar 1983b, 237). Theorized as a means by which women might come together and recognize their unrecognized herstory, the matrilineage then served to bind performer and audience member through a ritual of testimony.

The development of the *Daughters Cycle* took place over the course of ten years, and its methods and themes so greatly affected women dramatists that other feminist theater groups undertook similar projects. In the now historical reception of these matrilineage pieces one can see how the practices of dramatists found direction in feminist theories of patriarchal oppression. The feminist practice of women-centered theater provided a unique context within which the theory of affirmative action could be practiced and the practice of affirmation could be theorized. In light of the developing feminisms of the 1980s, however, it is not surprising to find that, within communities of feminist scholars and performers, critiques of "our" work in the "early" years of feminism have been voiced. The major critique of theaters focusing solely on the recuperation of women's experiences is that the singular focus on patriarchal oppression produces its own kind of indifference. Jill Dolan argues that, while matrilineage pieces evidence consciousness in regard to the differential oppression*s* experienced on account of race, class, and sexuality, in fact, the emphasis is on sameness—or on how the "commonalities" of women "override racial and class differences" (1988, 86). Dolan explains: "The genders of the performers and spectators have been switched from male to female, but they are still working through a representational situation defined by (absent/present) men. . . . The traditional white, middle-class, male transcendent spectator has been replaced with a generally white, middle-class, female transcendent spectator positioned as 'the daughter'" (1988, 91–92). While the critique of patriarchy brings to light issues of women's oppression, it nevertheless maintains a singular focus on male-female differentiation and elides the differences among women.

In light of these differences feminist organizations have struggled with the complexities that arise as identity becomes politics. With attention completely focused on affirming the experiences of women, (white) feminists have found themselves faced with critiques voiced by women of color. The Combahee River Collective in the early 1980s put it this way: "As Black feminists we are made constantly and painfully aware of how little effort white women have made to understand and combat their racism, which requires among other things that they have a more than superficial comprehension of race, color, and Black history and culture. Eliminating racism in the white women's movement is by definition work for white women to do, but we will continue to speak to and demand accountability on this issue" (1982, 13). These sentiments are echoed by dramatists like "Cherríe Moraga, who has written that "in failing . . . to take race, ethnicity, class into account in determining where women are at sexually, many feminists have created an analysis of sexual oppression . . . which is a political dead end" (1986, 187). Not surprisingly, her work focuses on who she is in a culture layered with multiple issues of oppression. In her words: "As a Chicana Lesbian, I write of the connection my own feminism has had with my sexual desire for women. This is my story" (189). This story is the material of her "teatro" *Giving Up the Ghost* (Moraga 1984), which presents Marisa, a Chicana lesbian in her late twenties, and Corky, Marisa's younger self at eleven and seventeen years old. *Ghost* traces the way in which Marisa struggles to maintain and affirm her identity, and this struggle takes place for and with "The People," "those viewing the performance" (ii). While patriarchy is woven into the fabric of Marisa's world, the immediate issue is that of survival in a culture that would literally beat her down for her desires. Survival becomes equated with telling and remembering her story, by identifying her desire for Amalia, who is "soft just in the ways that Marisa is hard" (i), and by speaking that desire in the poetry of her Chicana heritage. The play closes with this desire, with Marisa, who says, "I cling to her in my heart, my daydream with pencil in my mouth, when I put my fingers to my own forgotten places" (58).

The notion that feminism would find its direction by affirming identity is still a vital and fundamental point of coalition among feminists. Moreover, because theater is essentially tied to identity and identification, or tied to seeing who we are in flesh and blood, feminist theaters and dramatists have found themselves dealing concretely with issues of identity politics. But we have found that affirmation is a complex business and that our prescriptions for the ills of gender oppression are often fraught with contradiction. With the early feminist strategies of women-centered texts, forms, and practices the ideological constraints of patriarchy were exposed and resistance was made possible. Ideology itself, however, was not addressed. Consequently, testimony was considered unmediated, and women-only contexts were considered ideology free. But, if ideology is pervasive and its very nature is to mask the force of its power, can one trust "herstory" to be any less influenced by ideological assumptions than "history"? Can one assume that women-centered contexts are safe from the forces that institute privilege, hierarchy, and oppression? In other words, can one "enter here" and leave her ideology on the doorstep? These are the questions that feminists have had to ask, especially in light of critiques leveled by lesbians and women of color. These are also the kinds of questions that have propelled feminism into new directions and guided feminist dramatists to grapple with new problematics on the stage.

The Woman of Dramatic Representation

While feminist dramatists continue to focus on the legitimation of women's experiences and the underrepresentation of such experience, some feminists have augmented that focus by undertaking analyses of how gender is ideologically constructed. In this case the direction of feminist investigation has taken us into the realms of philosophy—and into the study of subjectivity. Emanating in large part from theories developed by European scholars, this critique has sometimes been defined as "postmodern" or "deconstructive." In 1978 Ruby Rich distinguished between the feminist impulses that derived from this European tradition and that of the American grass roots movement. She identified "two voices" of feminism. According to Rich, the American voice emphasized the legitimation of women's experiences and contributions and resulted in a "tendency toward getting information out, a tendency to offer testimony as theory." On the other hand, the European voice was committed to the use of the "most advanced tools of critical analysis," such as psychosemiotics and deconstruction. The emphasis upon critical theory led these feminists to "move beyond regarding the image, to analyzing the structure, codes, and general subtexts of the works." In other words, instead of asking "what does that image mean,?" they asked, "how is meaning produced?" (Rich 1978, 3–4). While the one voice accepted gender as a given, that in the case of women must be affirmed, the other voice asserted that gender is not biologically determined but, rather, an effect of ideology that could be imposed and transparently "naturalized" via representational apparati such as cinema and theater. This inquiry into gender as a construction resulted in a distinction between women and "Woman"—or the distinction between real, historical beings who are women and the fictional Woman who has been drawn in and by dominant ideology supposedly to represent them. According to theorists such as Teresa de Lauretis, while this Woman has been taken as a representation of women, she more accurately represents "other-than-man," "site of sexuality and masculine desire," and "object of men's social exchange" (1984, 5). Incorporating this new direction, the project of deconstructing Woman has been undertaken by feminist scholars and dramatists in order to evidence its oppressive ideology—an ideology that causes women to think of themselves as "objects" rather than "subjects," as passive rather than active, and as an effect of meaning rather than a producer of meaning.

Just as the dynamics of CR infused the work of many feminist theater groups, psychosemiotic theory and critiques of that theory have greatly influenced the practices of European and American dramatists. Extrapolating from Jacques Lacan, psychosemiotic theory is taken to be an examination of subjectivity that is grounded in the primal, psychological impact of the subject's entry into language, or the oedipal experience. According to Lacan, in order to achieve discursive mastery a subject relinquishes its experiential access to the world, or the "real," when that access becomes mediated by language, or the "symbolic." Inasmuch as entry into the symbolic is predicated upon an exchange of "fullness of being" for "fullness of meaning," this exchange is metaphorically symbolized by Lacan as relinquishing the sign of masculine fullness, the penis, for symbolic fullness, the phallus (Silverman 1983, 183). Feminists look to Lacan's explanation of subject processes in order to understand how the world is defined in a way that privileges some subjects over others. Such investigations then proceed into the realm of discourse, and they examine the effects of discursive practices in the formation of gender identifications and privileges. In doing so, such critiques question Lacan's process of definition. While Lacan stresses the metaphoric character of the penis/phallus image, even as an abstraction the phallus invokes explicit notions of possession: one either has the phallus or one doesn't. In this case privilege is established by the process of oppositional definition: there is only the one difference of having or not having, of being the subject *or* the object, of penetrating/producing *or* being penetrated/objectified. Kaja Silverman points out that "the male subject 'pays' for his symbolic privileges with a currency not available to the female subject" (185) and furthermore that "male subjectivity is defined in terms which rigorously exclude women both at the anatomical and cultural levels." Silverman goes on to argue that this characterization bespeaks a "cultural projection by means of which man can always be assured of having the phallus" as well as "justifying the exclusion of the female subject from symbolic authority and privilege" (188). Consequently, in her difference Woman comes to represent everything other than and opposite to Man. Woman is constructed as something to be acted upon as contrasted to the masculine actant, as a space or territory to be penetrated as contrasted to the masculine penetrator, and as a sight to be gazed upon as contrasted to the Man who does the gazing (de Lauretis 1984, 121, 133). Inasmuch as real women come to identify with this representation of Woman, de Lauretis argues that women are "coerced" into submissive, deprivileged experiences, and while "women's consent may not be gotten easily [it] is finally gotten, and has been for a long time, as much by rape and economic coercion as by the more subtle and lasting effects of ideology, representation, and identification" (134).

The work of Simone Benmussa, a French playwright and director, exemplifies the way in which this theoretical direction has influenced theatrical practice and, cooperatively, the way in which theater has produced theoretical considerations of gender. Her work also inhabits an important position in the history of American theater and feminism, in that her New York productions of French plays have formed a bridge between what Rich has called the "two voices" of feminism. Many of Benmussa's productions appear on the surface to be traditional narratives and "apolitical" in relation to the kinds of "political" performances produced by American feminist theater groups of the 1970s. Benmussa, however, describes her work as political because she aims at disruptions of ideological processes. Her directorial concept for Hélène Cixous's *Portrait of Dora* was one of narrative investigation (Benmussa 1979, intro.). Rather than focusing solely on a narrative of oppression, she set out to examine the role of narrative itself in the act of oppression. With this text she dramatically staged the way in which masculine desire generates a narrative structure that is open only to the construction of Woman but inhospitable to real women. Benmussa states that plays such as *Dora* have the potential to disrupt "the everyday, restrictive ordering of space and time imposed on us by the powers that be," but she stresses that, if this kind of theater devoted to ideological disruption is to succeed, "then it must exist and assert itself as political theatre, [for] it is radically opposed to the great edifying and reproducing machines that we see all around us at the moment" (11).

Engaged in textual politics, Benmussa exposes narrative and gender as just such edifying and reproducing machines in her own play *The Singular Life of Albert Nobbs*. Elin Diamond points out that this play is "dispersed over a textual field" that brings together the many accounts of Albert Nobbs's life (1985, 279). From a 1920s newspaper article that tells of a woman who had posed as a man for most of her life, George Moore adapted the incident into a short story, which appeared in his book *Celibate Lives*. Approximately sixty years later Benmussa adapted Moore's story into her play and used her adaptation to foreground the interaction of the various texts and authors of "Albert Nobbs." This foregrounding is accomplished by incorporating Moore as the narrating voice. Although Moore never appears on stage, he nevertheless structures the movement of the play and at times even appropriates the inner monologues of Albert (Case 1983, 23). In this way authority and patriarchy are represented in the coercive structuring of the male narrator, and, as with *Dora,* narrative itself comes to represent an ideological imposition rather than a natural phenomenon. Diamond calls attention to Benmussa's textual politics, stating, "[Her] achievement in *Albert Nobbs* is to induce narrativity in the audience while insisting on the coercive effects of a male narrative that (inevitably) refuses or diminishes and distorts the experience of female subjects" (1985, 283).

Within this narrative the construction of gender is foregrounded. Sue-Ellen Case points out that the play revolves around a woman "in drag." Albert dresses in male clothes in order to get a better-paying job and finds that she is "read" as a man due to the signs of her

apparel. But this cross-gender dressing eventually traps Albert, forcing "her female self to go into hiding" (Case 1983, 22–23). In this
case Albert is not a victim of any one man; rather, she is victimized
by the "patriarchal economy" and her own "male-identification, her
internalization of the patriarchal modes of production." As Albert
applies cross-gender dressing to her existence, the play exposes gender as a construction and, in Case's words, "provokes us to question
the basic assumption that gender characteristics are 'natural'"(24).

In large part the momentum to understand how ideology functions has come from Europe by way of Marxist and poststructuralist
theory. But the project of figuring out how consciousness is conditioned by the messages that are ideologically implanted in our minds
has certainly not been ignored by American scholars and dramatists.
In relation to this project Adrienne Kennedy's work comes to the
foreground with plays such as *Funnyhouse of a Negro, The Owl Answers,* and *A Movie Star Has to Star in Black and White* (1988). Like
Benmussa, Kennedy focuses on the way in which characters are constructed by the texts and contexts of their lives. Unlike Benmussa,
though, Kennedy's work presents the complexity of identity that has
been claimed as well as ideologically affixed to African Americans,
and particularly African-American women. From a reading of Kennedy's plays and her comments about them their autobiographical
nature becomes evident. She writes of growing up black in a racist
and sexist society, but, as Herbert Blau points out, she also writes of
her experience, which is the "*Negro* experience, the desire for assimilation, emotionally, intellectually, psycho-sexually, something more
than integration" (1984, 532). The development of character(s) in her
plays reflects this split personal/political identity and identification in
her life. The people of her plays develop through the layering of
signs, symbols, and internal monologues rather than through linear
plot structure. Furthermore, these people, like Benmussa's characters, are "dispersed over textual fields"—that is, they are developed
and redeveloped in subsequent plays, and they are literally embodied
in the words and images of other texts such as movies, classic plays,
and poems. This is particularly evident in her play *A Movie Star Has
to Star in Black and White.* In this piece the central character, Clara,
speaks of her life and desires, but she does so only by hearing the
words in the voices and images of idolized movie stars. She speaks
of her father, but these words come from Bette Davis in *Now Voy-*

ager; she tells of her brother's illness, but the scene is a shot of Jean Peters in *Viva Zapata!;* and she calls for help but through the voice of Shelley Winters in *A Place in the Sun.* These very white scenes are placed in the midst of Clara's very black life, where color is an absolute deprivileging difference. And across both black and white scenes the filter is that of a woman trying to see herself as a writer and producer of meaning, in spite of cultural encodings that relegate her to object status. The result is a complex rendering of identity that foregrounds the role of dominant culture in shaping how this particular black woman has come to recognize and/or misrecognize herself.

Because Kennedy's characters reflect the constructedness of ideological conditioning rather than subscribing to coherent characterization, critics have often searched for descriptives that might elucidate her "textual politics." Her work is often categorized as "contemporary surrealism" (Cohn 1982, 108–9). Visually, she juxtaposes images and contexts that redefine one another by their unorthodox pairing, and, textually, she prioritizes subtext rather than "realistic" dialogue. Unlike early surrealists, however, who relied upon sexual bipolarity as the paradigmatic emblem for Man's inability to reconcile the conscious and subconscious worlds, Kennedy foregrounds sexual bipolarity as a cultural construction fostered by desire-producing industries such as "Hollywood" and "great literature"—industries that have made it clear that to be a movie star you have to be white and to be great you have to be a man or be desired by a man. In her "acts of the mind" she focuses on how race and gender are produced rather than natural (108), therefore exposing ideology and its power to overtly and covertly discriminate against all "others." The psychosocial consequence of this discrimination surfaces in Clara in *Movie Star:* "Each day I wonder with what or with whom can I co-exist in a true union?"

With plays such as *Albert Nobbs* and *Movie Star* playwrights and producers provide models of how drama can expose the workings of ideology and, more specifically, how theater can be used to reveal the oppression that results from traditionally fixed notions of gender. This is an important development in that such ideological oppression has often found its means of indoctrination in "great" theater and "classic" drama. By taking theater itself to task the direction of feminist theory and practice has led to the deconstruction of Woman and the creation of vital dramatic forms with which to reveal that critique.

The Subject of Feminism

The various feminist examinations of subjectivity and gender construction have led to the expansion of the feminist project, and they have provided direction in the field of feminist drama. Such critiques of ideology have expanded our awareness; however, in a strange way they have also had a paralyzing effect. If ideology is assumed to be everywhere and always pervasive and its powers absolute, the best that any of us can hope for is consciousness. For feminists who continue to ground their theory/practice in the affirmative stance that action can be taken to change circumstances, the belief in an unalterable and omnipotent ideology is untenable. Without ignoring the force of ideological conditioning some feminists are now beginning to assert the existence of margins in which women, in particular, are both inside ideology, being objectified according to the construction of Woman, and outside ideology, noting that they are not the Woman of dominant discourse. It is in these marginal spaces that some feminists are placing the possibility for affirmative theory/practice and for disruption of the more centrally dominating forces of ideology.

In identifying such margins, however, once again we have had to question our own critiques in order to understand how such margins exist as well as the way in which we have been blind to them. This direction takes Teresa de Lauretis back to earlier feminist theory in which examinations of gender oppression focused on sexual difference and the differential privilege afforded to men. De Lauretis notes: "[the] emphasis on sexual difference did open up a critical space—a conceptual, representational, and erotic space—in which women could address themselves to women. And in the very act of assuming and speaking from the position of subject, a woman could concurrently recognize women as subjects and as objects of female desire" (1988, 155). At the same time, though, feminists were forced by their own increasing understanding of ideology to question the single-mindedness of analyses that focused solely on sexual difference. De Lauretis addresses the specific indifference that a feminist critique provokes when it is formulated primarily in regard to sexual difference, saying, "the first feminist emphasis on sexual difference as gender (women's difference from man) has rightly come under attack for obscuring the effects of other differences in women's psychosocial oppression" (1988, 155). That is, while women focus solely on the effects of patriarchal oppression and the effects of gender ideology, they deemphasize the many different forces that impact and oppress women—forces that produce class structure, racism, homophobia, and the like. As has already been stated, for some time women of color have theorized the ways in which these forces are interrelated, as is exemplified in the statement of purpose written by the Combahee River Collective about being black and feminist: "[We] are actively committed to struggling against racial, sexual, heterosexual, and class oppression and see as our particular task the development of integrated analysis and practice based upon the fact that the major systems of oppression are interlocking. The synthesis of these oppressions creates the conditions of our lives" (1982, 13). Informed by the critique that women of color have brought to (white) feminism, de Lauretis argues that the "subject of feminism" now needs to move beyond an analysis of gender as an exclusive, oppositional difference—whether that be an analysis of women's experience of patriarchy or a deconstruction of Woman. In advocating a move beyond an investigation of sexual difference, and even away from an emphasis on deconstructing Woman, de Lauretis reflects a growing awareness of how both of these critiques generalize and level the differing experiences of women. Consequently, the subject of feminism proposed by de Lauretis is the theorizing of how differences structure perception, with particular emphasis placed upon the notion that this "subject" is one "whose definition or conception is in progress, in this and other feminist critical texts" (1987, 10). Her admonition, then, is to move in the direction of analyzing how gender interacts with other differences, turning our attention to the "subject of feminism," as distinguished from a "female subject."

Remembering that de Lauretis is primarily concerned here with how feminists might "act" in light of ideology's omnipresence, her process of rearticulating the subject of feminism focuses on the potential to bring about change. She notes that, in our recent past, feminist concepts of empowerment and agency have been thought of in terms of "resistance"—resistance to culturally constructed ideas of female inferiority, resistance to being objectified, resistance to ideology in general. Moreover, these notions of resistance have always been affixed to ideas of making the entire world a better place as well as assumptions that we could know what a better world might be. In order to think about the various forces of socialization that differentially affect people from one context to another de Lauretis directs feminists to rethink notions of agency in terms of "micropolitical practice" or "local resistance." Rather than taking the position that one might change the world—a position that assumes an authority to know what's best for the world—de Lauretis encourages a radicalization of agency on the level of micropolitics. In that differences between women are realized in specific contexts, or in the "micropolitical practices of daily life," de Lauretis argues that it is at this level that resistance must occur. Without disavowing the existence of ideology de Lauretis posits that there is a space created at the point at which we recognize that we are not what ideology would have us be. Such awareness exists in margins that provide a vantage from which to understand our differences—that is, our difference from ideological constructs and imperatives as well as the differences that constitute community and individual identities. Micropolitical practice is that activity that aims at understanding the margins, empowering those who inhabit such margins to represent themselves, and encouraging critiques that account for the ways in which ideology works first and foremost at home. This new feminist direction serves to provide both a "critical negativity," in that it foregrounds the influence of ideology, as well as an "affirmative positivity of its politics," in that it offers a course of action rather than a conscious submission to ideology (1987, 26).

While marginalized experience has served as the thematic thrust of several feminist theater groups and many feminist plays, a micropolitical practice implies more than plots that deal with racism, sexism, and homophobia. It involves the investigation of discursive practices—ways of seeing, defining, and understanding experience—and their relationship to marginalized experience and micropolitical agency. Keeping this in mind, I turn to *Beauty and the Beast,* a production that was created by the Split Britches company beginning in 1983. In describing the Split Britches company Sue-Ellen Case notes that "the name of this company, Split Britches, connotes the split pants of both poverty and comedy, the splitting of male gender wear, and suggests puns such as split bridges/split breaches" (1988b, 141). Having performed across Europe and the United States, this company is noted for its "no-frills" approach to dramatic representation. It is also distinguished by the backgrounds of its members as well as by the feminist themes that they approach in production. Case states: "The company consists of three women: one heterosexual Jewish woman [Deborah Margolin], one 'butch' working-class lesbian mother [Peggy Shaw], and one southern, working-class 'femme' lesbian [Lois Weaver]" (141). Both Shaw and Weaver have worked with other feminist companies such as "SpiderWoman," for which issues relating to women's differences serve as the dramatic impetus for theatrical enterprise. Split Britches is further distinguished for having established and maintained a theater space devoted to the production of women's artistic endeavors. This space, the WOW Cafe, has been described as a "force more than a place." Alisa Solomon explains: "Unlike many East Village performance spaces, WOW, at 330 E. 11th Street, did not begin as a location seeking work to produce but was born the other way around. Women who had been producing a vast variety of work all over the East Village sought a permanent home" (1986, 305). Until 1982, when Split Britches moved into WOW, various other locations were tried and subsequently vacated; nevertheless, the force of this project acquired specificity. Lois Weaver recalls that they wanted "to create a multimedia environment" (Solomon 1986, 306). Although their primary goal was to acquire a "women's performance space," they also wanted "a hangout, a girl's social club" (309). The desired sociality of this project influenced the design of the actual physical spaces, the hours of production, and the methods employed to finance its operation. In addition to literally "begging on the streets," or, as Peggy Shaw explains, "guilt-tripping our friends into writing checks" to cover the rent, WOW founders would throw benefits to raise money (313). Characterized by Solomon as costume or theme parties, such benefits have included a Freudian Slip party—to which guests came dressed in lingerie, a Medical Drag Ball, and Butch-Femme nights (308, 313). Even in its meagerly funded production capacity WOW has enabled the work of artists such as Holly Hughes, Alina Troyana, and Split Britches itself. Offering "talking slide shows," variety nights, and fully mounted plays, this venue has opened itself to a number of female artists and a range of dramatic projects. Asserting feminism and lesbianism as "givens" rather than "issues," the WOW Cafe has provided a margin within which women's work can be realized, affirmed, *and* analyzed (312).

Within this context of varied and various productions, as well as varied and various experiences, Split Britches created *Beauty and the Beast; or, The One and Only World-Famous Vaudeville Revue.* Representative of WOW's variety, *Beauty and the Beast* conflates dramatic genres and asserts its difference not simply as a classic fairy tale nor as a vaudeville show. Described by one reviewer as a "Dada burlesque," the production does reflect the Dada evasion of definition (Stone 1983, 105). The play opens with a Salvation Army troupe attempting to dramatize "Beauty and the Beast" in order to raise money. Tina Margolis describes the ensuing action: "To fill out the bill—and escape the grave seriousness of their morality tale—the troupe performs specialty numbers as entr'acte material. The characters and roles include a pious-yet-repressed Salvation Army sergeant/elocutionist/Beauty (Lois Weaver); a Hassidic rabbi/father/stand-up comic, who is performing to pay for new Torah scrolls for his shul (Deborah Margolin); and an 86-year-old hoofer, the Beast, who thinks she's James Dean (Peggy Shaw)" (1983, 76–77). Through the course of the play, the tale of "Beauty and the Beast" is broken up with a reading from *Macbeth,* an impersonation of Tony Bennett, songs such as "Kitty from Kansas City" and "It's Impossible," and a section of classical ballet featuring the Beast and the Jewish rabbi, who sports a tutu.

Case argues that in this interrupted narrative, acted out in the context of the WOW Cafe, a different subject position is realized. Theorized as a "collective subject," this subject is not characterized by the traditional attributes of wholeness and coherence, nor is this subject constituted/contained within or even across the texts of the drama (1988b, 143). Rather, a subject position is established that collects significance from the text, context, and personae of the performers in the specificity of their intentional margin. The collecting of subjectivity is most obvious in *Beauty and the Beast,* as performers collect characters one on top of the other. In one scene this collection is visually marked as the performers suspend dresses on hangers from around their necks to indicate that they are representing other characters. In this menagerie of collected characterizations gender is foregrounded as a sociopolitical application, or construction, instead of as an essential or biological trait. Each costume functions as a sign calling up stereotypical meanings. A woman wears a suit, so she signifies "father." This same woman puts on a tutu over the suit, and she signifies "ballerina." Throughout the play the performers are literally layered in gender apparel, a visual statement that emphasizes constructedness rather than naturalness. Further, gender as a *bi*polar opposition is called into question by the personae of the performers, as they bring the butch-femme tradition of "consciously played out" roles to the stage (Case 1989, 291). Case explains: "The butch-femme couple inhabit the subject position together—'you can't have one without the other,' as the song says. The two roles never appear as . . . discrete. . . . These are not split subjects, suffering the torments of ideology. They are coupled ones that do not impale themselves on the poles of sexual difference" (1989, 283). From the streets to the stage, and in a context in which spectators witness both performances, these performers assume roles in real life, and, conversely, they abandon characterization onstage, displaying their own personalities and desires. As Case notes, "Rather than the way a single, whole, protagonist functioned in earlier works to represent 'Woman' as a homogeneous category," the collective subject appears as strategies, positionings, and deconstructions which emphasize the multiplicity and heterogeneity of the subject of feminism (1988b, 143). Case states, "Whereas, in the earlier years, women were regarded as similar to one another, but different from men, [here] the focus [is] an internal one, noting the differences among women of class, 'race,' and sexuality" (143–44). In a dramatic venue the subject of feminism is realized as the personal becomes the "dramatically political," as performers layer character upon character and as personae and role are conflated. Loaded with highly contextual signs that mark the specificity of this marginal space, *Beauty and the Beast* does not offer the possibility of an unspecified, universal subject nor even the possibility of a universalized female subject. It is the subject of feminism that one finds in this kind of theater—a subject marked in both theory and practice by its micropolitical intent.

In trying to understand the very existence of feminist directing and feminist drama, it is essential to understand the direction(s) of feminism. While portrayed in the popular press as solidified and codified, feminism continues to exist more as strategies and contextualized actions rather than as a fixed entity. With this essay I have presented one interpretation of how those strategies have developed in theory *and* in practice. I stress, however, that it is just that, an interpretation influenced by the contexts and issues that have shaped me. Rather than setting out characteristics and methods with which to absolutely identify feminist directors from those of other persuasions, I have chosen to highlight the dialogue and debate that goes on among those of us who continue to identify ourselves as feminists. In doing so I hope to have provided a critical and historical position from which to view and analyze the work of contemporary feminist directors. In this volume their work speaks specifically about the many complexities, contradictions, and divergent directions that characterize our theory, which is our practice, and vice versa. To those directors I say, "Take it away, have at it, enter stage *left*."

NOTE

1. The *Daughters Cycle* has not been published in its entirety. The first play of the trilogy, *Daughters,* was published in the *Massachusetts Review* (Coss, Segal, and Sklar 1983a). Some excerpts from the cycle appear in essays by WET founders (Coss, Segal, and Sklar 1983b; Sklar 1983).

REFERENCES

Benmussa, Simone. 1979. *Benmussa Directs.* London: John Calder.
Blau, Herbert, 1984. "The American Dream in American Gothic: The Plays of Sam Shepard and Adrienne Kennedy." *Modern Drama* 27, no. 4: 520–39.
Brown, Janet. 1979. *Feminist Drama: Definitions and Critical Analysis.* Metuchen: Scarecrow Press.
Brunner, Cornelia. 1980. "Roberta Sklar: Towards Creating a Women's Theatre." *Drama Review* 29, no. 2: 23–40.
Case, Sue-Ellen. 1988a. *Feminism and Theatre.* New York: Methuen.
———. 1988b. "From Split Subject to Split Britches." In *Feminine Focus: The New Women Playwrights,* edited by Enoch Brater. New York: Oxford University Press.
———. 1983. "Gender as Play: Simone Benmussa's *The Singular Life of Albert Nobbs.*" *Women & Performance* 1, no. 2: 21–24.
———. 1989. "Toward a Butch-Femme Aesthetic." In *Making a Spectacle: Feminist Essays on Contemporary Women's Theatre,* edited by Lynda Hart. Ann Arbor: University of Michigan Press.
Cohn, Ruby. 1982. *New American Dramatists: 1960–80.* New York: Grove Press.
Combahee River Collective. 1982. *All the Women Are White, All the Men Are Black, but Some of Us Are Brave.* Edited by Gloria Hull. Old Westbury, Conn.: The Feminist Press, 1982.
Coss, Clare, Sondra Segal, and Roberta Sklar. 1983a. "Daughters." *Massachusetts Review* (Spring): 141–77.

———. 1983b. "Notes on the Women's Experimental Theater." In *Women in Theatre: Compassion and Hope*, edited by Karen Malpede. New York: Drama Book Publishers.

———. 1980. "Separation and Survival: Mothers, Daughters, Sisters—The Women's Experimental Theater." In *The Future of Difference*, edited by Hester Eisenstein and Alice Jardine. New Brunswick, N.J.: Rutgers University Press.

de Lauretis, Teresa. 1984. *Alice Doesn't: Feminism, Semiotics, and Cinema*. Bloomington: Indiana University Press.

———. 1988. "Sexual Indifference and Lesbian Representation." *Theatre Journal* 40, no. 2: 155–77.

———. 1987. "The Technology of Gender." *Technologies of Gender*. Bloomington: Indiana University Press.

Diamond, Elin. 1985. "Refusing the Romanticism of Identity: Narrative Interventions in Churchill, Benmussa, Duras." *Theatre Journal* 37, no. 3: 273–86.

Dolan, Jill. 1988. *The Feminist Spectator as Critic*. Ann Arbor: UMI Research Press.

Gillespie, Patti. 1977. "Feminist Theatres in the 1970s." *Theatre News* 10, no. 2: 5, 17.

Hanna, Gillian. 1978. "Feminism and Theatre." In *Theatre Papers, Second Series*, edited by Peter Hulton. Devon: Department of Theatre, Dartington College of Arts.

Kennedy, Adrienne. 1988. *Adrienne Kennedy in One Act*. Minneapolis: University of Minnesota Press.

Leavitt, Dinah. 1980. *Feminist Theatre Groups*. New York: Jefferson McFarland.

Margolis, Tina. 1983. Review of *Beauty and the Beast*. *Women & Performance* 1, no. 1: 75–78.

Moraga, Cherríe. 1986. "From a Long Line of Vendidas: Chicanas and Feminism." In *Feminist Studies/Critical Studies*, edited by Teresa de Lauretis. Bloomington: Indiana University Press.

———. 1984. *Giving Up the Ghost*. Los Angeles: West End Press.

Rich, Ruby. 1978. "The Crisis of Naming in Feminist Film Criticism." *Jumpcut* 19:3–11.

Roth, Martha. 1983. "Notes toward a Feminist Performance Aesthetic." *Women & Performance* 1, no. 1: 5–14.

Segal, Sondra, and Roberta Sklar. 1987. "The Women's Experimental Theater." In *Women in American Theatre*, edited by Helen Chinoy and Linda Walsh Jenkins, rev. and exp. ed. New York: Theatre Communications Group.

Silverman, Kaja. 1983. *The Subject of Semiotics*. New York: Oxford University Press.

Sklar, Roberta. 1987. "Reflections." In *Women in American Theatre*, edited by Helen Chinoy and Linda Walsh Jenkins, rev. and exp. ed. New York: Theatre Communications Group.

———. 1983. "Sisters, or Never Trust Anyone Outside the Family." *Women & Performance* 1, no. 1: 57–70.

Solomon, Alisa. 1986. "The WOW Cafe." In *The Drama Review: Thirty Years of Commentary on the Avant-garde,* edited by Brooks McNamara and Jill Dolan. Ann Arbor: UMI Research Press.
Stone, Laurie. 1983. "Vixen Fire." *Village Voice.* (9 April): 105.

PART 1

Interpreting the Text

A feminist play can slip out from under, even when the director is herself a feminist. This section, entitled "Interpreting the Text," is about feminist directors working on feminist scripts, plays that, to use Nancy Miller's words, "protest the available fictions of women's becoming." *Portrait of Dora, Top Girls, Blood Relations,* and *Unfinished Women* are all plays that protest, but here we offer a warning: in no case does a production of one of these plays guarantee a feminist statement. There is the ever-present danger that, without certain checks, we will reflexively reproduce the very gender and racial stereotypes that we ought to be challenging.

A crucial resource in this process is feminist theory. The contributors to this section have all made use of theory as a way to think through a show before the old representations begin to assert themselves. Plays in production are slippery; meaning is produced not just by the spoken word but also by all the nonverbal aspects of the mise-en-scène and the performances. A handful of wrong choices, and the social critique can begin to blur and disappear. *Blood Relations,* for example, can easily diminish into a romanticized treatment of a sensational crime, a voyeuristic study of personality, a whodunit. It's all so delicate—which scenes get emphasis, how our attention gets focused on or off certain characters, what visual pictures are created and how they "speak." Note, for example, how closely and carefully the director and the dramaturg work with each other on *Portrait of Dora* and how closely both of them work with all the designers, for set, costumes, and aural effects.

Perhaps the lesson is that, if theory is going to be introduced into a production process, it needs to become the common property of every member of the creative team. The same thing pertains to a show like *Unfinished Women,* in which the critique of gender is coupled with a critique of race. Any time a production undertakes to challenge fundamental ideological assumptions, and theory becomes part of the arsenal, the entire production team needs to be included in the discussion. Not just informed—included.

JEANIE FORTE AND CHRISTINE SUMPTION

Encountering *Dora:* Putting Theory into Practice

In the spring of 1985 Christine Sumption chose Portrait of Dora *by Hélène Cixous as her Master of Fine Arts thesis directing project at the University of Washington, and Jeanie Forte joined her as dramaturg for the production. Since neither Chris nor Jeanie had worked on a production in that kind of relationship before, the whole process of directing and dramaturgical advising emerged experimentally, albeit in the context of a well-established friendship and easy respect for each other's talents and abilities. Although Chris was accustomed to doing her own research for her productions, she agreed that Jeanie should identify specific issues for research, locate texts or articles pertinent to a feminist discussion of the text, and conduct discussions with Chris and/or the cast, if needed. In addition, as an experienced director, Jeanie was encouraged to provide input (directly to Chris) regarding the implementation of theory once the rehearsal process began. Beyond these augmentations Chris continued to hold primary responsibility for the production as a whole, overseeing all design and acting details, consulting with Jeanie as she desired. What follows are their efforts to record both the process and the findings: first, in Jeanie's discussion of the theories that influenced the interpretation and staging; and, second, in Chris's examination of the specific challenges for a feminist director of this play.*

Encountering *Dora* in Theory by Jeanie Forte

Among the many branches of contemporary feminist theory, the one that Chris and I found most useful in its analysis recognizes its intersections with so-called postmodernist discourses, employing them where productive but also evidencing and debating points of resistance or contradiction. One such contradiction concerns the postmodern concept of a decentered subject: postmodernism deconstructs the Cartesian/postenlightenment notion of a unitary self—an independent individual who acts out of free will—positing instead a decentered subject, a creature shaped by discourse, the receptive intersection of cultural practices. This concept provides a basis for understanding the cultural construction of gender. The displacement of self into a subject also operates, however, to deny women status as speaking subjects, particularly in the psychoanalytic paradigm, which predominates throughout much postmodernist discourse. One of the most basic issues, then, in contemporary feminism concerns the construction of female subjectivity within a postmodernist context. Searching for female subjectivity is different from occupying a subject position, or the space of a decentered subject. It is the search for a feminist frame of reference that can provide a context for articulating one's experience of the world, one's desire.

In the psychoanalytic paradigm, derived from Freud but further elaborated within postmodernist discourse by Jacques Lacan, Woman is articulated as Other in relation to a male subject. She exists only as a mirror to reflect male desire, her position determined by where she is required to be in order to effect the male oedipal passage. Remember that when Freud asked his famous question, "What do women want?" he actually excluded women from the inquiry: "Throughout history people have knocked their heads against the riddle of the nature of femininity. . . . Nor will you have escaped worrying over this problem—those of you who are men; to those of you who are women this will not apply—you are yourselves the problem." His question thus refers only to men; that is, the answer is for men, reverts to men, has solely to do with male desire (de Lauretis 1983, 111). Woman is not the subject of her own inquiry but is, rather, the object within a closed male discourse.

Hélène Cixous's *Portrait of Dora* (1979) deals directly with these questions of female subjectivity and sexuality, challenging the psychoanalytic paradigm and frustrating its efforts to define or categorize. Even the title provides an indication of her project: Not "a," or "the," but simply "portrait"—undefined, unsituated, opening up possibilities rather than pinning them down. Also *portrait* indicates a picture, or visual image, not language—a picture drawn in the gaps produced by what language does not describe, which is in fact Dora.

The attempts to describe Dora, to encompass her with story by the other characters in the play, fail. Dora frustrates any effort to "narrate" her. She is not a single character in the play, even when you read it. Often the text will indicate that Dora says a line then will immediately follow that with another statement to be made by Dora, which, in the conventions of play transcription, gives the distinct impression that there are multiple Doras onstage. Nor is she definable by any of the other characters' perceptions of her. There are too many contradictions, differing versions, events perceived through dream or the fuzziness of memory, or literally and figuratively through smoke. In Freud's own description of the hysteric's account of things the narrative is incoherent, inconsistent, full of gaps and blind alleys. This frustration of narrative provides one of the bases for understanding the play in relation to current feminist/postmodernist theory.

Jean-François Lyotard defines the postmodern as "incredulity with regard to the master narratives" (1979, 7). (In French, the term is *grands récits,* literally "big stories," which supply explanations or perspectives for organizing our perception of the world; examples include narratives of speculation, such as Freud's, and narratives of emancipation, such as Marx's.) According to Lyotard, we can't know the origin of this incredulity or disbelief, but we see and feel its manifestations. Alice Jardine says, in turn, that this is experienced primarily as a loss, or at least a breakdown, of narrative (1985, 65). She notes that the human sciences' recent obsession with metaphor and metonymy—the twin cornerstones of narrative—demonstrates a panic surrounding narrativity as well as a "reimagining of the status of the image itself" (69). This crisis in narrative is experienced culturally as a "loss of legitimation," a destabilizing effect in structures of knowledge (structures that promote and sustain relations of power).

Roland Barthes observed that narrative is universal: "Caring nothing for the division between good and bad literature, narrative is international, transhistorical, transcultural: it is simply there, like life itself" (1977, 79). This gives some sense of the scope, or seriousness, of the implications of its loss, or breakdown. Barthes also characterized narrative's function: narrative is essentially a "logic, there exposed, risked and satisfied. . . . Logic here has emancipatory value—and with it the entire narrative" (124). He calls it a model for the process of becoming—but on whose terms? and at whose expense? In Barthes's analysis narrative is a vanquishing, a conquering force. It is the victor over mere repetition, which presumably cannot engender progress. Furthermore, narrative is monological, does not permit another voice. For feminists, however, the connection between narrative and oedipal desire is most compelling: "it may be significant that it is at the same moment (around the age of three) that the little human 'invents' at once sentence, narrative, and the Oedipus" (124). This implies an agency of desire that operates the narrativist logic; moreover, it is a desire grounded in the oedipal Object-ification of Woman.

This connection between oedipal desire and narrative is extensively explored by Teresa de Lauretis, whose work proved valuable in understanding *Portrait of Dora* (1984, 103–57). In "Desire in Narrative" she quotes Laura Mulvey's now famous remark, "Sadism demands a story," a statement that insinuates its own reversibility, or "A story demands sadism." To quote Mulvey in full: "sadism demands a story, depends on making something happen, forcing a change in another person, a battle of will and strength, victory/defeat, all occurring in a linear time with a beginning and an end" (1975, 14). Are we then to infer, de Lauretis asks, that sadism is the causal agent, the deep structure, the generative force of narrative?

De Lauretis asserts that subjectivity is engaged in the cogs of narrative and indeed constituted in the relation of narrative, meaning, and desire, so that the very work of narrativity is the engagement of the subject in certain positionalities of meaning and desire. She then demonstrates the connection between narrative and desire, showing that the desire motivating narrative is oedipal, or masculine, desire (1984, 106). Barthes also noted this: "The pleasure of the text is an Oedipal pleasure (to denude, to know, to learn the origin and the end), if it is true that every narrative is a staging of the (absent hidden or hypostatized) father—which would explain the solidarity of narrative forms, of family structures, and of prohibitions of nudity" (1975, 10).

To return briefly to Freud's question "What do women want?" we can now see it as a question of desire, which in turn generates a narrative, a quest. Like Oedipus, who starts with a question, not only is a quest a question of desire (a story is also thus a question of desire), but it is always oedipal desire (de Lauretis 1984, 111). Freud states this unequivocally in his "case study" of Dora: speaking of the sexual attraction between parents and children at an early age, which he feels informs all subsequent libidinal developments, he writes, "the myth of Oedipus is probably to be regarded as a poetical rendering of what is typical in these relations (Freud 1963, 73). This statement proves particularly ironic in the context of Dora's case, since she abruptly ends the therapy only three months after it begins, dismissing Freud's services and ignoring all entreaties to return, rendering Freud's attempt to prove his point fruitless.

So why is narrative sadistic? If narrative is governed by an oedipal logic, it is because it is situated within the system of exchange instituted by the incest prohibition, wherein Woman functions both as a sign (representation) and a value/object for that exchange (see Lévi-Strauss 1969, 1984; and Rubin 1975). Woman properly represents the fulfillment of the narrative promise (made, in Freud's model, to the little boy) and that representation works to support the male status of the mythical subject. The female position is always that of object/objective/obstacle, the figure of narrative closure (de Lauretis 1984, 140).

But if male desire is the question that generates narrative as oedipal drama, that question is an open one; the closure is only promised, not guaranteed. Oedipal desire requires that its object identify with the feminine position—in other words, women must either consent or be seduced into consenting to femininity. This is the sense in which sadism demands a story or story demands sadism and which points up the continuing need in feminist theory for a politics of the unconscious. As de Lauretis says: "for women's consent may not be gotten easily, but is finally gotten, and has been for a long time, as much by rape and economic coercion as by the more subtle and lasting effects of ideology, representation and identification" (1984, 134).

So narrative presents big stakes for feminism and is a crucial issue in *Portrait of Dora;* Freud repeatedly imposes the oedipal narrative on Dora's dreams and utterances. He has already determined Dora's story and interprets everything accordingly. In one exchange Dora is describing a dream:

> *Dora:* Frau K. puts Herr K. on the phone. He tells me he can't do very much. I'll have to wait until next year. I laugh. He tells me, "You know that. . . ." But I don't let him finish. I hang up.

Freud: In fact, you don't let things finish. Your ankle swells. You give birth. Nine months after the scene at the lake. So despite everything you manage to have a child by Herr K. Something happened during the scene at the lake.
Dora: Nothing happened!
Freud: Precisely. It was there that you took that false step, etc. etc.

He in fact reduces her to silence with his narration, after which she says "Is that all? You're giving birth to a mouse." Shortly thereafter she ends the treatment, saying in what seems like a non sequitur, "This desire still this desire. Yes" (Cixous 1979, 65). We might wonder, in the swimming referents of the play, whose desire—hers? Freud's? the play's? But ending in the affirmative "Yes" seems to invoke her own desire, which motivates her to release herself from a narrative that is not hers.

Freud, as the representative of narrative, is the spokesman for the "sane" world, the nonhysterical world, which is logical, predictable, unambiguous, solvable. He frequently expresses himself in aphorisms, conventional wisdoms, such as "Where there's smoke there's fire," "He whose lips are silent speaks with his fingertips," and a corollary statement made by Freud in his case history but given to Frau K. in the play, "I call a cat a cat." These pronouncements, meant to invoke simplicity, clarity, and the stability of tradition, actually do the opposite, invoking figural language, the presumably stable meanings coming undone by their own openness to double entendre. Lips correspond to the female genitals, which indeed are very "chatty" in the play and refuse to be silenced, and in French slang *chat* connotes certain features of female anatomy, as if to say "I call a pussy a pussy" (see Gallop 1982, 140).

Another important through-line of imagery concerns doors and whether or not they're open or shut. Even the title suggests doors in both French and English: *porte/portrait, door/Dora.* For the male characters in the play it is quite clear that doors represent female genitals, and in the male exclusion of opposites they must be either open or shut (contrasted with Dora, who says, "I may open/I can open a little bit. Something may or may not be open. Events may or may not have happened"). Freud's statement in this regard is that "naturally one can't be indifferent as to whether a girl is 'open' or 'closed.' It's obvious which key would be used to 'open' in such a case" (Cixous 1979, 46). Jane Gallop notes that the smug certitude of Freud's "naturally" and "well-known" offends Dora by denying the specificity of her signifiers in the same way that she is offended by Herr K.'s beginning his declaration of love with what she knows were the same words he had used to seduce a governess. As Gallop points out, what woman wants to be opened by a skeleton key (1982, 137)?

Dora also recognizes this "open-door" policy of the men as one of aggression and domination: whoever holds the key wields the power in the relationship. She says of Herr K., "I have no doubt he intends to open the door; It's either Him or Me" (Cixous 1979, 36). She also knows that to be opened means annihilation, to be made into nothing the way the wives and ex-governesses have been. Cixous says that Dora sees women executed to make space for her. "She knows that she will in turn be massacred" (Cixous and Clément 1986, 153). Once she is possessed sexually, she is annulled, and the void thus created can then be filled up with another woman, and so on— which demonstrates once again the exchange value of women.

In the end Freud has been put in the position of the seduced and abandoned governess; when Dora ends the therapy he protests, "That's the notice you give a governess" (Cixous 1979, 65). He's the object in relation to Dora, an identification that he can't tolerate either. They both, in this instant, have to think/hope that there's still some place where one can escape the structural exchange/narrative enclosure of women. Dora apparently realizes on some level that she must escape the oedipal narrative that would be imposed on her in order to find her own subjectivity.

The play also suggests that the affirmative lesbian love Dora feels for Frau K. is posed as an alternative, a sexuality of pleasure and joy rather than murderous assimilation (see Gallop 1982, 148–50). This love, of course, has no place in the oedipal narrative, is perceived only as a perversion, an infantile displacement. But in Cixous's play it seems situated not merely in opposition to heterosexuality but more as a bisexuality, an ambiguity, one that makes open or shut a matter of indifference. Frau K. says that bodies have many resources, pointing the way to a multiplicity of opportunities, of subjectivities other than the one imposed by dominant culture.

Cixous communicates this with the very form of the play, which is a hysterical play, in its ambiguity, its rupture of narrative, its resourceful sexuality. This, then, is where Chris began her work as director—to create a piece that would transport the audience into that space of hysteria—open, discontinuous, and without narrative closure.

Encountering *Dora* in Practice by Christine Sumption

Certain plays give directors a sense of closure. *Masterpieces* by Sarah Daniels, *Never in My Lifetime* by Shirley Gee, and *Hedda Gabler* by Henrik Ibsen are among those I count as my most complete directing experiences. Yet years after having directed *Portrait of Dora,* Hélène Cixous's play lingers in my thoughts like a troubling dream . . . elusive, wondrous, haunting, incomplete. I am obsessed by the directorial choices that I made, choices that I *should* have made, and choices that remain outside my imagining. From time to time I go back to the play, thinking: "At last! Now I finally know enough. I will be able to untangle the knot, to hold the play in my hands." And yet, time and again, I find that the play slips through my grasp. It defies attempts to contain and control it.

While most texts define the limits of performance possibilities, *Portrait of Dora* opens them. It presents the director with rich, startling, and seemingly endless opportunities for theatrical invention. It invites, even demands that the director go beyond merely interpreting the text to taking on a truly creative role. The director has to write her own performance text.

My earliest connection to the play was personal as well as political. I was drawn to Cixous's portrait of the family as a suffocating model of oppression in the larger society, a closed unit that seeks to envelop the dangerous secrets of its members. I encountered Dora not as a fixed character but, rather, as a welcoming friend, a troublemaker, a mysterious stranger, and a guide. Her world seemed both familiar and foreign. It both laid out the welcome mat and flashed *Danger!* The play was a terrifying and irresistible challenge.

"Metaphor breaks free; all that belongs to the realm of fantasmatic production, all that belongs to the imaginary and smashes language from all sides represents a force that cannot be controlled. Metaphors are what drive language mad" (Cixous, qtd. in Crowder 1983, 142). I was intrigued by Cixous's use of metaphor as a textual strategy to interrupt the reader's relationship to the text, to unseat logic and provoke imaginative response. Objects, events, actions, places, and even the characters themselves operate on constantly shifting metaphorical levels. Logic is further confounded by swirling questions of identity, contradictions, and uncertainty about what is real, dreamed, imagined, and remembered. The play challenges the logic of cause and effect and of sanity itself.

Central to Cixous's text is the image of a door that transcends simple binary notions of "open" and "closed." It is entrance, exit, passage, and obstruction; it is open *and* closed, active *and* passive. It articulates movement inward *and* outward. When Dora closes the doors of her eyes she simultaneously opens into herself. When Dora exits analysis she enters into the world.

As I prepared to enter into the world of *Portrait of Dora,* I struggled with the insistent question "What performance text shall I write?" The directorial challenge was not simply to stage the play but also to respond to it metaphorically. If the door of the text were a transcendent door, how could I evoke that door on the stage? If the Dora of the text were multiple, contradictory, and unknowable, how could I evoke that Dora on the stage? My questions multiplied as I dug deeper into the play. Finally, however, I took comfort in the realization that I would need to collaborate in a profound way with other artists, since a hierarchical approach was clearly at odds with the text. When the question became "What performance text shall *we* write?" it made all the difference.

Jeanie Forte and I began our work together by exploring Cixous's text, maneuvering through its dream logic, wrestling with its jarring contradictions, and envisioning its theatrical possibilities. Our discussions were wandering and associational. We found it difficult to confine ourselves to logical, point-by-point analysis and began to delight in the way that the text sent us on one fruitful tangent after another. We relished the subversive quality of Cixous's writing and took the first steps toward framing a production that would embody that sensibility.

When the designers joined the working process—Lynn Graves (set and projections), Patty Mathieu (costumes and lighting), Holly Reinhorn (sound), and Scott Lakin Jones (composer)—the collaboration caught fire. We refused to place boundaries on our imaginations but, instead, allowed ourselves to strike sparks off each other. One idea engendered others in a free-fall through the world of dreams, memory, trauma, fin de siècle Vienna, Freud, and Dora. We brain-stormed theatrical parallels to the layers of reality in the text, fanta-sized about using holograms to represent Dora's dreams, projections to represent her memories, and live action to represent physical real-ity. We riffed on notions of scrim and smoke and walls that actors could walk through in order to evoke the play's surreal dreamscape. We discussed amplifying the stage to give the set a voice of its own. We imagined underscoring the production with atonal music and sometimes giving the performance over to music entirely. No idea was ruled out at this early stage, no matter how outlandish, elaborate, or ridiculously expensive. What was important was to unlock our imaginations and allow free-flowing exchange.

For a time the design process wandered. We shared personal experiences and memories triggered by the play—family relation-ships, therapy, sexual assault, conflict with authority figures, and so on. We talked about our dreams. We brought in short stories, poetry, and theoretical articles that shaped our thinking. And we looked at photographs, paintings, architecture, and sculpture. Gradually, a production aesthetic began to emerge.

The set design formed the foundation of that aesthetic. It was to be a space in which opposites could hold true simultaneously, a space that could represent interior and exterior and be instantly, silently, and smoothly transformable from one kind of space to another, just as the text unfolds the layers of dream, fantasy, memory, and present time. Within this space we wanted the door—the play's central im-age—to have the potent metaphorical presence that objects have in dreams . . . quoted from reality, floating in space, with multiple, mysterious meanings.

Lynn Graves, a visual artist designing her first theatrical set, created a sculpture of venetian blinds hung in a modified wing-and-drop formation. Some slats in the blinds overlapped, creating silhou-ettes of nineteenth-century women. These figures could be empha-sized by closing the blinds or made virtually invisible by opening them. And, although the series of blinds seemed to be two-dimen-sional, actors walking through them ruptured that sense of flatness, reminding the audience that they themselves had constructed the im-ages. Lynn framed the venetian blind sculpture within the center of three archways. Upstage she placed an expansive rear projection screen onto which evocative images could be projected so that the environment was constantly transforming. And the venetian blinds served as an additional projection surface on which images could be layered one over the other.

The notion of projections proved productive in our thinking about the costumes. The costume design process traditionally begins with defining character, an act that we felt was inappropriate to Cixous's text, which defies the notion of character as an immutable truth. Consequently, we had to find a way to create costumes that expressed a point of view on fin de siècle Viennese society and the roles of men and women within that world, without constructing characters in the conventional sense. Patty Mathieu designed a collection of elegant garments that quoted the silhouette of the period, while stripping away color and detail. Dora, Freud, and the rest appeared as fluid white forms onto which color and patterns of light could be projected. They were not visual representations of characters but, rather, elusive, ever-changing figures.

Scott Lakin Jones and Holly Reinhorn created a hauntingly beautiful and ultimately disturbing aural world for *Portrait of Dora*. Harp, cello, clarinet, and percussion suggested the familiar, and yet the musical voices were combined in utterly unfamiliar ways. Ordinary sounds were presented out of context: the rhythmic cry of lake birds underscored Freud's analysis of Dora's dream, and the gentle sound of pearls falling to the ground became an ear-splitting clatter.

The success of the design collaboration was a result of the luxury of those months of discussion and experimentation. While the work with actors should have enjoyed the same opportunity to allow ideas to unfold gradually, we were limited to a traditional four-week process. The enormity of the task of approaching this text, developing an appropriate rehearsal process, and engaging with the actors as equal collaborators was something for which we were not fully prepared.

Rehearsing the play was a rewarding but difficult task that required breaking through years of training in psychological acting process. Jeanie helped develop a series of exercises that introduced the actors to the world of the play on a visceral level. Guided meditation, automatic writing, and storytelling games were among the techniques we used to help the actors tap into their imaginations and the "hysterical logic" of the play.[1] Preliminary text work, however, drew on more traditional concepts. We worked in terms of actions and objectives but eliminated the idea of superobjectives. The actors were encouraged to develop choices that encompassed a moment, without connecting one moment to that which preceded or followed. Transitions were lightning quick, to create an exhilarating cascade of contradictions and opposites.

Rehearsal further involved collaboration with the actors to find intersections between the strategies of the text and the staging. We selected key events in the text, explored them physically, and created physical gestures to signify them. The "scene by the lake" for example—in which Mr. K. makes a sexual advance on Dora—developed into a gesture in which Mr. K. approached Dora from behind, encircled her neck with his arm, and kissed her. The gesture became one that we could quote throughout the action, sometimes emphasizing the sexual nature of the gesture, sometimes emphasizing the violence. It appeared when the text specifically referred to the "scene by the lake" and at other times when the gesture stood in counterpoint to the language, as when Dora described to Freud her dream of fire. The gesture seemed to take on a life of its own, disrupting the flow of action with its own insistent voice.

In response to Cixous's textual use of substitution to transform one event into another we developed theatrical substitutions to point up patterns of relationships. The men in the play were often seen grouped together, dressed identically, silently smoking in a kind of male ritual. As each uttered the words "My wife means nothing to me," it became clear that their societal position rendered them virtually interchangeable. When Freud asked Dora to "tell me about the letter," a chain of substitutions unfolded in which Freud was replaced by Mr. B., who was replaced by Mr. K., and so on. The substitutions suggested the associational chain of Dora's invasion by men.

Our exploration of the image of the Sistine Madonna evoked the multiplicity of Cixous's text. Dora says: "I stood for a long time. In front of that painting . . . I stood alone. Completely absorbed. In that painting. For two hours. In its radiance." In our production Dora stood downstage, facing the audience, bathed in warm light. At the same time an image of the Madonna, in the same warm colors, appeared on the projection screen. Dora and the painting seemed to both reflect and emanate light. And when Mrs. K.'s silhouette appeared before the painting it was unclear whether it was she, Dora,

Dora (Cindy Basco) struggles to free herself from the grasp of
Freud (Chuck Noland) in *Portrait of Dora*. Photo by Patty
Mathieu.

or the Madonna who spoke. Dora was inside the painting and outside of it. She was adoring the painting and being adored at the same time.

As the play's central image, the door became a test of how many different ways we could use it: as a port of entry, as an exit route, as a frame, as an object that reveals or conceals, as an object that separates people or brings them together. Sometimes we exploded its function. The door was open, but Dora could not pass through. Mr. K. was hidden behind the door, which suddenly became translucent and revealed his looming shadow. Or the door simply opened of its own accord, no longer a passive object but now a willful, active force articulating its own movement.

At the end of the play Dora exits through the door. But the play does not come to a close in the conventional sense. Dora goes out *and* enters. Her action is an end *and* a beginning. When Dora leaves she ruptures the closed system of patriarchal culture. At the end of our production Dora exited through the door, the eyes of Freud and the others following her departure. She then reemerged through the venetian blind sculpture images of women. As Freud and the others receded into the frame, Dora proceeded downstage toward the audience, never stopping her movement as the lights faded to black.

> These events appear, like a shadow, in dreams, often with such lucidity that one seems actually to be able to grasp them. But despite that effect, they evade any definitive clarification; and if we proceed without particular skill and caution, we find ourselves unable to determine whether or not such an incident has really taken place. (Cixous 1979, 29)

Directing *Portrait of Dora* was for me a continual unfolding of images, ideas, and discoveries. And yet the experience was inconclusive and strangely unsettling. The very openness and discontinuity that had initially attracted me to the text overwhelmed me at times in rehearsal. Each choice, instead of paving the way to the next, illuminated the countless other choices that might have been made. I sometimes found myself paralyzed when working with the actors because I so clearly recognized what I should *not* do, that what I *should* do seemed out of reach. At other times I imposed choices on the actors that intuitively seemed right to me but which I could not articulate. In those instances the actors' physicalizations appeared bound, as if their bodies were obeying directorial command but their minds were rebelling.

Of the production a reviewer wrote, "Director Christine Sumption . . . brings a measure of clarity and coherence to *Portrait of Dora*." At the time I took it as a compliment. Now I imagine that that's where I went wrong.

Perhaps the very act of directing goes against the grain of Cixous's text—that *Portrait of Dora* must be undertaken in a truly collective working process. For to try to direct this play with anything resembling a conventional approach is to attempt to construct the narrative that Dora so resolutely defies.

NOTE

1. For good examples of rehearsal games, see Clive Barker's *Theatre Games: A New Approach to Drama Training* and Keith Johnstone's *Impro: Improvisation and the Theatre*.

REFERENCES

Barker, Clive. 1977. *Theatre Games: A New Approach to Drama Training*. London: Methuen.

Barthes, Roland. 1977. *Image-Music-Text*. New York: Hill and Wang.

———. 1975. *Pleasure of the Text*. New York: Hill and Wang.

Cixous, Hélène. 1979. *Portrait of Dora*. Trans. Anita Barrows. In *Benmussa Directs*. London: John Calder.

Cixous, Hélène, and Catherine Clément. 1986. *The Newly Born Woman*. Minneapolis: University of Minnesota Press.

Crowder, Diane Griffin. 1983. "Amazons and Mothers: Monique Wittig, Hélène Cixous and Theories of Women's Writing." *Contemporary Literature* (Summer): 115–44.

de Lauretis, Teresa. 1984. *Alice Doesn't: Feminism, Semiotics and Cinema*. Bloomington: Indiana University Press.

Freud, Sigmund. 1963. *Dora: An Analysis of a Case of Hysteria*. Edited by Philip Rieff. New York: Collier Books.

Gallop, Jane. 1982. "Keys to Dora." *The Daughter's Seduction: Feminism and Psychoanalysis*. New York: Cornell University Press.

Jardine, Alice. 1985. *Gynesis: Configurations of Woman and Modernity*. Ithaca: Cornell University Press.

Johnstone, Keith. 1979. *Impro: Improvisation and the Theatre*. New York: Theatre Arts Books.

Kemmel, Nancy Lee. "Portrait of Dora Would Make Freud Turn Over in His Grave." *The Daily of the University of Washington,* 24 May 1985.

Lévi-Strauss, Claude. 1984. *Anthropology and Myth.* London: Basil Blackwell.

———. 1969. *The Elementary Structures of Kinship.* Boston: Beacon.

Lyotard, Jean François. 1984. *The Postmodern Condition: A Report on Knowledge.* Trans. Geoff Bennington and Brian Massumi, Minneapolis: University of Minnesota Press.

McCaffrey, Philip. 1984. *Freud and Dora: The Artful Dream.* New Brunswick, N.J.: Rutgers University Press.

Morton, Frederic. 1979. *A Nervous Splendor: Vienna 1888–1889.* New York: Penguin Books.

Mulvey, Laura. 1975. "Visual Pleasure and Narrative Cinema." *Screen* 16, no. 3 (Autumn).

Rubin, Gayle. 1975. "The Traffic in Women: Notes on the 'Political Economy' of Sex." In *Toward an Anthropology of Women,* edited by Rayna Reiter. New York and London: Monthly Review Press.

SUSAN CLEMENT AND
ESTHER BETH SULLIVAN

The Split Subject of *Blood Relations*

Sharon Pollock's *Blood Relations* reads like a good mystery. The audience is faced with a heinous crime, and the drama seems to promise intimate insight into the events surrounding that crime. But this particular telling is not just candy for those of us with an appetite for great detective stories. It is also a play laced with feminist concerns and critiques. In approaching *Blood Relations* for production we committed ourselves to developing a production concept that would support and enhance the feminist message inherent in Sharon Pollock's script rather than erasing or ignoring those intentions. As we established our director/dramaturg team, we used much of our preproduction time for both theoretical and historical research. It was this research that helped us to identify feminist issues in the script and feminist potential in its structure. In thinking about *Blood Relations*—a play that splits the characterization of its central figure, Lizzie Borden, between two performers—we became particularly interested in the critique of the "split subject," which has emanated from feminist film theory. We then set out to relate the notion of a split subject to our production of *Blood Relations*.[1]

Blood Relations takes place during an afternoon in the life of Lizzie Borden, the infamous woman accused and then acquitted of brutally murdering her father and stepmother with an ax in the late 1800s. The play opens ten years after the Borden murders as Miss Lizzie and her lover, the Actress, share tea and conversation. Eventually, the conversation touches upon the one question that continues to plague Miss Lizzie and which the Actress has broached many times before this. In reference to the murders the Actress asks, "Did you, Lizzie? Lizzie, did you?" (95). Miss Lizzie refuses to answer the Actress's question outright, suggesting rather that they play a game. Together they will act out various events that led up to the murders, and from this reenactment the Actress can formulate her own opinion about Miss Lizzie's guilt or innocence. In this game, however, Miss Lizzie insists that the Actress play the title role. *Blood Relations* then progresses through scenes depicted as a play-within-a-play in which Miss Lizzie plays her former housemaid and the Actress plays Lizzie.

In the performance of this play the portrayal of the central figure is one that is split: two different women inhabit the role of "Lizzie." Complicating this split representation is the fact that these two women never fully abandon their original identities. Miss Lizzie never leaves the stage. She steps in and out of bracketed scenes, sometimes playing the role of her housemaid, sometimes commenting upon the events that transpire, and sometimes literally watching her life pass before her eyes. The Actress also remains onstage and shifts between role-playing her lover in a past life and conversing with that same woman in the present. The effect of this split representation is to create a central character that is not physically bound to any one performer onstage. While the split representation of Lizzie is written into the script, the playwright, however, gives few indications about how actually to stage the portrayal of multiple Lizzies. The practical questions that immediately arise are ones regarding the character of Miss Lizzie. In that she remains silent or absent through much of the play-within-a-play, should she be positioned inconspicuously or somehow remain present in the ongoing drama? Through production and research we decided to find ways to emphasize the split representation. We grounded this choice in our reading of feminist film theory. Because this field of study has focused on the dynamics of the "gaze" and the relationship of the spectator to a spectacle, rather than on literary texts, we found this kind of investigation particularly applicable to an analysis of theater. Moreover, in that film theory has developed as a critique and a means with which to intervene, it clarified our feminist understanding of this particular piece of theater. Most important, however, this theory gave us a way of understanding the feminist implications of both the content and the form of *Blood Relations*.[2]

The Split Subject in Theory

Within the field of film theory feminists such as E. Ann Kaplan, Laura Mulvey, and Kaja Silverman have taken on the project of understanding how both the form and content of classic Hollywood cinema are inscribed with gender ideology. Such theory has been articulated in relation to poststructuralist interpretations of psychoanalysis. Envisioning psychoanalysis as a description of how patriarchy continues to acquire significance, Kaplan states, "It is extremely important for women to use psychoanalysis as a tool, since it will unlock the secrets of our socialization within patriarchy" (1983, 24). Employing psychoanalytic concepts as deconstructive "weapons," these particular theorists have established a critique of classic Hollywood cinema. This project includes an investigation into the relationship between the cinematic narrative, the spectacle of the film, and the genderization of its spectators. In other words these theorists have focused on the process of identification, noting the way in which spectators identify with characters in a film and the way in which that process is not gender neutral.

As described by Kaja Silverman, the process of identification that occurs in classic Hollywood films involves a shifting from one "subject position" to another. She locates three subject positions in classic cinema. The "speaking subject" is equated with the power to produce (1983, 197–98). The speaking subject effects the organization of images and is located at the site of production. Rather than attributing this position to the perspective of any one person, be that the director or writer, this position refers to the gaze of the camera and the ideological conditions that would determine what is to be seen. In the classic Hollywood film this gaze controls what is made visible in the film at the same time that it denies its own existence. In this way the movie appears to represent reality rather than an edited and constructed point of view. The second subject position in such films is identified as the "subject of the speech." This refers to the fictional character of the film and is located in the narrative. In classic cinema the subject of the speech is developed as a coherent self, an ego ideal, a person who seems to charge the narrative with purpose and unity. The last subject position described by Silverman is that of the "spoken subject," or the spectator who watches the story unfold (197–99).

Identification occurs between these positions. In classic film this process is driven by desire, or the realization that there is something more to be had. The authority of the speaking subject inspires a desire on the part of the spectator in that the speaking subject possesses the power to articulate and produce meaning. In the position of desiring that authority the spectator is subjugated by a realization of its "lack" of power and productivity. From this position of lack the spectator seeks something more than it now possesses to "fill that lack." In classic cinema that "something more" comes by way of the narrative. According to Silverman, in narrative there is the "intimation of something which has not yet been fully seen, understood, revealed" (215). The spectator then identifies the subject of the speech, or the central figure of the narrative, as one who is in the position to reveal the rest of the story. Not wanting to be cut off from such potential, the spectator "identifies" with this character. Narrative brings about identification by providing ego ideals that not only seem to control the direction of the gaze but which incite action and produce meaning. Despite the "fiction" of this kind of authority, the spectator of classic cinema emerges as a spoken subject. Through identification the spoken subject becomes absent to itself by permitting a fictional character to "stand in" or speak for it (205).

The problem that feminist film critics address in regard to narrative identification in this traditional model is its propensity to define all the subject positions by maintaining their difference from object positions. Within classic cinema this differentiation is often realized by the different ways in which male and female characters are filmically envisioned. Laura Mulvey notes that in such movies the male character is often portrayed as having the capacity to look; the story is shot from his perspective. He is identified through processes such as shot/reverse shot, as the active manipulator of the gaze. The female character, on the other hand, functions to attract the male gaze. She exists to be looked at. Through close-ups she is taken out of the surrounding environment, inspected, and seen as parts—elbows, knees, breasts, etc. Consequently, the female appears as a fetishized object for the voyeuristic pleasure of a male-identified gaze. The construction of male and female characters visually empowers the male subject of the speech by creating him as the originator of the gaze, the possessor of power, and the authoring source. Mulvey argues that this visual distinction and empowering differentiation is then inscribed in spoken subjects as they come to identify with the narrative (1977, 418–21). She further indicts narrative as "sadistic" by arguing that it provides the perfect medium through which to voyeuristically investigate and objectify women. According to Mulvey, "This sadistic side fits well with narrative. Sadism demands a story, depends on making something happen, forcing a change in another person, . . . all occurring in a linear time with a beginning and an end" (422).

Silverman also notes the sadistic sense of narrative. She argues that in the standard format of classic film the narrative begins with some disruption of an existing order. This disruption dislocates the subject by challenging the "subject's ideals of coherence and fullness." As the story reaches its conclusion, a new order is established. Of course, that "new" order is usually a reestablishment of the original order, positions, and ideals (1983, 221). This pattern of reaffirmation, reenactment, and reinscription troubles Silverman in that its ultimate aim appears to be to recover "a sense of potency and wholeness for both the male character and male viewer" (222). As the male spectator "sutures" to the male character through the process of narrative identification, this process creates a discursive privilege. Identification, as it is structured in a "traditional" and "phallocentric" model, establishes subject positions that are different from object positions and empowered on the basis of that difference. In this case sexual difference visually symbolizes this difference. Feminist film theorists recognize the privilege of the sutured subject—a subject joined in narrative and identified as masculine—and call for feminists to effect the disruption of that privilege. According to Claire Johnson, "It is this imaginary unity, the sutured coherence, the imaginary sense of identity set up by the classic film which must be challenged by a feminist film practice" (qtd. in Silverman 1983, 222). The challenge that Johnson articulates for film practitioners is one that is being taken up by dramatists as well. As noted by Elin Diamond, many contemporary female playwrights are "refusing" the "romanticism" of narrative identity and identification by way of "narrative intervention" (1985, 273). Following Diamond's observation that "feminist artists in theatre are well placed to exploit the coercive structure of narrative" (276), we sought to realize the possibility for such a challenge in *Blood Relations*.

The Split Subject in Practice

From our reading of feminist film theory we recognized the importance of employing theatrical means that would foreground the dynamic of the split subject in *Blood Relations* so that the aforementioned pattern of identification might be disturbed. As our production took shape, we sought to accentuate the presence of multiple Lizzies onstage, to use that presence to preclude traditional identification, and to call attention to the male gaze, which usually constructs Woman as an object of desire rather than the subject of action.

We first made a number of directorial choices in order to reinforce the split subject dynamic. Miss Lizzie was always lit with a spotlight as she observed Actress/Lizzie interacting with other characters in the play-within-a-play. There were specific areas on the stage from which she observed the action. All of these were framed in some way: she stood in doorways, on the landing of the staircase, or in the aisles leading into the thrust theater. These technical choices afforded us a way to include Miss Lizzie in every scene by pointing to her presence. As these areas shared the dramatic space with the reenacted scenes, Miss Lizzie was never allowed to fade out of the drama, even as she watched in silence. We also pointed to the dynamic of the split subject by finding ways for Miss Lizzie and Actress/ Lizzie to communicate.

At many points the play seems to focus solely on the reenactment of Lizzie's life. Some lines resonate in multiple ways, however, considering that the Actress is playing the part of her lover and being directed by that same woman who remains onstage. By looking for lines that offered the potential of communication between the two Lizzies, even when none was indicated in the stage directions, no clear boundaries emerged between the play-within-a-play and the present time within which Miss Lizzie observes her past. To create this communication we found it helpful to envision Miss Lizzie in a position similar to that of a director side-coaching an actor. An example of this kind of side-coaching occurred in a scene in which Actress/Lizzie first encounters her sister Emma Borden at the breakfast table. In the play Emma has been disturbed by Lizzie's unladylike voice, which could be heard throughout the house. She reprimands Lizzie:

Emma: If mother heard you, you know what she'd say.

Lizzie: She's not my mother or yours.

Emma: Well, she married our father; if that doesn't make her our mother—

Lizzie: It doesn't.

Emma: Don't talk like that.

Lizzie: I'll talk as I like.

Emma: We're not going to fight, Lizzie. We're going to be quiet and have our breakfast.

Lizzie: Is that what we're going to do?

(98–99)

In a strictly textual reading of this scene the focus is on the interaction between the two sisters. Emma appears as the dutiful daughter. She wants to maintain peace in the household and is concerned that Lizzie mind her manners. As a result of this interchange, both the audience and Actress/Lizzie discover that there are strict rules about behavior within the Borden home. Beyond the boundaries of the written text, however, the dynamic between Actress/Lizzie and Miss Lizzie opens up other possibilities for interpretation and staging. The Actress needs information in order to "get into" her character, which means that she would want to find ways to ask for expositional material from Miss Lizzie. With that as a "given circumstance," when Actress/Lizzie asked, "Is that what we're going to do?" she delivered the question to both Emma and Miss Lizzie. Miss Lizzie nodded yes at the same time that Emma responded yes. These two affirmative answers presented an interesting complexity. Actress/Lizzie found out that she was to sit and be quiet at the breakfast table. That would be the accepted and demanded behavior in this situation. She also learned that this was how Miss Lizzie, her lover and side-coach, had had to behave within her own home. Simultaneously, then, Actress/Lizzie discovered how she should "act" in this scene as well as learning more about Miss Lizzie. With this kind of communication the audience's attention was split, and the relationship between the Actress and Miss Lizzie confounded a coherent, unitary construction of "Lizzie."

Furthermore, in establishing this double communication between the two women the performance commented on the construction of gender and the role of the male gaze in that construction. In the script, these dynamics are at work as Actress/Lizzie encounters

Dr. Patrick, a married man who surreptitiously visits Lizzie on a daily basis in order to flirt with her. Miss Lizzie sets the scene by describing Dr. Patrick to the Actress. When Dr. Patrick enters he calls good morning to Actress/Lizzie, and there is a moment of panic as she realizes that she is not yet ready for this scene to proceed. She responds, "I haven't decided whether it is or it isn't" (102). In our production she addressed this line to both Miss Lizzie and Dr. Patrick. Miss Lizzie then gave the Actress a visual cue to propel her into the Lizzie role as she related to Dr. Patrick.

While Actress/Lizzie is unsure of herself in this scene, Dr. Patrick is absolutely certain about himself and his situation. He knows that he has entered a danger zone. He is a married man flirting with an unmarried woman. His first action is to create an image of Lizzie that is reassuring and safe rather than threatening. Reminiscent of fetishized visions of women in classic cinema, he molds her and builds up her ladylike beauty in order to find a way to alleviate his fear.

> *Dr. Patrick:* The proper phrase is, "Good morning, Dr. Patrick," and then you smile, discreetly, of course, and lower the eyes, just a titch, twirl the parasol—
> *Lizzie:* The parasol?
> *Dr. Patrick:* The parasol, but not too fast; and then you murmur in a voice that was ever so soft and low, "And how are you doin' this morning, Dr. Patrick?" Your education's been sadly neglected, Miss Borden.
>
> (102)

Dr. Patrick seems to authorize the scene by describing an idealized and fetishized version of a woman. This woman is envisioned as if a camera were closing in to gaze on her beauty—a discreet smile, lowered eyes, a twirling parasol. The doctor directs her responses, indicating when she is successful in recreating his vision of femininity. In close reading, however, it is clear that Lizzie is not following the doctor's instructions to perfection, as he needs to correct her with "discreetly, of course," and "but not too fast." In working through this scene we chose to have Lizzie find ways to play with and against the social codes dictated by Dr. Patrick. Gestures were incorporated to comply with each of his commands, so that Actress/Lizzie literally constructed the doctor's idealized woman before him but with an attitude of disbelief. When Dr. Patrick corrected her with the proper greetings she mouthed the words silently, ironically, considering their importance. She smiled when he asked her to smile, but her smile was too demonstrative for him; it was not discreet. Although she was baffled by his suggestion to twirl a parasol when none existed, she conceded to the direction, but her playful gesture was too wild. In the script Dr. Patrick dictates lessons on womanly deportment, and with his gaze he comes to represent the subject empowered to objectify women. *Blood Relations,* however, foregrounds this dynamic rather than assuming that it is natural. As Actress/Lizzie temporarily and playfully complies with the doctor's desires, the real Miss Lizzie witnesses the scene without compliance. In our production this noncompliance was emphasized by placing Miss Lizzie on the stairway landing, which was center stage and elevated. She was lit by a spot and therefore always part of the scene. As Dr. Patrick flirtatiously played around, Miss Lizzie watched in seriousness. This act of observation disrupted the mechanism of suture that usually would allow audience members to identify with Dr. Patrick and his objectification of Lizzie. Because Miss Lizzie was a constant presence in the scene, the audience witnessed the way in which a woman is objectified, but they also saw Miss Lizzie silently resisting that process with her noncompliance.

In *Blood Relations* the play-within-a-play convention provides the opportunity to foreground the gaze, which would traditionally go unnoticed. This dramatic device also makes it possible to foreground the voyeuristic investigation of women that narrative usually imposes. In the script several episodes reenact excerpts from Lizzie's trial. These scenes present the defense lawyer interrogating a witness, questioning the defendant, and delivering his summation speech. In each case the defense attorney exists only as a voice-over, and the drama spotlights a woman onstage. The effect of these scenes is always to put Lizzie within the gaze of the implied jurors, who voyeuristically attempt to ascertain her guilt or innocence. Two of these scenes pose particular staging challenges, inasmuch as the stage directions are minimal or ambiguous at best. In one such scene, which occurs toward the end of act 1, the voice of the defense attorney delivers his summation speech. This speech opens as the defense attorney figuratively places his defendant in the spotlight: he orders what is an implied all-male jury to "look to Miss Borden" (105). He then proceeds to explain all the reasons why she could not have committed the crime: she is from an upstanding family; she could not have wielded the murder weapon; at least she could not have wielded it thirty-two times; and, being a gentlewoman, she could not have killed her stepmother then calmly proceeded to kill her father. The defense lawyer concludes by saying that these are acts of madness, not those of a gentlewoman. Moreover, if the jury were to find Lizzie guilty of such crimes, he warns, "look to your daughters . . . which one of us can lie abed at night, hear a rustle in the hall, a creak outside the door, which of you can plump your pillow, nudge your wife and sleep?" (105).

In order to stage this scene the given ambiguity created by the presence of two Lizzies was emphasized rather than elided. The first words of the defense attorney's speech direct everyone, including the jury, audience, and performers, to look to Lizzie—but to which Lizzie? In this case the two women were directed to look to each other. By responding to the defense lawyer's command in this manner, each woman named the other as the defendant and pointed to the split characterization of Lizzie. Once they were both "on the stand" and literally in the spotlight they listened to the defense lawyer's speech. His case rests on the premise that a gentlewoman could not commit such heinous acts. Consequently, if Lizzie does not behave in a ladylike fashion, the jury might find her guilty. To highlight this condition we developed a series of gestures that indicated the essence of a Victorian gentlewoman. Performed by both Lizzies mirroring each other in stylized movements, these gestures ran as a visual track corresponding to the defense attorney's speech. Each Lizzie carefully wiped her brow, bowed her head, hid her eyes, and came close to fainting at the mention of the murder weapon. By mirroring the gestures while in the courtroom—a place where one is placed to be looked at, investigated, and tried—the gestures took on a level of pointed performance. With this presentational style the scene foregrounded femininity as a construction, more specifically as a construction that a patriarchal culture would go to all ends to defend.

In another of the legal scenes occurring in act 2, the defense lawyer calls on Miss Borden and asks her to recount the events that transpired on the day of the murders. In this case the script does offer some stage directions. It indicates that both Lizzies turn to respond to the defense lawyer, but the subsequent lines are assigned only to

The Actress (Ellen Pritchard) prepares to murder Mr. Borden (William Kennedy) as Lizzie Borden (Sharon Huff) observes the scene in *Blood Relations*. Photo by Patty Mathieu.

Actress/Lizzie. Even though the script says that both women turn to respond, it offers no direction about Miss Lizzie's action while Actress/Lizzie is being interrogated. By incorporating this ambiguity into the piece, however, it creates the possibility of focusing on the kind of meaning that might be produced by the presence of Miss Lizzie as she watches both her own interrogation and the audience witnessing that interrogation. Eventually we blocked this scene so that, as the defense lawyer called Lizzie to the stand, both women turned and positioned themselves with Actress/Lizzie standing directly in front of Miss Lizzie. This position was faintly reminiscent of the mirroring performance in the previous legal scene. When the defense attorney began his questioning Actress/Lizzie responded, leaving Miss Lizzie passive and seemingly on the outside of her own story. Once Actress/Lizzie started to answer the defense attorney's questions Miss Lizzie moved away. She moved only on Actress/Lizzie's lines, a directorial choice that deliberately and technically split the focus. The movements consisted of Miss Lizzie crossing to one side of the stage, scanning the audience in order to see how they were responding to the interrogation, then crossing to the other side of the stage, where she again witnessed the audience's response. These simple yet pointed actions called attention to the voyeuristic qualities of the interrogation—a male voice interrogated a female figure; at the same time an implied all-male jury and the audience sat offstage in the darkness peering in on the scene. On one level this split focus implied that the audience along with the jury was sitting in judgment of Lizzie, participating in the continued defense not of a woman on trial for murder, but, rather, of the patriarchal construction of femininity. Additionally, on a discursive level the split focus precluded the structuring power of the male gaze. Miss Lizzie's presence constantly disavowed the gaze that would construct her as object of desire or as the female figure in need of voyeuristic investigation.

When the spectator of a classic Hollywood film comes to the end of the narrative having identified with the central character, the spectator experiences an illusory sense of completeness. The narrative itself has been overcome, the spectator seems to know all there is to know, and the lack-inspiring mystery no longer exists. Mulvey notes that this closure usually depends upon a conclusion to the male voyeur's interrogation of a female figure. As her guilt is ascertained and her punishment or forgiveness is rendered, the story comes to a close. *Blood Relations* contains a seemingly similar narrative, but the play lacks any neat closure. A traditional oedipal story unfolds in this play: a riddle must be solved, a father has been murdered, and the drama will reveal the murderer. In this case a woman is accused of the murder, and the drama serves as a means to ascertain her innocence or guilt. The performance text, however, confounds a final solution to the mystery. Once again the end of the play-within-the-play is ambiguous. While a murder is indicated by the visual picture of Actress/Lizzie poised and ready to strike her father with an ax, the very next moment robs the audience of that closure. Following a short blackout the script moves from the play-within-a-play to the present, and the Actress is seen to be holding an ax, but no father figure is there. It really has been an afternoon of role playing. When the Actress jumps to the conclusion that Miss Lizzie did kill her parents Miss Lizzie protests. As she points out to the Actress: "I didn't do it. You did" (122). The Actress has been playing Lizzie, and, as such, Miss Lizzie never actually commits the murders. Consequently, as the lights finally go down, there is ambiguity instead of closure. At this moment the performers played with the idea that both women might truly enjoy this ambiguity, and therefore the lights faded slowly with Miss Lizzie and the Actress verging on laughter, taking delight in their time together.

In the shape of an unsolved mystery *Blood Relations* exposes the socialization of women in a patriarchal society. It does so by using the device of a play-within-a-play, which realizes a split subject on-stage. As we worked on this play, we found that the split subject theatrically represented the contradiction of the female subject: while she struggles to be named the producer of meaning, she finds herself enmeshed in a system dependent on her object status. Consequently, we sought to give life to this contradiction by foregrounding the split characterization of Lizzie. Our dramaturgical examination of feminist film theory led to specific directorial choices that we feel more fully represented the feminist potential of this play.

NOTES

1. For this production Susan was the director, and Beth served as the dramaturg. Throughout this article we use the collective voice to discuss our production, since much of what we are focusing on here relates to decisions that were specific to the implementation of theory into practice.

2. Trying to find a way to discuss the layered characterization in this article is as complicated as it was to stage. We will use the name "Miss Lizzie" to indicate the performer/character who is identified as the "real" Lizzie Borden in the script. "The Actress" will refer to the performer who plays Miss Lizzie's lover, but this name will be specific to her "real" identity, and "Actress/Lizzie" will refer to her when she is role-playing the part of Lizzie. We will use the name "Lizzie" to refer to the general character of Lizzie Borden, independent of which performer is playing that part.

REFERENCES

Diamond, Elin. 1985. "Refusing the Romanticism of Identity: Narrative Interventions in Churchill, Benmussa, and Duras." *Theatre Journal* 37, no. 3: 273–86.

Kaplan, E. Ann. 1983. *Women and Film: Both Sides of the Camera*. New York: Methuen.

Mulvey, Laura. 1977. "Visual Pleasure and Narrative Cinema." *Women and the Cinema: A Critical Anthology*. Edited by Karyn Kay and Gerald Peary. New York: Dutton.

Pollock, Sharon. 1984. *Blood Relations*. In *Plays by Women: Volume Three*, edited by Michelene Wandor. London: Methuen.

Silverman, Kaja. 1983. *The Subject of Semiotics*. New York: Oxford University Press.

JULI THOMPSON BURK

Top Girls and the Politics of Representation

In the fall of 1987 I directed Caryl Churchill's *Top Girls* (1982) at the University of Hawaii as part of the Department of Theatre and Dance's mainstage season. The play presents an interesting challenge for the materialist-feminist director. Read from the point of view of the dominant ideology of Western culture, *Top Girls* is a play about a successful if somewhat heartless career woman, Marlene, and her bitter working-class sister, Joyce. Read from the perspective of this materialist-feminist, however, the play shifts its focus to the sacrifices Marlene has had to make to achieve success and the choices women like Marlene and her sister, Joyce, don't have in contemporary society. I knew that the production would have to ask the audience to read against their normal patterns, those of the patriarchal social system, to see this play from within a different framework.

I had read and much admired Nancy Hartsock's *Money, Sex, and Power* (1983), and, as I began to plan my production, I decided to explore her contention that class society is the means by which women participate in their own oppression (262). In other words the power relations that define success in the capitalist world are a *result* of the oppression of women. In order to maintain and preserve society as it is known in the Western world today both men and women participate in the oppression of women. Using Hartsock's model, I saw *Top Girls* as a play that provided a framework wherein the theoretical critique of success in the Reagan/Thatcher era illuminated the underlying oppression of the capitalist economic system. What I wanted to achieve in this production was a performance text that presented the script as a question about the cost of Marlene's success, where Marlene was neither villain nor victim but, instead, a combination of the two. In this way I could examine how success is often oppression in disguise. What follows is my analysis of the play and a discussion of the ways in which I attempted to incorporate my conclusions on the stage in terms of characterization, staging, and production design.

The Analysis

At the level of plot Churchill's *Top Girls* examines the life and relationships of Marlene, a politically conservative, dynamic, single career woman who has just been promoted to managing director of the Top Girls Employment Agency in London. She is juxtaposed with her politically progressive, bitter, divorced sister, Joyce, who has spent her life in the domestic world raising a child and working in her own home and those of the wealthy women in her small, dying English town. The opening scene is Marlene's celebration of her promotion to managing director of the employment agency, a party at which she is the only contemporary character (other invited guests include Pope Joan, Patient Griselda, Lady Nijo, and Isabella Bird, all characters from history, literature, folklore, and art). Following her promotion celebration the scenes of the play move through exchanges with her office mates the following Monday, some interviews with applicants to the agency, and a scene taking place in Marlene's hometown, where her sister still lives and is raising Marlene's illegitimate daughter. While Marlene does not appear in every scene, the progression of events is chronological following the celebration. The final scene of the play departs radically from the chronology, taking place at Joyce's one year before Marlene's promotion. As a result, it informs all the events presented before it, standing in counterpoint to the dominant ideology that would label Marlene a successful, if heartless, businesswoman.

The characters attending the opening party embody various historical myths of women's success, but the disaffection and alienation apparent in each woman's tale provide the necessary framework in which the opposite positions of Marlene and Joyce are constellated. The temporal dislocation of the earliest of the narrative events—the confrontation between the sisters—focuses attention on some of the costs associated with Marlene's success. Other structural elements that support my interpretation include the exclusion of men from the stage, the use of multiple characterization to emphasize socially influenced character traits, and the designation of the figure of the child (in this case Angie) as the theatrical locus of the intersection between the personal and the political.

In presenting *Top Girls* I wanted to question the nature of Marlene's success and its consequences for herself and others. Instead of creating a drama that glorified or crucified this career woman, I attempted to demonstrate how Marlene can only be considered successful within a market-driven sphere. Hartsock sees the capitalist system as a set of power relations revolving around the buyer and seller as points of reference. This buyer and seller need one another to survive but at the same time seek to consume one another, a relation that alienates one from the other. Within the market-oriented system Marlene's appointment to managing director over a male colleague of greater seniority appears to be a banner of achievement for women, what some might call a feminist victory. Her new position prompts her to comment in the first scene, "Well, it's not Pope . . . [but] it's worth a party" (13). Close examination of Marlene's victory celebration in the first scene reveals an unusual situation: all of her guests are from the distant past—none of them coworkers, real-life friends, or family. This lack of personal relationships is irrelevant to the consideration of market-oriented success. The resonance of Marlene's lack of contemporaries at the celebration is based on a paradigm located in another sphere of activity.

Having watched Marlene proceed through the weeks following her promotion, the final scene takes place out of chronology, before the events of the play began. Marlene travels to the town of her birth to visit her sister, and during this encounter we find out that her sister, Joyce, has raised Marlene's illegitimate daughter, Angie. Coupled with an earlier scene in which Marlene nervously questions Angie about the nature of her surprise visit, it becomes clear that the path to Marlene's success has been paved with Joyce's labor. Within the market-oriented model this situation has no relationship to Marlene's success.

While the terms of Marlene's success would appear completely justified within the market-oriented model, the oppression Marlene both suffers and participates in to achieve success became the object of examination in my production. As the play progressed, I wanted to show that her success rests on her acceptance of patriarchal capitalist structures, the power relations they create, and the self-evacuation necessary to exist within their boundaries. Hartsock's theorization of the relationship between class and gender provides a methodology to account for these costs. First, in accepting patriarchal-capitalist structures Marlene must accept her life activity as a commodity with the concomitant dehumanization that ensues. Second, in accepting the power relations created by the market-oriented model of the patriarchal-capitalist structure Marlene must construct and internalize what Hartsock calls a masculine self, which exists "in opposition to the concrete world of daily life, by escaping from contact with the female world of the household" (241). Third, in accepting the self-evacuation necessary to achieve and maintain success in the patriarchal-capitalist system Marlene must resign herself to the estranged relations with others that result from her own estranged labor. From this vantage point the price of success for Marlene appears incredibly high and demonstrates that, in the process of obtaining success in this system, she not only participates in it by oppressing others but becomes a victim of its oppression as well.

Accepting one's life activity as a commodity, and the concomitant separation from others, Hartsock contends, is related to the rejection of the concrete world of daily life, which is located squarely in the realm of traditional female labor. This rejection of material reality begins in the family, where children (particularly male children) learn that nothing is to be gained from the concrete world of the household and everything is to be gained from the abstract world of politics, or public life (241). Substituting Marlene's success for what Hartsock describes as masculinity reveals another price she must pay. Marlene has learned that the female world of the household is a useless one that must be rejected in order to obtain success in masculine terms, the only terms available. Her interview with a young job applicant in act 1, scene 2, is an example of this attitude. Early in the interview Jeanine reveals that she is saving to get married, though she is not wearing an engagement ring. Despite Jeanine's protestations, Marlene assumes that Jeanine will work only until she marries or until she begins to bear children. Both her treatment of Jeanine and her discussion in the last scene of how vehemently she desired to free herself from the situation of her mother (and other women in her hometown) illustrate that Marlene completely rejects any possibility of value in the concrete world of daily life. Believing that their mother had a wasted life, she tells Joyce, "I had to get out, I knew when I was thirteen, out of their house, out of them, never let that happen to me, never let him, make my own way, out" (Churchill 1982, 85).

A major result of rejecting the female-inhabited world of daily life is the establishment of one of the principal components of success, the role of what Hartsock, following Martin Hollis and Edward Nell, calls "the rational economic man." Accepting this role carries with it a forced self-evacuation, a price Marlene has paid. This rational economic man operates as a perfectly rational agent, unrestricted by emotion. Hartsock describes these frequently isolated people who drive the market-oriented model as "individuals whose very humanity is based on their independence from the wills of others . . . since they owe nothing to the community as a whole, either for who they are or for the resources they possess."[1] Associations between rational economic men can occur only through the exchange of things, objects, and not through personal relationships. Marlene, in her quest for success, accepts the role of rational economic man and suffers the resulting self-evacuation. Her encounter with her sister in the final scene of the play illustrates both the means and the end of the acceptance. In this scene the community to whom she feels she owes nothing survives in the remnants of her immediate family: her mother in the nursing home; her sister, Joyce; and her child, Angie. Marlene's alienation from these individuals is complete, and the basis of her relationship with them is characterized in the presents she brings. Whiskey for Joyce and a dress for Angie satisfy what Marlene rationalizes as a perfectly justified exchange of holiday gifts and assuage her guilt for not delivering them in a timely manner. Joyce rarely drinks, and the dress for Angie, while it is the correct size, is unfortunately more appropriate for the nine-year-old whom Marlene last visited than for the sixteen-year-old she now finds. The difference is illustrative: Angie at sixteen must soon, like Marlene, face the possibility of reproduction and, like Marlene, is unprepared.

Marlene's success can only be a positive achievement when viewed from the perspective of the market-oriented model she has accepted. The play's focus shifts, however, when it is read from the perspective of a materialist-feminist model of reproduction. As such, it identifies the ideology Marlene has accepted and reveals that, within the market-oriented model, success can be achieved only at the expense of both Marlene and the women she oppresses. The first scene of the play, the celebration, ends with the line "How marvelous while it lasted," although the party has completely degenerated (Churchill 1982, 29). The final moment succinctly expresses the critique offered by the play: after Marlene has rejected Angie the last line consists of Angie's single word, "Frightening" (87). The price of success in the Reagan/Thatcher patriarchal-capitalist world, perhaps great while it lasts, is ultimately truly frightening.

The Realization

I was convinced that the structure and details of the text supported my interpretation of *Top Girls* as problematizing Marlene's success. The challenge now was to create a performance text that did not rely completely on the last scene to establish for the audience that Marlene is as much a victim as she is victimizer, that she is as alienated as alienating, and that her spectrum of opportunity has been severely limited by the options available to her as a woman. The following provides examples from characterization, staging, and production design that I used in order to prevent my audiences from relaxing into a traditional patriarchal reading of the play, which would render Marlene little more than a "bad mommy" who abandoned her child for life in the fast lane.

Characterization

The text of *Top Girls* provides the audience with almost no moments in which Marlene is other than her impersonal businesslike self. Even when she is "entertaining" in the play's first scene, she is calm, cool, and in control. There is only a brief section of her exchange with Joyce in the final scene in which Marlene lets down her powerful demeanor to reveal a desire to be wanted by her sister, needed in some unarticulated way. Structurally, this moment occurs very late in the text, so it was important for me to provide a double edge to Marlene's hardened exterior throughout the production. Instead of relying on this moment to erode her tough image entirely because of her tears, I worked to question her take-charge attitude.

My first step in this effort was to cast against Marlene's hard exterior. I cast a talented actress, who had to play against her own distaste for the kind of woman Marlene had become. It played as a distaste on *Marlene's* part for that part of herself that was still vaguely aware of how she had sold out. In addition, Marlene was comfortable only when she was in a business rather than personal situation. This included the play's opening scene, which I interpreted to be a sort of professional survivors' hall of fame created by Marlene.

While refusing to vilify Marlene, I also felt it necessary to resist the temptation to idealize Joyce or portray her simply as a victim. While neither sister is ultimately sympathetic, Joyce has fed, clothed, looked after Marlene's illegitimate child, and remained in a less-than-stimulating environment out of family loyalty. Her politics are diametrically opposed to Marlene's, who thinks Maggie Thatcher is great, saying, "I'd give her a job," to which Joyce replies: "What good's a woman if it's her? I suppose you'd have liked Hitler if he was a woman. Ms. Hitler. Got a lot done, Hitlerina" (Churchill 1982, 84). But to portray Joyce simply as the victim ignores her emotional battering of Angie, her acceptance of her father's physical battering of her mother, and Marlene's challenge: "You could have left" (76).

Instead of portraying Joyce as a martyr to the needs of her family (which the traditional "bad mommy" interpretation demands), I worked to emphasize her bitterness at the failure of her martyrdom, as it is expressed in her anger toward Angie and Marlene. Accepting the traditional role of wife and mother has brought Joyce nothing but hardship. In withholding a positive protagonist for the audience to identify with, I hoped to problematize the choices both sisters made. At the same time I wanted to emphasize the fact that, once each woman chose between career and family, there were few options open to her regardless of the current myth that anything is possible. For women in the 1980s as well as those in the historical past presented in the play's first scene there are far fewer choices than Western culture would have us believe.

The opening scene in which Marlene celebrates her promotion with women from cultural and social history presents a series of challenges. Among them is how to portray each of the women and how to characterize Marlene's relationship to these figures. What I tried to do was to position them as successful people (for the most part) in Marlene's opinion. But I also wanted the audience to see how each woman's apparent success rested upon her ultimate oppression. Thus, we portrayed the historical characters as contradictions, not successes. They rarely even appeared to listen to one another, happier to relate their own stories than to try to understand one another's experiences. And their party, as if to predict the ultimate quotient of satisfaction in Marlene's life, degenerates into complete chaos.

In casting the historical women I was able to make one point clear, which resulted directly from producing the play in Hawaii. Because these women were for me Marlene's fiction, created from her sense of what is successful, I deliberately cast a Caucasian woman as Lady Nijo, the woman from tenth-century Japan. The ethnic mix in this university made it obvious that if I had wanted an Asian woman to play Nijo I could have cast her easily.

Staging

There are several moments that I would like to cite as examples of how this play can be produced from the materialist-feminist perspective to question the price of Marlene's success rather than vilify her for her choices. Some have criticized the play for what they see as a lack of consistency in the portrayal of Marlene as oppressed victim rather than simply oppressor. They see the final scene as some sort of *deus ex machina* that does not deliver the necessary challenge to Marlene's apparent success.

I began questioning Marlene's success as early as the opening scene in which she celebrates her promotion with the historical characters. Not only did I want to make it clear that she had included no family or workplace friends in the gathering, I also wanted to point out the fact that these historical characters are Marlene's heroes, not necessarily those I or anyone in the audience might choose. As such, they are alienated from one another; they do not listen to one another very carefully and are constantly interrupting to tell their own stories rather than hear out one of the other guests. To emphasize this point a long rectangular table was used at which the women sat only on one side, allowing the interactions to be staged so that they were more like monologues than conversation.

This same strategy was carried over into the interview situations in the employment agency. There are three interviews during the course of the play. In the first Marlene interviews young Jeanine, a woman about to get married, who wants a better job; in the second Win interviews Louise, an older woman, who is tired of seeing the young men she has trained promoted; and in the third Nell interviews

Shona, a fast-talking, streetwise woman whose whole file turns out to be false. In all three situations the interviewer seldom looked at the woman she was talking to, while each of the three interviewees desperately tried to make eye contact. Of the three Marlene pointedly was the most alienated from the human being opposite her, had the least eye contact with her interviewee, and frequently checked her watch to see how much time was left. Marlene's success at the employment agency is directly related to her lack of sympathy for the interviewee and her ability to quickly size up a person as a commodity in her own advancement.

In the play's chronologically displaced final scene we see Marlene in a personal environment for the first time. (Her party to celebrate her promotion was not in her home but, instead, in a restaurant, the traditional location of networking and business meals.) She is not comfortable in this place, which reminds her of her own upbringing, of the family she has tried to reject and forget, and of the messiness of personal entanglements. After Angie has gone to bed Joyce and Marlene argue over the progression of events at the time of Angie's birth, and Marlene finally dissolves in tears, her feelings hurt that Joyce is not bothered at all by the six years since her last visit. Joyce responds by saying: "Don't grizzle, Marlene, for God's sake. Marly? Come on, pet. Love you really. Fucking stop it will you?" (Churchill 1982, 81). I staged this with Joyce coming across the set to Marlene and sitting by her to pat and comfort her. Even though Marlene's feelings were hurt when Joyce appeared indifferent to her absence, I directed Marlene to recoil from Joyce's caresses, uncomfortable with physical contact beyond the businesslike handshake.

The final moment of the play, when Angie comes back downstairs after Joyce has gone to bed, calling "Mum?" further illustrated Marlene's discomfort with physical closeness. She decides to continue the ruse that Joyce is Angie's mother by refusing to answer to Mum and responding: "No, she's gone to bed. It's Aunty Marlene" (Churchill 1982, 87). At this point Marlene was seated on the upstage edge of the sofa, wrapped in a blanket, having a last drink before sleep. Angie came into the room, crossed to the sofa, sat beside her for the last exchange of conversation, and after her final word, "Frightening," laid herself across Marlene's lap. This image was deliberately staged to ironically invoke Michelangelo's Pietà,[2] visually confirming Marlene's historical inability to maintain close family ties and her complete alienation from the experience and commitment of motherhood.

This choice was particularly successful in this heavily Catholic state. It was an image that called to mind the sacrifices women make and the extent of Marlene's alienation from herself and from her child. She did not cuddle up with or to Angie in this moment but remained quite stiff, very different from the sculpture of the Virgin, who cradles her son lovingly in her lap. I hoped that the image would have a double edge and was pleased that one of the male reviewers did in fact make the connection.

Production Stage Design

In addition to characterization and staging I sought to bring resonances of my production concept into the visual elements on the stage, to create an atmosphere of little comfort and few options. Four aspects of the stage design that directly related were the use of hard right angles, gray tones in almost all furniture, sparseness of objects, and no distinction in style between the furniture in the employment agency, the restaurant, and Joyce's flat.

Each of the locations of the play—the restaurant, the employment agency (an office and an interviewing room), Joyce's backyard, and Joyce's flat—were scaled down to the least number of objects necessary for the action. I felt this would underscore the barrenness of Marlene and Joyce's lives, that they lived to survive rather than enjoy, having no other options. While Joyce had no money for decorations or small comforts, Marlene had no interest in them. The only location in which there were objects not directly related to the action of the scene was in the restaurant. There we used a few objects related to the historical characters, placing them carefully so as to suggest as little ambience as possible. Joyce's backyard was completely devoid of vegetation, and the fort built by the two young girls consisted of a grocery cart on its side, a tattered sheet, and a few bricks. The emptiness of each location suggested the sense of emptiness in life when there are few options and great responsibilities.

We built all the furniture for the production, using nothing commercially available (as those pieces are generally designed for comfort and ease). The chairs, desks, and tables onstage were without round edges or cushions. The unforgiving right angles were heightened by cross pieces that were in full view. What these lines did to the bodies of the actors who used the furniture was evident: nothing was comfortable, and it looked it.

We also used exactly the same furniture design for the employment offices and Joyce's flat, as a means of equating the two environments. While Joyce's "home" was not more comfortable than the employment agency, neither was the office more sophisticated and high-tech than Joyce's flat. It was important that neither location become identified as a haven; both appeared as alienated and alienating spaces.

The furniture was all painted gray, and the floor treatments were also in a shade of gray. We made no attempt to try to create wood grain finishes, which would have looked rich and natural by comparison. The lack of color was intended to reinforce the lack of choice, just as the lack of different kinds of places to sit suggested the lack of real options for the women in the play.

Using Hartsock's model as the underpinning for my analysis of *Top Girls* helped me to find ways to theatricalize the price of success for women in a capitalist society. For me and, I hope, for the spectators who attended this production Marlene was not simply a heartless woman who had abandoned her child for life in the fast lane of the business world. Instead, her life as presented by Churchill in *Top Girls* illustrates the dangerous and complex situation faced by many women in advanced capitalism, in which the consequences of success are almost as frightening as those of failure.

NOTES

1. Hartsock paraphrasing C. B. MacPherson, *The Political Theory of Possessive Individualism* (New York: Oxford University Press, 1964), 263.
2. I realize that calling up the image of the Pietà was a dangerous choice for a feminist who does not accept the oppression of any organized religion, let alone the Catholic mythology. I used it, however, as a relatively well-known image, to counterpoint the traditional role of mother with Marlene's situation.

REFERENCES

Churchill, Caryl. 1982. *Top Girls*. London: Methuen.

Hartsock, Nancy. 1983. *Money, Sex, and Power: Toward a Feminist Historical Materialism.* New York: Longman.
MacPherson, C. B. 1964. *The Political Theory of Possessive Individualism.* New York: Oxford University Press.

ELLEN DONKIN

Black Text, White Director: Issues of Race and Gender in Directing African-American Drama

In the fall of 1986 I directed a production of Aishah Rahman's *Unfinished Women Cry in No Man's Land while a Bird Dies in a Gilded Cage*. This project framed itself as a question, one that I think is urgent and which I hope will get the attention it deserves from the academy at large. The question is twofold: first, whether or not an academic white director can or should direct nonwhite drama; and, second, to what extent the lessons of feminist theory, and of women's liberation, which was itself originally shaped and formed by African-American liberation, can throw light on the process of a white director encountering an African-American dramatic text.

Put a slightly different way, there is a critical shortage of directors of color right now in academic institutions. Students of color in these same institutions, many of whom are already under pressure to bypass the arts for preprofessional programs of study, are often doubly reluctant to undertake a storming of the barricade. In the meantime the campus theaters continue to generate representations on the stage that reinforce the public perception of *student* as white and *minority* as minor. Faculty directors respond to a situation that is in good part of their own making by declaring that there are no minority actors and that, as a consequence this year, again, there can be no minority show. The campus theater becomes a locus for erasure of the minority student presence and for that reason carries a special burden of responsibility for figuring out a way forward.

The issue has to be carefully contextualized: a white director needs to be clear that the immediate project at hand is to actively

Rehearsing the final birthing scene from *Unfinished Women Cry in No Man's Land while a Bird Dies in a Gilded Cage* by Aishah Rahman. Monica Stancil as Wilma, Ellen Donkin directing. Photo by David Daigle.

intervene in the exclusionary cycle of canonical shows and to invest in a new generation of directors who may someday enter academic theater as colleagues. It is not a substitute for having directors of color; it is a transitional measure toward training those directors. Traditional white liberalism warns that the white director working on a black play may be preempting a director of color, or that she or he will impose white cultural values on a black text. I suspect the first issue can only be resolved at each individual institution on a case-by-case basis. On the second issue I want to offer some thoughts about the way my work on *Unfinished Women* forced me to rethink the role of the director as it has been handed down to us by traditional director training programs in the academy and by professionals outside the academy. A director's personal style is one element among many in the complex system called mode of production, which sees to it that whatever is produced ultimately reproduces dominant ideology. The way we direct is part of that system, and we need therefore to become conscious of our own processes. It is exactly at this juncture that feminist analysis can intervene.

To begin with the model of director as "interpreter" of the text is full of the kinds of bogus neutralities and veiled authority that feminists have been exposing in literature and literary criticism for the past twenty years. In the instance of a white director working on an African-American play text the real functions of the position of director become even more blatantly exposed as a form of colonialism. I call it the Stanley/Livingstone syndrome: the true job of the director is to come into the dark continent of the text and bring civilization: name the waterfalls after the Imperialist Queen, lay down some roads for easy access to treasure, confine big game to parks to make hunting easier, and bring religion and smallpox to the natives. Gertrude Stein understood plays as landscapes, and the metaphor is a useful one here. Houston Baker, Jr., in his article "Caliban's Triple Play," describes the ways that European travel narratives of the nineteenth century tend to sentimentalize and romanticize the landscape and to describe it devoid of its inhabitants.

> What never appears in such narrations is the I/Eye itself, or the indigenous inhabitants as people *in a functional relationship to the landscape* [my emphasis]. Instead, an objective voice domesticates and normalizes the landscape, recording it with an eye always in the service of European "science." The I/Eye as an organ and agent of state power—an advance prospector revealing dramatic economic advantages available from a pliant landscape—is always bracketed. Similarly the indigenous people are bracketed—separated from chapters of landscape narration into descriptive chapters labelled "Manners-and-customs of the natives." (386)

If, as white director, I understand the play as a landscape and enter it as pliant territory to be shaped, I will have bracketed the indigenous voices, replaced those voices with my own, and, before rehearsals even begin, damaged the relationship of the actors to their landscape by imposing the rhythms, expectations, and pacing required by white audiences. The putative black audience will not even have been considered.

This kind of directing is a form of plunder; it raids the text of the play for the state by using theater production to temporarily put *liberal* back into the liberal arts. The black assistant director is exploited as a kind of native guide who teaches the white explorer the language, shows her the path to water, and later is either discarded or sent off to colonial schools for further indoctrination.

As white director, I may only enter the text of an African-American play in a position of inquiry (as distinct from the missionary position). This is vitally distinct from the kind of neutral passivity that characterizes white liberalism and which ultimately is only a postponement of aggression on both text and actors by a disappointed and furious white director; Alice Childress's play *Trouble in Mind* is an explicit reenactment of this kind of aggression.

This position of inquiry raises a second point, which is another long-term feminist concern, the issue of difference. One of the precepts of liberalism, as I inherited it, was that equality meant collapsing difference, looking for the universal humanity in all of us. Cultural feminism, which is becoming increasingly controversial, looks for the universality of womanhood in similar ways. As an alternative, I want to suggest to white directors that being white is not a transparency, not a neutral and benevolent stewardship, but that it is a very specific position that has to be clarified relative to gender, sexual preference, and class. This clarifying of the director's position does two things: it shifts authority for the life of the play onto the playwright and the actors living inside of that text. It also sets up a prototype for difference within the black community itself.

To be more specific Aishah's play addresses itself directly to issues of class difference within the black community, so it became important to let difference surface, especially in our informal socializing and warming up before rehearsal or during breaks. We talked about Keely Respass's growing up in the rural South and the influence the church had on her growing-up years. Wendy Elliott talked about growing up in the West Indies in which the dominant culture was (at least nominally) black, and Aida Allen talked about her plans for finishing school as a single mother. Monica Stancil described growing up in Newark and never seeing a white face except on television

Monica Stancil as Wilma, as she goes into labor: "Oh God it hurts! I wish I could sing!!!" Photo by David Daigle.

until she was almost ten years old; I talked about growing up in Connecticut and never seeing a black face, especially not on television, until I was about ten years old. Julio Dicent, one of the two men in the production, who was also of Puerto Rican descent, was cast as the play's curiously liminal master of ceremonies, Charlie Chan, a "black man in blackface," as Aishah says in her script (205). Of all of us he was the most vocal and articulate about the ways in which racism links arms with sexism, homophobia, and ageism; his political analysis in our discussions set a note for our collective awareness and for his character's shaping presence in the play.

The third point has to do with the issue of collaboration. Our designer for the show, Wayne Kramer, who also directed one of the twelve scenes for me, commented to me once that he had seen more collaborative directing on this show than he was used to. It may have been in part because the show grew out of a class on black drama, that the students in rehearsals at night were the same students in class in the mornings, and that the play was constantly being absorbed and rethought by all of us. Toward the middle of the rehearsal process, when I had exhausted my ideas for solving the final moments of the play (in which one character dies and a second gives birth), a visiting performance artist and dancer came to rehearsal one night and spontaneously offered to try to restage the final scene. The results were magical. I also had two assistant student directors, and all three of us regularly gave notes after each rehearsal. I brought in visiting lecturers for the class to rehearsal, I consulted over the phone with Aishah, and, for the final production, both Aishah and the founders of Boston's New African Company, Lynda Patton and Jim Spruill, came to critique the show.

In other words collaboration was part of the process of disinvesting the director of authority over the text, of decentralizing that "interpretive" process. Here it is helpful, however, to insist on a distinction between internal discipline (issues such as coming to rehearsal on time, learning lines, remembering blocking) and artistic authority. It is *artistic* authority that is at issue; *artistic* authority is what seeks collaboration and must decentralize if the mode is really to be one of inquiry. One characteristic of liberalism has been to collapse discipline and artistic authority, so that poor discipline in rehearsals gets equated with decentralization of authority. Ultimately, the pattern it sets up is to ensure failure of the production and of the working relations of the production, so that no further "minority" drama is seen to be possible because of unreliability, lateness, poor discipline—all the things that the director has in fact set up as expectations.

My last point has to do with dramatic structure. Aishah's play is about the day on which Charlie Parker, the great saxophonist, died. He is uptown at an expensive hotel under the care of a wealthy white jazz patroness named Pasha as the play opens, sick in body and spirit. In another part of New York, in a rundown "Hide-a Wee Home," a group of young single women, three of them African American, one Puerto Rican, and one white, wait to give birth to their babies. It is

1955. The immediate dramatic question is whether these young women should keep their babies. But Charlie Chan, the moderator, asks the larger structural question posed by the play: "Hide-a-Wee Home for Unwed Mothers, and Pasha's Boudoir. What is the connection between the two events? Simply that it all happened in the same moment. Time stands still. It is only we who are driven in distorted circles, and only those of us who have chewed water know it has bones!" (206). We understood these lines to mean that simple chronological development was going to be withheld from us in this play (we were right). The chewing of water and discovering it had bones was resonant for me with the invisible and inexorable workings of a dominant ideology. So the play—perhaps—was going to be about how ideology had worked to separate Parker from these pregnant women and what that meant for the future of these unborn babies. If the two events, Parker's death and the babies' births, *were* connected, then discovering that connection and reconnecting them, which is what Charlie Chan does in the play, would be a spatial enterprise and not a chronological one. The two worlds would have to touch each other again, be reconnected, for life to continue. Wilma, the central character among the young women, remarks once, "Charlie Parker played in tongues!" suggesting that she heard him as if he were speaking a language. The reconnecting of Parker with his community, with the women who can *hear* his work, is the moment for the artist of the song escaping the gilded cage; as Wilma's child is born, its first cries are the wails of a tenor sax. Parker's death gives life; his music gives continuity, coherence, and language to the community if they will hear it.

As Keely Respass pointed out in class, not only does the community need Parker's music in order to be able to find its way, but so does Parker also need the community. Without Parker the community splinters, gives away its babies, invests itself in upward mobility and assimilation; when the music plays again, people are regrouped as a community and become conscious again of their history and of its impact on the present. When Parker plays, the Ogun/Obatala division in Yoruba mythology is healed, and Obatala's music shapes the new child in the womb so that it can be born. But without the community, in his gilded cage, surrounded by whites who cannot hear the tongues, Parker sickens and dies. Without the community the artist becomes sterile; the community, without the artist, bears unfinished children who are given away and loses its collective sense of history and direction and purpose.

A friend once told me that she believed that jazz had little or nothing to do with "relaxation" or "recreation" after a day's work. For her, at least, it had everything to do with teaching at a predominantly white college and needing to be put back together again at the end of a day, as a member of an African-American community. Jazz put her pieces back together, reconstituted her. Her story threw some light on a moment of the play: one of the characters of the play, Paulette, who is from an upwardly mobile black family and is determined to get rid of her baby, says: "I grew up in my father's house and was never allowed to call him anything but 'sir.' 'Yes, sir.' You do understand that cultured Negroes listen to classical music, not jazz. 'Oh, yes, sir.' And now it's 'You will give up your baby for adoption so you can come home and be my daughter again.' Oh, yes, sir" (229). Rahman's script seems to be pointing to the dangers of assimilation by telling us that there is an important connection to be made between losing music and losing children and, with them, the sense of self. Paulette's weaning from jazz by her anxious father constitutes a loss of both self and community, and it is this loss in Parker and the women that the play reveals and explores.

Nothing prepared me for the thematic and intellectual complexity of this script, but feminism had at least formally prepared me for a text that was structured on spatial contiguities rather than on chronological continuities.[1] In an article on Hrosvitha in which she cites Luce Irigaray's essay "This Sex Which Is Not One," Sue-Ellen Case explores models for dramatic structuring that have to do with touching, rather than with the chronological causalities of realism (Case, 536–39). Only at the end does Parker's space intersect with that of the women; he moves toward Wilma as she goes into labor and, at the moment of birth, falls backward between her legs, dying and being born at the same moment. Some people who saw the play commented that it felt structurally flawed, that the connection between the two narratives was not clear until the very end, that its shape was that of an open-ended triangle. In the end I was unable to respond because I had difficulty viewing this landscape with any objectivity, but it seemed to me then, and still does, that this "structural problem" is exactly the point of the play and that the discomfort it causes is a space in which we are educated rather than tranquilized.

The model of "touching," of scenes touching rather than building on one another or explaining one another, is one that perhaps can also serve as a model for the project of feminist directing. We do not penetrate a script like a kind of territory to be mapped, renamed, mined, and conquered; we have to relinquish the security and safety of "tightly shaped scenes," and "climactic builds" in order to undergo some uncomfortable shifts, if we are going to let the script speak to us and educate us. If we don't, we enter the world of the play like Stanley, and, after tracking through miles of wilderness and past hundreds of silent indigenous people, we find exactly what we set out to find, the only white male in the forest. "Dr. Livingstone, I presume?"

NOTES

This paper is a tribute to Margaret Wilkerson, who first introduced me to Aishah Rahman's play, and to Aishah herself, who was throughout a guiding hand.

1. Alicia Kae Koger, in her very useful essay "Jazz Form and Jazz Function," offers jazz itself as a way to understand how Rahman structures her script (see Koger, 99–111).

REFERENCES

Baker, Houston, Jr. "Caliban's Triple Play." In *Race, Writing, and Difference,* edited by Henry Louis Gates, Jr. Chicago: University of Chicago Press, 1986. See also, in the same volume, Mary Louise Pratt's essay entitled "Scratches on the Face of the Country; or, What Mr. Barrow Saw in the Land of the Bushmen."

Case, Sue-Ellen. "Re-viewing Hrotsvit," *Theatre Journal* (December 1983).

Koger, Alicia Kae. "Jazz Form and Jazz Function: An Analysis of *Unfinished Women Cry in No Man's Land while a Bird Dies in a Gilded Cage.*" *MELUS: The Journal of the Society for the Study of the Multi-Ethnic Literature of the United States* (Fall 1989–90).

Rahman, Aishah. *Unfinished Women Cry in No Man's Land while a Bird Dies in a Gilded Cage.* In *Nine Plays by Black Women,* edited by Margaret B. Wilkerson. New York: New American Library, 1986.

PART 2

Subverting the Text

Subversion: the ruin or overthrow of something established. In theater the something established is the canon of classics, plays that overwhelmingly favor male characters, male narratives, male bonding, and male views of women. Women's lives and women's eroticism are submerged in favor of the defining and containing activities of men. So subverting one of these plays means first acknowledging that the plays have written women out, and then finding creative ways of writing women back in. We find it helpful to think of subversion *not* as a kind of militaristic overthrow but, instead, as a salvage operation—or, as in the case of Kendall's, the uncovering of what is covered, less a subversion of the text itself than a subversion of the culture that sought to sanitize it.

For the feminist director, as Gay Gibson Cima shows, subverting one of these plays is an attractive proposition for a number of reasons. One very practical reason is that it widens the field and makes it possible to rethink a preplanned season of classics in new and energizing ways. But there is another important reason for turning a classic inside out. If plays constitute an important part of gender training, then a disruption of those plays potentially gets to one primary source of gender information and challenges it. When a director undertakes to subvert a classic, or even a relatively obscure piece like *Agnes de Castro,* a thought-provoking space can open up between the audience's expectations of the text and what they actually are given to see. When subversion is working best it creates a space in which audiences catch themselves in the act of making assumptions and brings them to a halt.

Subversion, however, is not a hatchet job. Directors can't tear into the classics in a reactive frenzy and expect their audiences either to enjoy themselves or to venture forward with them. We think there has to be playfulness and pleasure as well as analysis and indignation. Or, as Lois Weaver puts it, "in order to do this kind of work, you have to go to a place that's a lot about love." Otherwise, in the process of abusing the abuser we simply recreate a new version of "gender trouble."

GAY GIBSON CIMA

Strategies for Subverting the Canon

> . . . it is not the text which reflects female experience that best serves feminist interests, but rather the work which disrupts the very structures of symbolic discourse through which patriarchal culture is constituted.
>
> —Rita Felski

Act 1, scene 2, of *The Merchant of Venice*. Shakespeare: at the heart of the theatrical canon. The scene depicts Portia and her waiting woman, Nerissa, chatting about the various unacceptable suitors who have come to Belmont to try to win Portia's hand. In keeping with her father's will, she must be won by the correct reading of inscriptions on three separate caskets, or jewelry-size boxes: one gold, one silver, one lead. The appropriate partner for Portia, it is assumed, will choose the lead casket, whose inscription indicates a willingness to risk everything for love of her. (According to the script, only Bassanio chooses correctly, two acts later, setting the stage for Portia and Bassanio's marriage and the coupling of Nerissa with Gratiano, one of Bassanio's close friends.)

Let me recount one particular feminist staging of act 1, scene 2: the set represents Portia's private chamber, with flowers everywhere, a fireplace, a theatrical portrait of Portia's father on the upstage wall, a bed, a table downstage on which are placed the three caskets. Early morning light pours into the room as Portia and Nerissa relax lazily on the bed, Portia reclining with her back on Nerissa's chest. Half-dressed in her white slip and camisole, Portia seems part-lover, part-friend, only half unaware of the effect she has on her roommate, who is comfortably dressed in tailored black. As Nerissa revels in Portia's ridicule of her suitors, Portia retires to the dressing room offstage, casually continuing their conversation as she dresses for the day. Nerissa, in Portia's absence, moves down center to the caskets. She reads their inscriptions, selects the leaden box, and releases Portia's picture from its casket. Portia returns, playfully mocking the idea of unmediated patriarchal power: "I will only be won by my father's will." This Portia and Nerissa share a comfortable, sustaining, playful love; they later marry best friends Bassanio and Gratiano in name only, in order to secure a continuing life together.

Tony Shum, an eighteen-year-old Asian-American male without any previous training in theater or directing, produced this scene three weeks into my required English 015 (Introduction to Poetry and Drama) course in the fall of 1990. He worked collaboratively with his classmates Erin Sweeney (Portia) and Melissa Spoharski (Nerissa), responding to my challenge to grant the female characters the same strong connection with one another that the men, particularly Bassanio and Antonio, seemed to enjoy. I am pleased that they gave me permission to outline their blocking strategy here: through a couple of simple choices they undermined the basic assumption of the casket (romance) plot. I offer a description of their work together not because it serves as a flawless model of subversion, but rather because it shows the imaginative leaps that feminist directing can grant.

I teach survival training—feminist directing not only as a separate and worthy profession but also as a crucial skill for negotiating one's way through the landmines of mainstream culture. In addition to introducing students to new ideas of theater and new scripts from outside the canon, I try to teach them to discern the ideological bases of traditional works, in this case the heterosexist bias of act 1, scene 2, of *Merchant,* and help them formulate politically enabling staging strategies, strategies of intervention and subversion. For me, feminist directing functions as a life-sustaining skill—for female students, surely, but also for many of the males, who, because of their ethnic, class, or racial background, their sexual orientation, or their nonmachismo personalities, may experience themselves as marginalized by mainstream culture.

As feminist directors, many of us consider the theater a laboratory in which we prove the validity of experiences previously excluded from or subordinated on the stage. We direct new or recently rediscovered feminist scripts and create our own collectively built plays. Some believe that this is the only way to accomplish feminist goals, that directing the canon—no matter how subversive the director's tactics—simply reinscribes patriarchal values. Others, like myself, think it necessary to adopt *both* strategies: directing the new and redirecting the old. These two projects can proceed simultaneously, enabling us to reach the widest possible audience and allowing us to contribute to the process of creating real material change. Directing productions for an already committed feminist audience solidifies an important sense of community and empowerment and may suggest the important differences among us; however, it does not necessarily provide the only or the best avenue for bringing about actual social change. To paraphrase Susan Lanser, I do not believe that theater alone can make a revolution, but it can help to make the revolutions in consciousness that lead to change (Lanser 1987, 22–23).

Teresa de Lauretis sees a dialectical process operating within feminism, "a tension towards the positivity of politics, or affirmative action on behalf of women as social subjects, on one front, and the negativity inherent in the radical critique of patriarchal, bourgeois culture on the other" (de Lauretis 1985, 154). Directors can contribute to this critique by provoking audiences to rethink traditional values and begin to formulate new ones. Through our feminist productions we can "expose the universal as masculine, the natural as cultural, the textual as political," revealing the ideological and material bases of what is there, demonstrating what is not there, and adding what is silenced or marginalized (Lanser 1987, 6).

I accept Alison Jaggar's concept of feminism as any and all theory and practice that devotes itself to ending the subordination of women, so my comments on directing are not meant to be all-inclusive or univocal (Jaggar 1983). I do hope that they will coalesce current trends, act as catalysts, and contribute, along with the other essays in this book, to the ongoing and ever-widening theory and practice of feminist directing. I also hope that they will help us reexamine our own assumptions. Rita Felski, for example, contends that there is no *necessary* relationship between feminism and experimental form, or between the "masculine" and narrative form. She thereby questions two of the seemingly solid philosophical bases of feminist directing strategies, especially for subverting the canon.[1] Her arguments force us to rethink our goals, to consider not just the formal aspects of our directorial work but also their relationship to the actual conditions of their creation and audience reception:

... it is impossible to speak of "masculine" and "feminine" in any meaningful sense in the formal analysis of texts; the political value of literary [and performance] texts from the standpoint of feminism can be determined only by an investigation of their social functions and effects in relation to the interests of women in a particular historical context, and not by attempting to deduce an abstract literary [or directing] theory of "masculine" and "feminine," "subversive" and "reactionary" forms in isolation from the social conditions of their production and reception. (Felski 1989, 2)

To subvert the canon, then, we must examine the way we finance, house, cast, rehearse, and publicize our revisionist stagings, and we must think carefully about the reception of the work. What is the social function and effect of our directorial work? Which specific strategies—design interventions, cross-casting, textual changes, for example—might enable the particular audience of an individual production to see themselves anew? There is no universal formula or combination of strategies that will work best in every situation. Furthermore, it is possible for us to think we are subverting a script when we are not: sheer formal experimentation alone, such as interrupting a narrative, does not necessarily constitute a feminist directorial tactic. A glance at mass culture reveals that a film like *When Harry Met Sally* can employ narrative breaks, in fact, to emphasize the "rightness" of the patriarchal romance plot.

Contemporary Marxists have suggested that postmodernism has created such social and perceptual confusion that the politically engaged artist should provide the audience with cognitive maps, strategies that help us see the particular positions we occupy as individuals and as groups and enable us to regain our ability to act, to struggle toward productive change. As Esther Beth Sullivan makes clear in this book, these maps within feminism may be drawn in many different ways, of course, but many American academics ground their directorial work in materialist rather than cultural or radical feminist theory: the effort is not to represent or celebrate specific images of women so much as to articulate and dismantle the processes and apparatus that attempt to control theatrical representations of women and, in turn, real women. For that reason the epic theater of the Brecht Collective has proven particularly useful to feminist directors probing the *construction* of ideas about gender, race, sexual preference, class, and ethnicity. Some feminist directors have also turned to French feminist theory in their efforts to subvert the coherence of language and deconstruct the workings of spectatorial desire in the theater. Others seem to work in concert with theorists such as Teresa de Lauretis, whose theory of the technology of gender informs the feminist project; Audre Lorde and bell hooks, who have enabled us to think through issues relating specifically to women of color; and Sue-Ellen Case and Jill Dolan, who have foregrounded, among other things, the lesbian issues emerging within theatrical contexts.

The relationship between feminist directing and feminist theory is, in fact, more complicated than I have thus far suggested. While directors wanting to find ways to subvert the canon can surely find inspiration from theoretical texts, theorists frequently base their work on an awareness of certain directorial practices. The relationship between directing and theory is a complex and fluctuating one, but one thing is clear: we can *create* as well as test theory in the practice of our art. Feminist directors do not simply put feminist theory into practice but, rather, discover theory in practice. Our work forces us to question the binary opposition of the very terms *theory* and *practice,* an opposition that seems not only false but also unproductive. Elin Diamond, Michelene Wandor, and Marianne Goldberg, to mention only a few of the other writers specifically interested in feminist theater and dance, have articulated many of the issues feminist directors and troupes are simultaneously exploring onstage.[2] And, increasingly in recent years, directors and theorists (who may, of course, be the same persons) have drawn on the work of feminists from other disciplines, particularly literature and film, just as these scholars have drawn from the theater to create metaphors for their work. The phrases "performance of texts" and "representations of the body" are catchphrases in literary theory at the moment, revealing the interweaving of theater and literary theory. As feminist directors, then, we simultaneously stage theoretical concerns and theorize through theatrical practices.

Subverting the Canon: Show What Is There and/or Show What Is Not

1. Usurp the means of production, or, failing that, stage one or more of the major forces that financed your particular

show, selected the script, and set the parameters of its staging. Try to gain control of the money so that you can maintain artistic control. If that is not feasible, make clear in your
production what agencies you wrestled with. You may not
want to be so obvious as to stage a prologue in which someone demands that you direct *Hamlet,* but you can stage the
powers within the audience and the academy that have
placed *Hamlet* at the center of the theatrical canon.

2. Discover and stage the "social script" of the original production. Rachel DuPlessis borrows this term from the social
sciences because it "offers to social analysis what 'ideology'
offers to cultural analysis . . . to explain the existence of
strongly mandated patterns of learned behavior that are culturally and historically specific, and that offer a rationale for
unselfconscious acts" (1985, 2). What are the societal rules
followed in the script? Can you show their effects through
parody or other means? How did the lives of the actors who
originally performed the work (or the relationship between
those actors and their managers, directors, or producers) inform the original productions? Are there actual eighteenth-
century diaries or letters that could serve as counterpoints
to your heroine trapped in her sentimental comedy? What
forces or actual events led to the scripting of the performance
you are revisioning? Can you stage them?

3. This leads to the idea of restoring historical consciousness
to our work by staging the historical conditions, relationships, and influences that shaped it. As new historicists such
as Stephen Greenblatt and others have argued, art cannot be
separated from its historical setting. And, just as certain Renaissance court activities may be viewed as theater, the production of a script such as *The Masque of Blackness* must be
seen as politics as well as theater. Kim Hall has discussed the
race-related issues embedded in that script in such a way as
to encourage a new feminist production questioning Queen
Anne's political position in the court and on the stage.

4. Find stage images that raise questions about why the characters are represented as they are. Zelda Fichandler, in her 1990
Arena Stage production of Ibsen's *A Doll House,* hinted at
the nineteenth-century social script of that work through an

opening tableau: all the characters were represented as dolls, actor/mannequins stuffed with dusty, rigid ideas. Nora and Torvald resembled nothing more than the bride and groom dolls on the top of a wedding cake, and the minor characters were shown to gaze at them in dumbfounded silence. The remainder of the production, unfortunately, failed to fulfill the promise of that potentially subversive move. I found myself planning a Bunraku-style *Doll House* in contemporary dress, set in a paper-thin walled "doll house" shaped like a cross between Santa's workshop and a child's penny bank and produced in a suburban shopping mall on a Saturday afternoon.

5. This Bunraku *Doll House* could serve as an illustration of the next suggestion: look for the underlying myth and represent it as serving the patriarchy rather than acting as a psychological reality. A striking example of this strategy emerges in Avanthi Meduri's revisionist stagings of Indian dance-drama. Meduri dances the traditional stories in the customary costumes, but she divides her work into segments, interweaving new story lines into the ancient ones and adding a new audience and invisible actor—a daughter—to the traditionally all-male spectatorship. She seems to illustrate what Elin Diamond has called "looking-at-being-looked-at-ness." There are countless ways to accomplish the goal of exposing the underlying myth. With a contemporary script such as *Equus,* for example, which employs a presentational style of acting to mask the nature of homoerotic desire being performed onstage, why not unmask the male actor playing Alan Strang's horse/lover, Nugget, and show how patriarchal (and Freudian) directives channel the sexual energies in the script?

6. Another way of thinking about this process is to stage the original "interpretive community" that made meaning of the premiere production or of any subsequent production. Stanley Fish uses that term to describe the group of critics, academics, and others who control the parameters of meaning made from a given text or production. At certain points in history the "moral majority" has been especially vociferous in attempting to control the behavior of women on- and

offstage. It is especially tempting right now, with the debate raging over censorship and government funding, to stage the parallels between a seventeenth-century conservative such as Jeremy Collier and the reactionaries who are currently refusing funding to feminist performance artists such as Karen Finley and Holly Hughes. Through feminist directing we can highlight the ways in which various agencies attempt to monitor women in the arts, and we can explode the myth of their invulnerability.

7. Focus on demonstrating and critiquing the acting style of the period as it controls female bodies. Envision a production of Molière, for example, in which the actors alternately adopt and drop the mandated movement patterns of the original production. Use Sande Zeig or Marianne Goldberg's theories about exploring gender-free movement to experiment with how your actors get from one place to another onstage. If you are producing George Bernard Shaw, say, cast a narrator to read (part of) the stage directions then allow the actors to contradict them. Cast Webster's *The Duchess of Malfi* in accordance with Renaissance conventions, with male actors playing the female characters, and demonstrate that this is how a particular male writer thought a woman ought to be represented onstage, not how real women lived or wished to live.

8. Employ and critique, or parody, the historical blocking patterns that marginalized women in the premiere productions of classic scripts, productions in which the actors playing male characters customarily commanded center stage. Allow the female characters, however they seem to be silenced by the script, to take center stage in terms of placement and movement.

9. Represent in your production the women who enabled the male writers to create the works that have been canonized. Produce, for example, Brecht scripts in such a way that the major artistic as well as domestic contributions of the women in the Brecht Collective become apparent. In doing so a director would be "refocusing our attention on the power of the background and implicitly calling the woman

as 'stagehand' to center stage," as Lynda Hart and Marilyn Frye have suggested (Hart 1989, 2; Frye 1983, 170).

10. Write beyond the ending of romance plots. DuPlessis discusses this strategy in terms of the novel, but it is equally useful with the script. As in the *Merchant* scene that opens this essay, we can use blocking techniques or casting strategies or add scenes and epilogues that explode the myth that the "rightful end" of female characters is marriage (which commonly signifies successful incorporation into the world of romance) or death (signaling "sexual and social failure") (DuPlessis 1985, 1).

11. Cross-gender, cross-racial, and cross-generational casting tactics can also aid in the process of subverting the canon. Many feminist directors, including those represented in this book, have changed the way in which they cast shows, relinquishing the old dictates that increase the iconicity of the actor (the collapse of the actor into character) and substituting, for that tradition, practices that provide for a more elastic relationship between actor and character. The Mabou Mines's 1990 staging of *Lear,* with Ruth Maleczech as a Southern matriarch, and Split Britches's free adaptation of *Little Women* serve as examples of how classic texts can be transformed through tactics such as cross-gender casting and cross-dressing as well as textual interventions.

12. Produce a double bill: staging Joan Schenkar's *Koch's Postulate,* for example, alongside a traditional folktale such as *Hansel and Gretel* will surely undermine the patriarchal dictates of the latter.

13. Unusual sets, choreographic interludes, and vocal arias such as echolalic repetitions of select words or phrases can also subvert a script in performance. Several of the directors contributing to this book have explored the way in which the designer and choreographer can contribute to the feminist project onstage. Instead of building a Wagnerian-style unified work of art, these feminist directors employ dance and the set itself to intervene in the seamless creation of meaning on stage.

14. Produce your show in a nontheatrical space, using a public

place that comments in a feminist fashion on the setting of your script, or highlight the conventions implicit in the theater that you use, spotlighting the function of the proscenium arch, for example. Consider the spatial relationship between the actor and the audience carefully, as in performance artist Suzanne Lacy's work.[3]

15. Ask your dramaturg to seek out unusual means of access into the period of the play. Try to find out, for example, about legal and medical practices as well as social practices. Locate oral histories of women, when possible, or ferret out rare book room collections of women's documents to use in performance. In unearthing the cultural history and actual material conditions of the people or the types of characters represented in the script, the dramaturg can be of special help to the feminist director.[4]

16. Be aware of your rehearsal techniques: Do they promote a questioning attitude, empowering your actors, or do they turn your actors into powerless female characters? Talk to the actors about their relationships with the characters and draw on their inventiveness as you rethink, and perhaps refuse, the psychologically "real" acting style that frequently conflates a victimized character with a victimized live actor. Explain your particular rehearsal approach, its strong and weak points.

17. If you build your directorial work upon actors' improvisations, plan carefully, because improvisations can inadvertently reproduce the dominant ideological structures that you are trying to critique. Actors may spontaneously voice their own unrecognized biases or they may move in stereotypical ways, ways that reinforce rather than redirect the traditional values promoted in the canon.

18. Reinvent the audience-actor-director relationship, striving for a sense of "improvised directing." Perhaps the work of Split Britches most clearly illustrates this strategy: just as they have refused the singular director and, instead, build their work collectively, they also have repositioned their audience. Instead of mastering the audience, polishing the production to prove their brilliance as directors and the actors' docility (as well as their virtuosity), they have built into

their work the planned and carefully executed sense of spontaneity, which they call "letting the seams show." In productions such as *Little Women: The Tragedy* and *Honey I'm Home: The Alcestis Story*, they give the audience the opportunity to create a sense of community with the actors, to feel empowered rather than mastered by the theatrical presentation (see Sabrina Hamilton's article in part 2 of this volume). The obviously provisional settings, the cleverly manipulated sense of chaos in blocking, the audience's feeling that the actors really were not directed at all but, instead, simply decided to stage their own stuff—this is evidence of a careful directorial strategy of seeming improvisation. This is certainly one way out of the traditional hierarchy in which the director (subservient to the playwright) masters in turn the actors, designers, and the audience. This strategy can be usefully employed by the director staging a script from the canon, too.

19. As an antidote to the emphasis on the individual in most of the humanist drama within the canon, stage the wider social context of the conflict, the community out of which the characters emerge.

20. Be aware of the "hidden" semiotics of your production: of the theater architecture, the publicity, the lobby, the tickets, the program, the price of admission, the "casting" of ushers.[5]

21. Make your production into what Stanley Fish has called a "self-consuming artifact," a performance text that moves dialectically to contradict its own truths, and thereby challenge the audience to make meaning out of it.

22. Adopt strategies from feminist performance art. Artists such as Marianne Goldberg assume the roles of writer, director, performer, and designer simultaneously. Interestingly, Goldberg has attempted to subvert her own authority as writer, to avoid mastering the audience, by giving the audience the means through which they may produce their own images, as she did in *Hudson Rover* when she gave video cameras to various audience members. Goldberg also frequently produces her work in several formats simultaneously: onstage, on video, in "performance pieces for print," and in gallery showings of the mechanicals or cam-

era-ready materials for printing those "performance pieces." She thereby proliferates the artwork and subverts the notion of an authoritative version of it. Feminist directors can borrow tactics from Goldberg for their work within the canon (see Goldberg's essay in part 3 of this book).

As the present collection of essays proves, the strategies of feminist directing are as varied and eclectic as those practicing it. But one thing is clear: it is a powerful and effective means of producing a new view of reality. And in the coming years we may be able to build on this pioneering volume, even to rediscover, from the theatrical past, female directors who give our work in the present a sense of history as rich as our sense of the future.

We are living at a time when the director has wrestled much authority away from the playwright. Partly as a result of the work of visionaries such as Antonin Artaud, who called for "no more masterpieces," and Jerzy Grotowski, who elevated the status of the director to new heights, we increasingly regard the director as the agent responsible for determining how the meaning or experience of any given theater production is constructed for and by the audience. Whether the director works alone or collectively, the directorial role presumes the privilege of interpretive freedom. Directors no longer search for "the playwright's intention," a process that seems peculiarly outdated in a postmodern world in which theorists such as Michel Foucault and Jacques Derrida have gone so far as to declare the death of the author. For feminist directors, then, the prevailing winds prove particularly auspicious: we are granted, by the dominant cultural attitude toward directing in general, a certain license to experiment. Our revisionist productions of classics receive a validation of sorts from the general attitude toward directing. It is professionally acceptable, for example, if not commercially lucrative, to subvert the classics through cross-racial and cross-gender casting. Repertory companies across the country are hosting symposia on nontraditional casting; there is a certain cachet about some of the tactics crucial to feminist directing.

But a danger lurks here, one that we need to be aware of: when the strategies of feminist directing become mainstream they will lose their power to subvert traditional modes of perception. They will simply become "radical chic." For that reason the notion of feminist directing should not be conceived in static terms, nor can it be divorced from the political dynamics of actual performance situations.

There is another danger in the power that the director now enjoys in our culture. The feminist project itself seeks to find a way to explode the hierarchical methods of the patriarchy, so how can the feminist director assume *primary* power in the production of the artwork? Isn't this simply reinscribing the subjection of actors, designers, and audience in an "age of the director"? In fact, in the mainstream theater the director frequently now seems to fulfill what Foucault calls the "author function," the agent within the theater apparatus who delimits the meaning of the work. Precisely because of this danger, many of the directors represented in this book seek to collaborate with their actors, designers, and choreographers. Instead of replacing the playwright-as-author with the director-as-author, they hope to create an ever-shifting balance of power within the means of production.

But we have not yet validated the idea of the various contributors (actors, designers, choreographers, composers, etc.) working independently—we seem to want to retain the concept of the director as a filter. Part of the reason for our reluctance to scrap the director may very well be the need to build a politically engaged theater: we need a facilitator, someone to make sure the pieces fit, even if those pieces are purposely contradictory. At this moment in time the feminist director seems one of our best hopes in the work of changing our ideas of the theater and the world, whether within the canon or outside it.

NOTES

The chapter epigraph is taken from Felski, *Beyond Feminist Aesthetics,* 30.

    1. In her critique of Lacan, for example, Rita Felski explains that

> critical analysis of existing discursive systems and conventions of representation has played an important part in recent feminist theory. To move, however, from the recognition of an androcentric bias in language use as exemplified in existing hierarchies of meaning to the assertion that social and symbolic discourse is inherently phallocentric is a highly reductive jump. Such an argument simplifies the complex nature of the interaction of feminism as a counter-ideology with a dominant patriarchal culture, a relationship necessarily defined by both dependence and critique; in at-

tempting to avoid a voluntarism which assumes that language is a transparent instrument free of ideology, it falls into the opposite trap of a linguistic determinism, which interprets all discursive language as a reinforcement of patriarchal structures. Recent French theory has usefully reemphasized the point that discourse is not interest-free and has developed a number of analyses of the nexus of relations between language and power; but simply to *equate* language with power (that is, symbolic discourse with patriarchy) is to obliterate fundamental distinctions between the various functions and contexts of language use and to devalue subjective agency and critical intervention in such a way as to negate the very legitimacy of the writer's own theoretical position. (Felski, *Beyond Feminist Aesthetics,* 42)

2. I have found the following especially helpful: Diamond's essay "Brechtian Theory/Feminist Theory: Toward a Gestic Feminist Criticism," *TDR: A Journal of Performance Studies* 32, no. 1 (T117) (Spring 1988): 82–95; Wandor's *Look Back in Gender: Sexuality and the Family in Post-War British Drama* (London and New York: Methuen, 1987); and Goldberg's "Ballerinas and Ball Passing," *Women & Performance: A Journal of Feminist Theory* 3, no. 2:6 (1987–88): 7–32.

3. See, for example, the articles on Lacy in *TDR: A Journal of Performance Studies* 32, no. 1 (T117) (Spring 1988): 42–82.

4. Tracy C. Davis's "Questions for a Feminist Methodology in Theatre History" prompted this suggestion; her essay may be found in *Interpreting the Theatrical Past: Essays in the Historiography of Performance,* edited by Thomas Postlewait and Bruce A. McConachie (Iowa City: University of Iowa Press, 1989), 59–82. Several other essays in that collection have proven helpful, especially those by Erika Fischer-Lichte, Marvin Carlson, and Joseph R. Roach.

5. See Marvin Carlson, *Theatre Semiotics: Signs of Life* (Bloomington: Indiana University Press, 1990); and *Places of Performance: The Semiotics of Theatre Architecture* (Ithaca, N.Y.: Cornell University Press, 1989), for very useful analyses of these aspects of production.

REFERENCES

Carlson, Marvin. 1989. *Places of Performance: The Semiotics of Theatre Architecture.* Ithaca, N.Y.: Cornell University Press.
———. 1990. *Theatre Semiotics: Signs of Life.* Bloomington: Indiana University Press.
Davis, Tracy C. 1989. "Questions for a Feminist Methodology in Theatre History." In *Interpreting the Theatrical Past: Essays in the Historiography of Performance,* edited by Thomas Postlewait and Bruce A. McConachie, 59–82. Iowa City: University of Iowa Press.
de Lauretis, Teresa. 1985. "Aesthetics and Feminist Theory: Rethinking Women's Cinema." *New German Critique,* no. 34:154–75.

Diamond, Elin. 1988. "Brechtian Theory/Feminist Theory: Toward a Gestic Feminist Criticism." *TDR: A Journal of Performance Studies* 32, no. 1 (Spring): 82–95.

DuPlessis, Rachel Blau. 1985. *Writing Beyond the Ending.* Bloomington: Indiana University Press.

Felski, Rita. 1989. *Beyond Feminist Aesthetics: Feminist Literature and Social Change.* Cambridge, Mass.: Harvard University Press.

Frye, Marilyn. 1983. *The Politics of Reality: Essays in Feminist Theory.* New York: Crossing.

Goldberg, Marianne. 1987–88. "Ballerinas and Ball Passing." *Women & Performance: A Journal of Feminist Theory* 3, no. 2:7–32.

Hall, Kim F. 1991. "Sexual Politics and Cultural Identity in *The Masque of Blackness.*" In *The Performance of Power: Theatrical Discourse and Politics,* edited by Sue-Ellen Case and Janelle Reinelt. Iowa City: University of Iowa Press.

Hart, Lynda. 1989. *Making a Spectacle: Feminist Essays on Contemporary Women's Theatre.* Ann Arbor: University of Michigan Press.

Jaggar, Alison M. 1983. *Feminist Politics and Human Nature.* Brighton, England: Harvester.

Lanser, Susan. 1987. "The Feminist Transformation of Literature." Paper delivered at Georgetown University.

Wandor, Michelene. 1987. *Look Back in Gender: Sexuality and the Family in Post-War British Drama.* London and New York: Methuen.

KENDALL

Ways of Looking at *Agnes de Castro* (1695): A Lesbian History Play at WOW Cafe

One Way: Agnes enters in combat boots and a black leather jacket with a Silence = Death button. The Princess, in a soft sweater and a fashionably long skirt, reaches out to her and cries,

> Agnes, you've come!
> My griefs have lost already half their force,
> They vanish at your sight, like mists before the sun.

They embrace.

Another Way: Two sane women are surrounded by lunatics. Agnes and the Princess perform "realism," a fourth wall in place, their concentration riveted on each other; the rest of the cast romps and rages around them in camp, grotesque, and melodramatic excess, breaking out of character to address the audience in asides, which comment on the action and summarize scenes that have been cut.

Another: Agnes, a femme in butch clothing, enters to embrace her lover, a femme in femme clothing. Clearly, the two are in trouble, even before it's revealed that the femmy femme is really a married bisexual whose husband is in love with the butchy femme. Then an ultrafemme, Bianca, hops like a trained poodle around the evil Elvira, played by a woman playing a female impersonator, which figures, since she's the villain and, of course, male-identified. Elvira's covillain, Alvaro, is played by a traditionally "feminine" woman in gay male drag, a mustache neatly painted in eyebrow pencil above her meticulously crimsoned lips; s/he flirts with the "King," a butch in a double-breasted men's suit.

Another: Both the *gestus* and the audience become textual apparatus as the production *r*epresents a gay and lesbian gestural language, recognizable and comedic to spectators who can "read" it. The result is a postmodern lesbian romance in which scenes of lesbian realism are juxtaposed with scenes of character parody and conscious melodrama. The whole is intercut with disruptions of narrative, foregrounding the experience of the female actors as representers of a drama that is both real (their appearance as actors on a stage) and not-real (their appearance as "women" and "men" relying on the camp tradition to exaggerate the distortions inherent in these signs). The power of representation is given only to female actors who presume a lesbian gaze; that gaze completes the meaning.

Another: Eight white women, all but one enrolled in exclusive private colleges, perform a seventeenth-century play about royalty in a working-class venue touted as "lesbian space" in New York City. Only one of the actors identifies herself as lesbian. After a slow opening night the house is packed Friday and Saturday. Forty people are turned away at the door each night. All seats are taken, and additional spectators stand in the aisles, hang off ladders, and whistle, shout, and stomp their approval.

Another: Agnes de Castro is blatant lesbian chauvinist fantasy. The only fully developed character is the butch in combat boots; her bisexual lover comes second. All the "men" characters are cardboard fictions, and the two nonlesbian "women" are as shallow as the males. It's a complete reversal of the socially constructed fictions commercial theater holds so dear. The lesbians are normative, and everyone else is deviant, an antidote to ghoulish caricatures of lesbians as well as to dreary politically correct, erotophobic, lesbian coming-out drama.

Another: Alisa Solomon, a *Village Voice* reviewer, writes: "In its first production in 300 years, students from Hampshire College's theater department (fresh from an evidently inspiring workshop with Split Britches) point up the play's rad tendencies without, methinks, sacrificing its trad style. The all-woman cast twists the already-bent genders into new disruptions. . . ."

Another: A revival of Catherine Trotter's *Agnes de Castro* (1695), based on a novel by Aphra Behn, remakes history. *Agnes* was the first commercially successful English-language play to feature a lesbian heroine; it played to a fashionable public with a distaste for rigid gender identities. King William, the public figurehead of Whig morality, was privately both gay and outrageously effeminate. Princess Anne, soon to be queen, was described as "masculine" in demeanor, had an unusually low speaking voice, preferred horses to drawing rooms, and was passionately involved with another woman. A "cabal" of "ladies of quality" preferred each other's embraces to men's. Fops in wigs and high-heeled shoes thrived on what Luce Irigaray would later describe as "hommo-sexuality." Certainly some spectators of Trotter's day would have "read" the play as the lesbian love story it is. At Drury Lane the play was five acts of heroic tragedy in blank verse; at the WOW Cafe it is a fast-paced hour's worth of camped-up love story, which spoofs gendered relationships and the society that prescribes them.

Another: Style becomes content. Acting style—realism, camp, grotesque. Restoration style—direct audience asides, flowery language with balanced periods and inverted sentences, grand figure-eight movements and operatic poses that match the language. Design as style—the postmodern mismatch of costumes, the cardboard cut-out props, the wedding cake backdrop of hearts and doves, beneath which snakes twine around a white picket fence. Style emphasizes the superficiality of a society in which two women who love each other are doomed, "murdered."

There's no one way of looking at the sprawl of meanings to be reaped from this production, by these players, in this venue. Karena Rahall's production of *Agnes de Castro*—which romped and disrupted, schemed and decentered, teased and kissed sweetly and deconstructed its moment on the stage—is fit subject for more ways of looking than these, but it certainly deserves more looking. The show closed in April of 1990, Alisa Solomon's cameo review appeared in the *Voice,* Morgan Gwenwald took some photographs for the Lesbian Herstory Archives, and that seemed to be the end of it.

In my mind the production was a landmark in the history of lesbian theater. Despite centuries of nonrepresentation or misrepresentation of lesbians onstage, despite all the lives of lesbian actors, managers, playwrights, and designers denied, ignored, hidden, or diminished ("devoted companions," "lifelong friends"), here was lesbian theater history given breath again. Unearthing *Agnes de Castro* and the social context in which it appeared rips off the closet door behind which kings, queens, and a host of wealthy white gay people who had reason to resist gender limitation have been stashed through the centuries. It also proves that lesbian theater *has* a professional history in the English-speaking world.

When William Hoffman compiled his ground-breaking *Gay Plays* in 1979 he found only two lesbian plays and wrote: "there are very few plays about lesbians. This is probably so because the people most likely to write about them are women, and female playwrights, gay and straight, are rare" (x). In Britain in 1987 Jill Davis compiled what she thought was the first anthology of lesbian plays, three-fourths of which were written after Hoffman's collection came out. But she wrote: "In editing this volume I would like very much to have included a play by, about, for lesbian women written before 1945. I haven't found one" (9).

Here it is, and there is much to say about it. In 1986 the *Journal of Homosexuality* published a plodding scholarly justification I made of *Agnes* as a lesbian history play. At least nobody has to do that again, but there are plenty of unanswered questions. I hope a qualified theorist will analyze in depth the social context in which the play was first produced. I hope someone will compare its structure, its language, and its construction of gender with William Congreve's *Love for Love* or John Vanbrugh's *Relapse*. Even bearing in mind that Trotter was sixteen and self-educated when she wrote it and had neither financial support nor connections in the business, such comparisons will serve further to deconstruct the canon and to illustrate the social subversiveness of Trotter's tragedy.

How did the homosexuality of King William and Queen Anne influence the construction of sex, gender, and lust in their society and on the public stage? How did (or does) class correlate with homosexual behavior in Britain and the United States, and how does that influence the reception of lesbian representation then or now? How was *Agnes* received by Trotter's spectators? Are there letters or diaries in somebody's attic in Bath or York that mention the play's premiere in 1695?

Perhaps more important, the final script for Rahall's production may be compared with Trotter's original—changes noted, adaptations studied. The full "text" of Rahall's production, including its reception and its *gestus,* can be analyzed in detail. It is little short of miraculous that, after three hundred years of silence, two female lovers created by a gifted teenager found actor-bodies and voices to speak their love again. And they spoke to an audience that heard them and cheered. That miracle was preceded by two others. First, that I found a copy of the play in the University of Texas library and read, with a lesbian understanding, its meaning. Second, that Karena Rahall, with less than six weeks from start to finish, was able to assemble and train an ensemble company, develop an adaptation of Trotter's play in collaboration with that company, and bring the play to production.

Briefly, the first pre-miracle. Others before me read the play but missed its point. Edmund Gosse, who appreciated Trotter's playmaking more than anyone in our century before me, allowed that there was "a good deal of meritorious character-drawing in 'Agnes de Castro'"; he remarked on the "benevolent and tenderly forgiving Princess," "the fierce purity of Agnes," and "the infatuation of the Prince." But he didn't get it. He was amused by "a capital scene of exquisite confusion between this generous and distracted trio," admired what he thought was "not at all young-ladyish," but concluded, "It is a bad play, but not at all an unpromising one" (Gosse, 94). I might almost agree that it was a "bad play" if I had missed the central point, the meaning of the pivotal relationship, the revolutionary characterization of the title character.

Nancy Cotton, writing sixty years and two feminist movements after Gosse, found *Agnes* "weak blank verse" and complained it was "peculiar" (Cotton, 83). Looking for the good parts with heterosexist blinders on, she concluded with a judgment often made against lesbians, that Agnes is "frigid" (103). She *is* frigid toward men, which, of course, is hardly the same thing. Jacqueline Pearson takes more time than Cotton to examine the play and finds "women open the play, wholly dominate the first act, and speak more than half the lines, which is very unusual in plays of the period" (Pearson, 23). She is certainly on the right track there, but she falls into a rut by observing that all Trotter's heroines have "an agonised purity" (184). She mistakes Agnes's indifference to men for passivity and fails to note that it is only heterosexual passion that is, indeed, "criticised rather than celebrated" (185).

I found *Agnes* in the summer of 1983, at the University of Texas, as I was slogging my way through page after page of spleen and vapors, looking for a dissertation topic. I wanted a female playwright who wrote in English before the twentieth century, and I was willing to read through anything to find her. When I came across the pulsing, devoted, unmistakably erotic energy between Agnes and the Princess, I doubted my judgment, read again, knew, and still doubted.

I feared I was projecting, hallucinating. But there were the words on the mottled page: "My Agnes! Art thou come! My Souls best Comfort, / Thou dear Relief to my oppressing Cares" (3). Agnes, jealous of the Prince and infuriated by his puerile crush on her and his indifference to the Princess, rages: "Gods! Is it just the Prince enjoy this Blessing, / Who knows not how to value the vast Treasure" (7). This could be merely the effulgence of romantic friendship, I thought, fresh from a reading of Lillian Faderman.

But later Trotter scripts a scene in which Bianca, hot from spying on the two women, reports to Elvira: "They mingled Kisses with the tend'rest Words, / As if their Rivalship had made 'em dear" (20). From scene 1 Trotter has Elvira predict that competition for the Prince will make the Princess and Agnes hate each other. Trotter sets up the whole action of the play to prove that prediction wrong, by showing that Agnes is indifferent to the Prince. She is anything but indifferent to the Princess.

I still doubted myself, still feared that I was only seeing what I wanted to see. So I went to the Aphra Behn novel from which Trotter took her play—sometimes lifting whole sheets of dialogue without so much as a change in beat. Behn's Agnes is a protofeminist, who refuses to marry Alvaro because "nothing is dearer to me than my liberty." Trotter intensifies this in her Agnes, who declares her "Heart" (frequently a euphemism for genitals) was not "design'd for such a Union" (13). Trotter's Agnes goes on:

> I feel no melting, no soft Passion there;
> None but for charming Liberty, and Glory;
> Then Sir, [she addresses the King] wou'd you controul the
>   Will of Heav'n
> Who made me not for Love?
>
> (13)

Not heterosexual love, anyway, which was the only kind Trotter's simple-minded King thought women feel, though she scripted him a flirtation with Alvaro.

I let this all soak in, then I looked at the structure of the play. If the relationship between Agnes and the Princess were not unusually intense, there would be no play. The single, unmistakable point of the play is that love between two women can overcome the intrusions of any man, can take priority over male approval, desire, dominion. To my lesbian way of thinking there is nothing peculiar in that, but in the history of English-speaking theater where else is that point made? So, I thought, that is why Cotton finds it "peculiar," Pearson mistakes the frustrations of the two women for "agonised purity," and Gosse finds the lovers "distracted." The three critics, bless their obtuse hearts, are all blind as bats to the possibility of passion between women. I sat back in my seat, dizzy with delight, and gazed at the ceiling. I had found the gem I was looking for.

Six years later I assigned it in a class I was teaching on Gay and Lesbian Theater. Karena Rahall was in that class. When she told me she wanted to direct the play it was my turn to be obtuse and bat-blind. "Karena, this play has massive historical and literary importance," I drawled, a little nasal and pompous, "but you can't *produce* it. It would run four hours, it has a ridiculous plot, and that seventeenth-century language will never come across. It couldn't possibly work," I told her. Somewhat intimidated by my idiocy, she spent a summer looking for another lesbian play she wanted to direct, but she couldn't find one.

"I just keep thinking about *Agnes*," she wrote. "It's the most romantic story I've ever read. Sure, it's long, and most of it is really boring, but I keep turning to the scenes with the two women and reading them over. I can't believe two women are speaking to each other in such beautiful language and talking about how in love they are in a seventeenth-century play." Inspired by her obsession, I began to see visions and to dream dreams.

"Let's cut the hell out of it and see what we come up with," I suggested. "After all, you're older than Trotter was when she wrote this play, and she was plagiarizing like mad from Aphra Behn. I don't think she'd mind if you took respectful liberties, if your purpose is to reveal her meaning." I was on a roll. "And why not add a few asides—perfectly in keeping with the style and the period—in which actors step out of character and address their twentieth-century audience, comment on their characters' predicaments, and summarize the long boring parts."

Later Rahall wrote: "This really scared me at first. But in the first rehearsals we did character monologues. . . . I told the actors we might use some of this to create scenes within the play" (Rahall 1990b, 7). The company was on its way to the disruptions of narrative that, paradoxically, held the cut play together and contextualized it. The first "aside" occurred after the Prince and Princess have one of the more absurd exchanges in the play, in which he begs her to kill him for falling in love with Agnes. Trotter's script calls for the Prince to rant for over a page. Lesley James, playing the preppie Prince, stepped forward as herself and confronted the audience with her dilemma as an actress trying to understand the motivation for her character. She spoke as both character and actor: "So, what do you think? Where did I go wrong?" She examined the psychology of the scene and concluded, "I guess I'll just have to suffer. Yeah, that's it: I'll *suffer.*" This provided a perfect segue to the conclusion of the endless soliloquy, "To atone my crime, I'll be exquisitely wretched" (Randall 1990c, 8).

My favorite aside was Bianca's, occurring near the end of the play, as she made crucial plot revelations just before she died. The scene begins in camp style with Trotter's blank verse: "Let me in dying clear my spotted soul, / By saving those whose ruin I designed"; then Joanna Settle, the actress playing Bianca, looked at her watch and reported to the audience, "And then I told them everything: about how it was Elvira who killed Constantia and how Agnes was innocent." Immediately back to the script, her Bianca-voice, and the melodrama, she concluded, "I'm going to heaven" (28).

Not only did the actors write their own asides; they also made cuts whenever they felt cutting would clarify meaning. After the initial "ruthless" cutting, which Rahall and I made together, the first read-through ran over an hour and a half. By the end, even with the addition of considerable stage business, the show was running sixty-four minutes. Rahall notes: "When we didn't like something or understand it we just cut it. Entire sub-plots were cut from the play as well as a few characters. We continued cutting and pasting up until the day before the show" ("Retrospective," 6). When I asked who should be listed as the author of the adaptation Rahall insisted it was "Hampshire College Theatre Collective." Under duress she agreed to be named as principal adaptor. The stage manager wrote down the changes and kept a record of the script, but the director, the cast, and the crew all shared in the adapting. The key to the process was the company's respect for Trotter's genius and its commitment to preserve the integrity of her script. *Thy* became *your,* Prince Don Pedro became Pedro—but the poetry of the love scenes and the parody of Agnes's society was pure Trotter. The result was a liberation of Trotter's strength from the faddish verbosity of her day. The result was also that the lesbianism in the piece came fully out of the closet. If any doubt remained in my mind about Trotter's intentions, the process of writing the adaptation relieved them. To bring the lesbianism "out" the company needed to add nothing. What they did was subtract what had fogged or obscured the meaning in the original.

Rahall never equivocated about her audience. "I had lesbians in mind. If men came and enjoyed the performance that was fine, but it was certainly not meant for them." Nor did she hesitate to credit Lois Weaver, Deb Margolin, and Peggy Shaw with giving her the tools, the chutzpah, the vision, and, the playfulness that made the play come together. She wrote: "They taught me how to relax and allow things to happen, how to trust the work. . . . They were used to learning lines the day of the performance. . . . The idea that it's only a show and if it fails you can always do another one, was really important for me" (Rahall 1990b, 4).

Avoiding the pitfalls of perfectionism, hierarchy, and directorial control, Rahall did "trust the work." She let the adapted play evolve as the actors developed their roles and their physicalizations and wrote their asides. She gave the actors exercises, improvisations, and games, but she trusted them to develop their own characters and most of the blocking. She remarks, "Once they trusted me they were more interested in my opinion and my help; give them power and they don't want it as much" (Rahall 1990b, 6). Did I mention she was twenty-two at the time?

Rehearsals focused on physicalization. She taught the actors to "choose a few lines to work with and coach each other to create stories that depended more on the body than the words. Working with verse, this was very important" (Rahall 1990b, 9). When Susan Mahoney's Alvaro began to be recognizably nelly, which was in fact hinted in Trotter's script, the characterization took flight; Mahoney's body work pushed camp to its limits in exactly the way that some gay men choose to do, so she wasn't ridiculing gay men but, in fact, joining in some gay men's ridicule of gender restrictions. This led Rahall to some ruminations on camp, drag, and transvestism, which showed up in her final analysis of the play.

"The choice of camp for *Agnes* was never a question for me. The first time I read the play the distinction between good and evil characters was so clear that it was absurd. If Trotter were alive today she might be writing for Split Britches" (Rahall 1990a, 25). Camp, Rahall explained to me, was the only way she could even consider portraying Trotter's "evil" characters, and, since camp has long been a style of gay theater and gay life, it helped to clarify "gay" meanings in the text. Furthermore, the use of camp as self-parody allowed the actors to explore the negative aspects of their characters in depth.

The choice of drag came from a different set of considerations. First of all, Rahall felt she would run into problems directing men in a lesbian play; she foresaw conflicts, tests of her authority or demands for extra attention and reassurance, and she didn't want to waste her time. More significantly, she wanted to work with an all-female cast, and she felt that having women play all the roles would subvert the construction of male power in the play. "We did not pretend to be male but we certainly imitated that image in order to subvert it" (Rahall 1990a, 30).

Alvaro, for example, rapes Agnes in Trotter's play. Had Alvaro been played by a man, the scene could only have been profoundly disturbing to women. Rahall represented the rape with a forced kiss, which, she says, "is not so disgusting" because the audience knows it is really watching Susan Mahoney, and not a potential rapist, acting the part of Alvaro. "What we were really seeing," Rahall explains, "was two women kissing. The subject of both characters was lesbian" (Rahall 1990b, 27). That subject multiplied as Alvaro, played by a woman impersonating a gay man, flirted with the King, played by Abby Kaplan, who performed "him" as butch.

Butch and femme are additional issues Rahall's company chose to play with, though they relied more on the education they got from the Split Britches workshop than on personal experiences of lesbians who express themselves as butch or femme. The role of Agnes was the only role Rahall precast, because she felt Agnes had to be played by a lesbian. The particular lesbian Rahall found for the role doesn't identify as either femme or butch but consciously or otherwise performs herself as a femme. This worked perfectly for Rahall's concept, which was that Agnes be "a femme in butch clothing" in order to reinforce what she believed was Trotter's intention: that Agnes be not only the subject in the play but also the object of desire "for all of the characters, even those who hated her" (Rahall 1990a, 26). Thus, the combat boots (actually black work boots from a local secondhand store). On a butch lesbian, combat boots would have made a monolithic statement; on Angelique von Halle, who created the role of Rahall's Agnes and had to practice before she got the knack of sitting with her knees apart, they were a little incongruous, intriguing.

The play went well in the tiny studio theater at Hampshire College in February, for an audience of the actors' friends and families, but Rahall felt it didn't mature until it reached WOW Cafe after a two-month hiatus. The New York audience "caught all the jokes," including ones the Hampshire audience failed to catch; the actors responded with more freedom and confidence in their roles, and, most important, Agnes and the Princess "connected to a point that they hadn't at Hampshire" (Rahall 1990b, 14).

Performing lesbian connection for a predominantly lesbian audience inspired (or intimidated) the actors playing Agnes and the Princess to invest their work with the fullest range of emotional depth and connection they could; this, in turn, made the contrast between their work and the camp roles sharper and freed the actors in those roles to take them to their limits. The performers, watching themselves be seen and seeing the seers, also "caught all the jokes." Spirals of cooperative seeing linked like intertwining mobius strips and reflected each other.

The majority opinion in the Smith College class I taught in Gay and Lesbian Theater (in which forty-six of the fifty-three participants identified themselves as lesbian) was that, although the number of lesbian plays that have been published since 1970 is encouraging and the knowledge that unscripted lesbian performances flourish in major cities is inspiring, they are not enough. Theater makers and would-be theatergoers suffer the same disappointments again and again: *Color-less:* so many plays about white, middle-class women "coming out." *Sexless:* fear of offending or threatening nonlesbian spectators, fear of politically incorrect expressions of desire. *Obscure:* encoded meanings, plays written to illustrate psycholinguistic or deconstruction theory. *Deadly. Deadly. Deadly.*

Poster advertising *Agnes de Castro*, Catherine Trotter's
seventeenth-century play. Karena Rahall's production was staged
in April 1990 at the WOW Cafe in New York. Poster by Peggy
Shaw.

One student said, "You'd think some of these playwrights wrote with their heterosexual mothers looking over their shoulders." Where is the sexual, racial, political, and social welter of the lesbian bar, bookstore, march, or even twelve-step meeting? Where is the raunchy, rebellious, loud, fucked-up, or punked-out foot-stomp and bellow of lesbian flesh and resistance? Feminisms, theories, and lesbian theater practices cross, intersect, and depart from one another in curious ways. Some evolving feminisms shut out the dyke on the street with academicized language; some react to men's violence against women by advocating a morality that some lesbians find sterile and restrictive; some artists, in an effort to transcend an oppressive sign system, make new signs whose meanings are accessible only to a "feminist" elite. Shut out, restricted, or excluded from feminist art making, those who would be spectators for new lesbian theater, those hungry for representations of themselves and their world, go dancing instead, in rooms full of mirrors.

One way through the bottleneck of theories and feminisms is a leap into the protofeminist past. *Agnes de Castro* offers no vision of Amazon nirvana, of the way things ought to be, or will be, come the revolution. Agnes and her bisexual Princess, never an ideal or liberated couple, end up dead. They inhabit an aristocratic white world both remote and, in the WOW Cafe context, absurd. But they love grandly and rebel fiercely against the lunatic social order that cannot see, and has no name for, what they are. The language of their love is breathtaking, gorgeous. They represent one of the faces of lesbian history. Lesbian history is, among other things, tragic. Camp. Goofy. Gorgeous.

REFERENCES

Cotton, Nancy. *Women Playwrights in England c. 1363–1750.* Lewisburg, Pa.: Bucknell University Press, 1980.

Davis, Jill, ed. *Lesbian Plays.* London: Methuen, 1987.

Faderman, Lillian. *Surpassing the Love of Men: Romantic Friendship and Love between Women from the Renaissance to the Present.* New York: William Morrow, 1981.

Gosse, Edmund. "Catherine Trotter, the Precursor of the Bluestockings." *Transactions of the Royal Society of Literature of the United Kingdom.* 2d ser., vol. 34. London: Oxford University Press, 1916.

Hoffman, William M., ed. *Gay Plays: The First Collection.* New York: Avon, 1979.

Irigaray, Luce. *Speculum of the Other Woman.* Trans. Gillian C. Gill. Ithaca: Cornell University Press, 1985.

Kendall, Kathryn. "From Lesbian Heroine to Devoted Wife: or, What the Stage Would Allow." *Journal of Homosexuality* 12, nos. 3–4 (May 1986): 9–22.

Pearson, Jacqueline. *The Prostituted Muse: Images of Women and Women Dramatists, 1642–1737.* New York: St. Martin's Press, 1988.

Rahall, Karena. "Queer and Feminist Theatre in Your Face." Unpublished MS, April 1990a.

———. "Retrospective Study of the Production of *Agnes de Castro* Staged at Hampshire College, February 1990, and at the WOW Cafe, April 1990." Unpublished MS, April 1990b.

Rahall, Karena, and the Hampshire College Theatre Collective, adaptors. *Agnes de Castro: A Tragedy by Catherine Trotter.* Unpublished play, 1990c.

Solomon, Alisa. "Cameos." *Village Voice* 35 (8 May 1990): 112.

Trotter, Catherine. *Agnes de Castro.* London: Performed 1695, published 1696. Reprint. In *The Plays of Mary Pix and Catherine Trotter,* edited by Edna L. Steeves, 2 vols. New York: Garland, 1982.

GAYLE AUSTIN

Resisting the Birth Mark: Subverting Hawthorne in a Feminist Theory Play

In Brief: No Suspense

This essay is about the process of conceiving, developing, and directing a feminist theory play. A deconstruction of Nathaniel Hawthorne's short story "The Birthmark," this play interrupted the narrative with short pieces of feminist theoretical texts and used various feminist and postmodern approaches to production.[1] The idea of a play that would be analogous to a theory film first occurred to me a year earlier, but this piece was conceived in August 1989 and over a period of five months was "written," rehearsed, and produced at Georgia State University in Atlanta. The rehearsal period included much improvisation and incorporation of the cast's ideas into the script. We put stress on process rather than product, and the ten-scene, half-hour-long script went through seven drafts.

Hawthorne's short story tells of a late eighteenth-century scientist who becomes obsessed with a birthmark on his wife's cheek. He subjects her to scientific observation and experimentation; at the end of the story the birthmark is gone, and the wife is dead. The feminist theorists whose texts I used are: literary critics Judith Fetterley and Elizabeth Meese, French writers Hélène Cixous and Catherine Clément, and theater writers Sue-Ellen Case, Jill Dolan, Marianne Goldberg, and Susan Yankowitz.

Director's Program Note

"Much of the text of this piece is taken directly from Nathaniel Hawthorne's short story 'The Birthmark.' First published in a magazine in 1843 (the year after Hawthorne's marriage), it was included in his collection *Mosses from an Old Manse* in 1846. Critics of the story tend to see it as a parable about the dangers of science overreaching itself, or about original sin or idealism. It is frequently anthologized and taught on the high school and college levels.

"This is a work-in-progress of what I call a feminist theory play. The idea is based on that of the theory film: a film that demonstrates in its form and/or content the theories that have been developed about the nature of film, its construction, how it works, and how it works upon the audience. To my knowledge, no one has tried to develop a play that would use feminist theories in a similar way to explore the nature of the relationship of performance and theatre to actual women as well as the image of 'Woman,' though some theatre directors use aspects of the related theory of deconstruction to approach classic plays.

"The piece has changed over the period of rehearsal, with helpful contributions made by everyone involved. It is not finished, may never be, but I do plan to continue to work on it. I consider it the first in a series. Audience feedback is welcome. I can be reached through the Department of Communication at Georgia State."

Am I a Feminist Director?

I am a feminist, but I do not have conventional director training. I took one course in directing as an undergraduate in a liberal arts program in which I stressed dramatic literature and criticism. Most of my work in professional theater has been as a dramaturg and literary manager, which has allowed me to meet and observe many directors, designers, and actors but which is generally considered more administrative than "creative." But, on the other hand, if I was untrained, I was also helpfully unconstrained.

I have been pulled between the binary oppositions of administrative and creative, academic and professional, theory and practice, for twenty years. For once I decided to stand still in the crack, extend one arm in each direction, and pull.

August 1988

At the Women and Theatre Preconference of the Association for Theatre in Higher Education in San Diego, in the midst of beautiful weather and emotional and intellectual upheaval, I thought and said aloud for the first time, "What about a theory play?" At least one person said, "*You* do it." Not me, I thought. I had written some short plays a while back, but this seemed a big undertaking. I did, however, start taking notes:

> Theory play:
> humor
> I don't know what this has to do with theory, but . . .
> I desire theory
> liminality
> narrative
> doubling/split subject/multiple subject

I felt informed by them all as I worked, but the first note—humor—was all but absent from the final work—Top of the list next time.

Inspirations

"A theory film." I could not remember, until months after this production, where I first heard the phrase, but it was in E. Ann Kaplan's book *Women and Film* (1983), read while I was taking a course at New York University in the summer of 1984. The name I associated with the phrase was Yvonne Rainer.

In 1987 *Women & Performance* published a Rainer filmscript. Marianne Goldberg wrote about feminist film theorist Laura Mulvey and the film: "Yvonne Rainer's 1985 film, *The Man Who Envied Women,* takes Mulvey's view to its logical conclusion. It radically breaks with conventional representational modes by refusing the visual image of the female protagonist and doubling the lead male" (1987–88, 97). In the script the woman is represented only through voice-over, and pieces of theoretical texts are used in various ways. I absorbed the general outline of this information but did not consciously refer to it until after my production. I interpolated her methods by inverting them, representing the patriarchal Hawthorne narrator only through a male tape-recorded voice, which was turned on and off by female performers, and doubling the role of the Feminist Critic with two actresses.

The spring 1988 issue of *TDR: A Journal of Performance Studies* contained two articles that must have entered my subconscious before the August 1988 conference: Elin Diamond discussed feminist uses of Brechtian theory, and Peggy Phelan discussed (among other things) Yvonne Rainer's film. Rereading the articles after my production, certain sections leapt out as inspirations for what I had done.

Diamond put Brecht back into my mind, from which premises he had been evicted for misogyny many years earlier. Obviously, the techniques of alienation he developed could be used for feminist ends, if we just worked on it. Phelan described a scene from *The Man Who Envied Women* that contained "a harrowing and hilarious rhetorical contest between Jack and Jackie; he quotes Foucault's *Discipline and Punish* (1977), and she responds with Morris's 'The Pirate's Fiancée' (1979)" (1988, 113–14). This became, in my play, the alternating voices of two feminist critics, one roughly "materialist," the other "cultural," who at one point arm wrestled. "Most avant-garde film works so hard to thwart narrative structure that the rigidity of the exclusion paradoxically increases the spectator's desire for its presence" (Phelan 1988, 114). I decided that ways needed to be found to keep the audience looking at the enactments, even while it was pushing them away in many ways. I kept in mind the Brechtian traffic accident idea for holding attention and combined short, unexpected scenes with the general line of narrative from the Hawthorne story. I thought: throw them a bone but point out in every way that it's poison.

August 1989

When I began writing a chapter for my book *Feminist Theories for Dramatic Criticism* using Judith Fetterley's *The Resisting Reader,* I was particularly taken with the passion in her writing and her anger at the way American male authors had portrayed women over the centuries. I found her work perfectly applicable to plays by Eugene O'Neill and wrote about that. Her remarks on Nathaniel Hawthorne's story "The Birthmark" remained in my mind. She calls it a success story—"the demonstration of how to murder your wife and get away with it." Other phrases stuck: "the only good woman is a dead one"; "the idealization of women has its source in a profound hostility toward women"; "the hand which shaped Georgiana's birth has left its mark on her in *blood*"; female characters "are projections, not people"; and "Georgiana is co-opted into a view of herself as flawed and comes to hate herself as an impediment to Aylmer's aspiration" (1978, 22, 24, 25, 29, 32).

During a phone call with Mary Karen Dahl toward the end of August I talked about the book chapter I had just written. I thought Fetterley's writing had a dramatic sense in its passion. Sometime during that talk I remembered the previous summer. I mentioned my idea of a feminist theory play and the directive from someone: "*You* do it." Mary Karen was encouraging. The pieces "Fetterley," "Hawthorne," and "theory play" fell together, and I speculated about a performance using Fetterley's words to interrupt Hawthorne's narrative. As had happened many times during other discussions with colleagues, the speaking and thinking and feedback combined to make something that wasn't there before. I was off.

I began with the idea of Hawthorne and Fetterley at podiums on two sides of the stage speaking their texts while scientist Aylmer and wife Georgiana act out the story in the space between them. At one point I saw Fetterley trying to stop Georgiana from taking the potion offered by Aylmer. She wants to rescue her. She rushes from the podium and grabs the goblet. Fetterley gets drawn into the action, despite the fact that she has asserted that "Georgiana" is only a male construct and doesn't really exist. In the production a form of this moment remained, but it was much more intellectualized and lacked the impact of the critic losing her "objectivity," since she had already interacted with Georgiana many times earlier in the play.

At first there was no immediate production slot at Georgia State for this piece, yet I felt from the first that, while I was "writing," I was also "directing." I began taking notes late in August:

—"Resisting the Birth Mark: Theory Play I" (in a series)
—male voice-over telling story, visuals commenting on it
—wife, after she dies, gets up and takes care of him
—frame with actors in rehearsal clothes, go into roles
—early on tell high points of story: no suspense
—the horror: draw audience in, then interrupt
—THERE IS NO MARK ON THE ACTRESS'S CHEEK
—the birthmark is her sex
—audience close to actors, raked seats, looking down as in a surgical amphitheater, harsh overhead light, crude table

—dueling discourses

—separate audience as they come in, male and female sections, on opposite sides of actors

—Georgiana has a double (her mother?)

—closure: any? what kind?

—Georgiana becomes a big handprint, or projections of one, maybe onto her body

—he tries to fetishize her; the birthmark interferes, so he negatively fetishizes it

—the mark is her life, the marks he has made in his lab book are his; he reads hers and is revolted and acts on it, she reads his and gains insight into him but no power to act on it and absorbs his revulsion

—her face rests on the book (the two marks meet); she bursts into tears

—Hawthorne, visible, writing? says both their lines for them? walks into scene and takes A's [Aylmer's] place while still speaking for G. (she mouths words?)

—or he reads narration, she is directed by NH [Nathaniel Hawthorne], who whispers into her ear before each speech

—at one point stress melodrama, woman in peril plot ("Gaslight"); she breaks character, says there's no point in trying to save her, she's going to die (she wants to?)

—double cast G. [Georgiana] and Aylmer with black and white actors, split subjects, but men work together similarly, women differently

—perhaps have both male and female play each role

—same four actors play all parts

—use unseen male voice-over only for Hawthorne

—perhaps insert myself: at offstage table, running lights and sound?

—first half male gaze constructs female image; second half deconstruct image, woman becomes active subject, takes over discourse as well as lights and sound

—use audience's desire for closure, until they realize they are wishing for the enactment of her death; point that out to them

—split female subject unites at some point; two actresses work together at something to make their fate better

—NH uses mike [microphone] throughout, can leave stage, not be seen, still do v.o. [voice-over] and dominate

—Fetterley never leaves stage, participates, is among characters

—NH gives G. her lines on cards or in her ear, except for her singing and gestures

—start with one actress laid out on table, looked at as audience comes in

—perhaps podiums down on auditorium floor level, "characters" on apron

—stage manager (female) visible with sound and light controls

—four actors, all in identical warm-up outfits, assume roles, toss costume pieces back and forth, arbitrary who gets which one

—actresses draw "beauty marks" on each other, like schoolgirls making up, or like a rite?

—project text onto set, walls; women walk into and out of, having text on them

—actress holds a sign: "this is not a Woman"

—A. asks G. to sing; she screams; he reacts as if she is singing.

Many of these ideas were not used, but some of them were. Some changed in the course of rehearsal. Some of them could be used in another piece. Looking back at these notes, I see that the ideas for directing this text evolved simultaneously with the text itself. The play was "written" by photocopying selected pages of text, pasting passages on separate 3 × 5 index cards, arranging the cards on a large flat surface, and letting them fall into a pattern of ten scenes. I used most of the sections of dialogue from the original short story, and a few sections of the original narration, in chronological order, interrupting them at frequent intervals with relevant passages of theory. Then the cards were photocopied onto pages and eventually typed into script form, but only at the latest possible minute. I thought of choosing the passages as script writing, and arranging the cards as something on the cusp of script writing and directing. This part of the process gave me a great deal of pleasure, the loose shaping of ideas and words in a way I had never done before. Even without the goal of a specific production, I felt I was making theater with my cards that would just have to be seen, somewhere.

Process

I made several more phone calls during the fall of 1989, trying out ideas on colleagues, asking for support and encouragement to continue with the project. My confidence grew and the script began to take shape. The first draft (14 September 1989) had a cast of four: Georgiana, Judith Fetterley, Aylmer, and Nathaniel Hawthorne. Along with the dialogue and narration from the story, there was only Fetterley's text as intervention. I also continued to envision the play as taking place in a performing space between two podia. I was given a performance slot in January 1990, and the need for a script became more pressing. By the second draft (November 1989), I added other feminist texts, designating the speaker of those texts "Feminist Critic," rather than Fetterley. The actors I wanted to cast were two females, one male, a female performing the job of stage manager, and a male to do a voice-over tape of Hawthorne's narration.

Draft 3 (15 November 1989), done after a cold reading, added a few specific stage directions and trimmed down the narration sections. This draft was used for auditions, held in November. At the auditions two actresses read well for the Feminist Critic, and I cast both. They were very different physical types, and I was seized by the idea of splitting the role of critic in two, giving one mostly materialist lines and the other lines that pertained mostly to the body, with each retaining some of Fetterley's text. This resulted in a rearranged draft 4 (20 November 1989), with the cast designated as Performers A through F, with which we went into the first phase of rehearsals.

After a week of rehearsals one of the actresses playing a Feminist Critic withdrew from the production. She felt she could not be "feminine" and "feminist" at the same time. She clearly felt embodying this role was more than playing a part. The remaining cast members and I discussed her departure, and I asked if anyone else had reservations about participating. No one else spoke of leaving. The commitment of the remaining students to the material was firm and growing. I was grateful that she had withdrawn at an early point. Pleased with the effect of having two Feminist Critics, I decided to retain the concept. The actress cast as Stage Manager moved into Feminist Critic and the Assistant Stage Manager into Stage Manager. The second Feminist Critic, which had been conceived of for one body, quickly took on new traits in a different body, one that was considerably larger and included an operatic singing voice. Suddenly she sang, and theory about opera was added. We had several sessions of reading the script aloud and began some improvisation with movement. Over the Thanksgiving break I did further revisions.

On December 6 Marc Lepine killed fourteen women at an engineering school in Montreal. On December 8 I had several conversations about the crime and about the fact that he had said, "You're all a bunch of feminists! I hate feminists!" as he killed the women. Just before rehearsal that evening I added a short section, in which the male actor jumps onto the table and says those words. The actress who most often plays Georgiana says, "I'm not a feminist," and the male actor mimes shooting the women. This new section completed draft 5 (8 December 1989), from which the actors began to seriously memorize lines.

The second phase of rehearsal began to resemble a more conventional rehearsal process. We worked scene by scene, but I continued to change movement, resulting in draft 6 (21 December 1989). I often asked the actors to perform a section in several different ways. They gave me feedback on what they felt worked and what did not. I almost always agreed with their perceptions. They were, indeed, co-authors of this work. Yet I reserved the right to make the final decisions and did the actual "rewriting" myself. I called on two professional women directors I knew in Atlanta and a male colleague at Georgia State to observe some rehearsals and particularly to help me and the actors with matters of stage movement, mime, and dance. I wanted these elements to be in the production, but was acutely aware of my lack of experience. Their help was generously given and aided tremendously.

We began the third and final phase of rehearsals just after New Year's Day and worked intensively up to opening on 11 January. Everyone now worked off book, and technical aspects were added, day by day. Even at this point some blocking changed. Blocking for the end of the piece was not set until shortly before opening. I continually stressed that this was a workshop, that the aim was to make the piece as good as it could be, not simply to showcase the acting skills of the performers involved. This was not the usual way of working for these students, but they performed beautifully. I tried to give as much stability and consistency as possible without boxing myself into not changing what needed to be changed. A balance was achieved, and the show went on. The final draft (7) is dated 20 January 1990, closing night.

Product

The production itself was my idea of "poor theater." From the beginning I was aware of stealing the basic mise-en-scène from the production of the Wooster Group's *Rumstick Road,* which I had seen at the Performing Garage in New York City. The flat black painted quality, the white light, the examination table with a woman's body on it, and the visible stage manager were imprinted on my mind, though I set the stage manager downstage left with her back to the audience, rather than up center, facing the audience. The actual control of lights, slides, and sound was performed at that table, which also held a keyboard and props. I was also aware that I was trying to use these avant-garde, deconstructive techniques toward an explicitly feminist end. I had not seen much feminism in the New York avant-garde work of the 1970s and 1980s, even by a woman director such as Liz LeCompte.

My favorite moment in the production came just after Georgiana took the potion, while Aylmer was observing her reactions and the taped male voice was narrating. I had the actor playing Aylmer move into the audience area and turn on a classroom-type overhead projector that threw a beam of light onto the woman's body on stage. As the voice told of Aylmer's observations, the actor began to "draw" on the woman's body, feet to head, using a red marker. By the time he reached the head, the tape had been turned off. One of the feminist critics spoke a piece of Fetterley's text, building to a crescendo of words, with Aylmer madly scribbling all over her body. Blackout.

The only review of the play, written by student M. Helen Bolton, appeared in the Georgia State *Signal* on 30 January 1990:

> *Resisting The Birthmark* [*sic*] was, well sorta strange. It was very interesting, just strange. . . . The acting was good although there were a few odd moments such as when characters started switching places with other characters. Or maybe that was just another thing that went over my head or between my legs or something like that. But all in all it was a good play I guess. I mean like I

said the acting was fine and a few actresses sang with beautiful voices but the whole point of the play was, well, beyond me.

Most audiences were very quiet. A majority of the audience members were black and had come to see the second play on the bill that evening, "Oh, Slavery Days," a piece compiled and directed by my colleague Shirlene Holmes, which was composed of slave narratives. Only a few people left during *Resisting the Birth Mark,* which surprised me. A few colleagues from the university and from the theater community were very supportive and encouraged me to continue with this line of investigation. One reaction that stayed in my mind was: "I didn't understand it all, but it held my interest, moment to moment."

Summing Up

To some extent this process was an experiment in spectator tolerance. How much can anyone take before her or his receptors close down? How much text, how much interrupted narrative, how much absence of humor and lack of familiar conventions can any spectator absorb?

Compromises:
I gave them narrative but interrupted it.
I gave them actors performing individual "characters" 80 percent of the time but had them switch roles the other 20 percent, including one instance of gender-reversal.
I sometimes had the theory being spoken also being "acted out" simultaneously but often the actions came before or after the words.

I tried to let boundaries blur between my critical/theoretical reading and writing, teaching, and "creative" writing and directing. The texts of theory became part of staging. The rehearsal period became a form of teaching, as did the videotape later. The show has led to ideas for future productions. And the production has led to ideas for future research.

After the initial production was over I began to envision an evening of short feminist theory plays, riffs on male texts about women, using feminist theory ideas and texts performatively. Male texts might include: anthropological fieldwork, psychological case studies, or histories of science, films, and even plays.

January 1992

In fact, the second feminist theory play I wrote was a longer one-act play deconstructing Ibsen's play, which I call "The Doll House Show." At the time of this writing it is in rehearsal, directed by my graduate student, Deb Calabria. The line between directing and writing is crossed constantly by both of us. I have enjoyed giving up some of the day-to-day practical problems to another person and gain from an additional perspective. We collaborate continuously.

The play has two women playing Nora, two playing Gracie Allen, one playing Laura Kieler (the "real-life" model for Nora, who was put in an asylum by her husband then returned to him and their children), one playing Barbie (the doll), and three men playing Ibsen, Torvald, Rank, Michael Meyer, a carnival barker, and a tour guide. All the women speak various feminist theories at different times in the play. The audience is separated according to gender and have two different environmental experiences.

So I end these "notes from the front" in the midst of rehearsing. And theorizing. And teaching.

NOTE

1. In creating a title for this piece, I deliberately broke up Hawthorne's title into its component parts, from "birthmark" to "birth mark."

REFERENCES

Fetterley, Judith. 1978. *The Resisting Reader: A Feminist Approach to American Fiction.* Bloomington: Indiana University Press.
Goldberg, Marianne. 1987–88. "The Body, Discourse, and *The Man Who Envied Women.*" *Women & Performance* 3:97–102.
Kaplan, E. Ann. 1983. *Women and Film: Both Sides of the Camera.* London: Methuen.
Phelan, Peggy. 1988. "Feminist Theory, Poststructuralism, and Performance." *TDR: A Journal of Performance Studies* 32 (Spring): 107–27.

Sabrina Hamilton

Split Britches and the *Alcestis* Lesson: "What Is This Albatross?"

The art of theater consists of knowing who to steal from. I am certainly not the first person to steal from Split Britches, nor will I be the last. This essay is partly about my work with Split Britches on *Alcestis,* but it is also about how that experience shaped my own direction on a completely different project in Berlin.[1]

The Split Britches Theater Company,[2] which consists of Deborah Margolin, Peggy Shaw, Lois Weaver, and their production manager, Heidi Blackwell, received funding in the fall of 1989 to do a college residency.[3] Under the terms of the grant they were to undertake a production of Euripides's *Alcestis,* working with the students enrolled in an introductory theater course called Feminist Theater. I cotaught that course and participated in the development of the show. My primary task was lighting design.

The following summer (1990) I was invited to devise and direct a production based on the Ikarus legend at one of Berlin's "off-theaters," Theater Zerbröchene Fenster (Broken Window). I decided that I didn't want to work on a solo piece, nor was I interested in working only with men, so the production interwove the myths of Eve and Lilith with the stories of Ikarus and Daedalus. It was a daunting experience working on an original script in a foreign country where I speak little of the language and in a culture that socially, politically, and theatrically was undergoing a period of intense change. While I was there, I transcribed a lengthy taped interview with the members of Split Britches (made shortly after the residency) about their views on women and directing. While these two theatrical experiences were quite distinct, there are similarities in the ways that they deviated from standard modes of direction and theater-making.

The experience of preparing for rehearsal in Germany while listening to the words taped in New York is something I would like to share.

Briefly, *Alcestis* is about a king, Admetus, whose time has come to die. But due to the intercession of Apollo, he will be granted a reprieve if he can find someone to die in his stead. His wife, Alcestis, volunteers to take his place, and he accepts. Initially, Split Britches felt very resistant to the script primarily because of its inherently heterosexual plot line. As a lesbian couple, Peggy and Lois saw no connection to issues that were important to them in their own lives. They remember sitting around and asking themselves: "Why are we doing *Alcestis?* What *is* this albatross?" Their response, finally, was to subvert the play and to find ways to write their interests and concerns into it. Their initial disappointment at not being able to "start from scratch" gave way to their belief that "there are no accidents."

One of the most important tools that Split Britches uses in the creation of their work is fantasy. They began by inviting class members to fantasize their roles in the production, both onstage and offstage. This was tremendously empowering to the students because it eliminated a lot of the competition for roles or production positions. Since the production was to be based on *Alcestis,* there were some clear ideas for possible characters, though characters could be added, deleted, combined, or altered to suit the needs and interests of the group. As a result, from the very outset of *Honey, I'm Home* (the title of our version of *Alcestis*), instead of there being a solitary playwright, everyone was involved in the writing of the piece. Even people who wanted to work on the production but who did not want to perform were included in the process of script development.

Similarly, the project in Berlin had some requirements attached to it. I was invited specifically to direct a member of the resident company, Johannes Hupka, in the role of Ikarus. Together we had decided what the other roles were and had fixed most of the production positions prior to my arrival. I still needed, however, to find the three other cast members. In casting the two women's roles, Eve and Lilith, I drew on the Split Britches technique of casting the ensemble before casting the specific roles. I chose the two women, Anya Kaul and Karin Plichta-Sölding, both for their performance skills and their potential for developing the piece. As with the *Alcestis* ensemble, they were involved in scripting their roles as well as performing them.

The initial rehearsals were devoted to imagining what our version of the Ikarus legend might be and how we would portray the characters we had selected. I chose to have everyone work on *all* the roles, including the designers and production personnel. This meant that the investment of the ensemble was in the piece as a whole, not just their assigned part in it. More cooks can sometimes result in more and richer soup.

Another aspect of the way Split Britches works is that the script, the performances, the design elements, the music, and the staging all develop simultaneously instead of following the standard theatrical sequence of script, music, design, staging, and performance. Work on one area is likely to lead to ideas for another. In addition to performance skills each of the company members has additional areas of strength that they bring to each session. Lois's primary function is that of director. Peggy is the group's primary designer and technician, while Deb is the company's wordsmith, the one who transforms the group's improvisations into the final script.

It is of particular importance that the directing process and the writing process for a Split Britches production are not divided but that they happen simultaneously. No one discovers a play and decides to direct it. As Lois says: "When we start a project, we don't have a very concrete idea of what it's going to be. We start with a few ideas in a great unknown and sort of let the play build itself." They believe strongly in using their personal feelings and responses as the taproot for their plays. They follow their own interests, using what's happening in their daily lives as grist for the mill and not worrying about whether the audience will "get it." Part of Split Britches' political strategy is based on the belief that audiences will recognize the global in their personal material.

After the initial nucleus of ideas has formed, Lois, Peggy, and Deb enter a phase of development that consists of sitting around, eating pasta, and making phone calls. They bring in any material that looks remotely interesting. It might be a book, a movie, a song, a story, a memory, or pictures. One idea informs another as they brainstorm. They begin to memorize and enact parts of things they have written, collected, or observed. But all the while they are "scribing" the process. In this technique one or more of the group takes notes at every session, and this material subsequently becomes the central "image bank" for the show. Each of them has a different

Ikarus, played by Johannes Hupka, being trained to fly by Eve, played by Karin Plichta-Sölding, in Sabrina Hamilton's Berlin production of *Wenn Vögel Flügel Hatten, Der Fall Ikarus*. Photo by Martin Ostrowski.

notational style: Lois keeps notes on the overall journey of the play; Deb tends to document ideas, images, and funny lines that people say; and Peggy is the one who records visual images.

In this process they also reserve the right to script themselves *out* of certain parts, or to not pursue material that may be of interest to the others. Lois says:

> It's a lot about desire. You've really got to ask "What do you want to say? [What is] the fantasy, what do you want to do on stage?" And then, [what are] the other desires, like, "I don't want a lot of lines," or "I did this last time," or "I don't want to do this." And usually when we express the "I don't," that's exactly what we end up doing. It works that way too.

Ironically, as Lois points out, what one is afraid to do onstage often becomes the most alluring.

In Berlin, when I asked the performers what they had always wanted to do onstage, one of them admitted that she wanted to work in a postmodern dance style of performance. This led me to cast her as Lilith, who was largely nonverbal and whose performance was interwoven with projections, special effects, and synthesized sound. By contrast, the woman playing Eve had come from a largely nonnaturalistic acting background and was interested in exploring dialogue, as was Johannes, the actor playing Ikarus. As a result, most of the dialogue in the show was between the two of them. Johannes was also interested in ballet as a form related to flying, and, just as Split Britches found a way to incorporate 1950s rock'n'roll classics into *Honey, I'm Home,* we managed to incorporate a "dream ballet" into our production. I found that the simultaneous use of different performance styles greatly enhanced the theatricality of the event.

Back to Split Britches. As a director, Lois sets up the exercises that will help generate the material. She usually decides what the company will talk about or work on in each meeting or rehearsal. After a time there is a phase of stepping back. This consists of putting the material into some kind of order and seeing what connective material is needed. Gaps may be filled through improvisations, discussion, or by asking Deb to write something. She frequently comes up with material based on what gets scribed in previous sessions. Deb says: "Lois has a dramatist's eye for sequence, for what follows what. She sees in advance of the moment what is required to keep the journey of the play moving on course. Lois says 'Here's a blank,' and I'm good at filling in that blank."

The classical director, though she or he can sometimes make cuts, is usually duty bound to find a way to make the script work, while Lois can simply work with the rest of her team to alter the script. While Lois is working as playwright to structure the material, she is also thinking as a director about the blocking, emotional beats, transitions, and pacing. In traditional theater practice the point at which the director usually gets involved for the first time is after the completion of the script. She or he is then faced with the task of trying to discover what the play is about and finding ways to represent that onstage. In the case of Split Britches there is a conflation of the scripting and directorial processes, which is possible because a creative team already knows what the material is about.

Deb speaks of how empowering their process is, emphasizing the joy of not having to consider the audience and whether or not they think she looks good or sings well. The company works instead in a process that validates all of their experiences as theatrically viable. By not allowing the audience to become censors or judges, they are left with a feeling of great privacy and depth in the work. The writing in *Honey, I'm Home* contains many images that are obviously very deep for the actors who conceived and performed them but may have been obscure to the audience. Initially, I was afraid that this type of writing would distance the audience, but I think it actually pulled them in. Not only were they made curious and interested, but they responded to the emotional integrity of the performance.

Split Britches allowed the production process to show during the performance. There was one scene in which Peggy, who played Admetus, leaned over Lois (as Alcestis) on her deathbed, and seemingly forgot her lines. Lois opened one eye and prompted Peggy. Peggy continued to need her help and Lois was soon assisted in the prompting by Deb, who, besides having written these lines, was playing the role of Death. Peggy finally broke in saying: "I can't take this! . . . I said I didn't want so many lines. And I didn't want to play a man." What ensued was a scene right in the middle of the play in which all three sat down on the steps center stage and stripped away the theatrical layers until what was left was three women discussing their roles, their process, their work, and theater in general. Later in the scene Peggy, Lois, and Deb cut short the discussion (and the scene) by saying:

> *Peggy:* What does that mean?
> *Lois and Deb:* I don't know.
> *Lois:* Look, let's just get on with it.

This scene provides a glimpse into how different the Split Britches style of performance is from prevailing theatrical process. They truly are the subjects of their work. Nobody makes a piece "on them," as often happens with dance companies, nor are they "interpreting" or "embodying" someone else's work. Deb, Peggy, Lois, and the students working on *Honey, I'm Home* retained responsibility and control, and the audience was made aware of this.

The scene described above is also of interest because with all

Deb Margolin as "Death" looms over Peggy Shaw as
Admetus and Lois Weaver as Alcestis in *Honey, I'm Home*.
Peggy has forgotten her lines and ad libs (*sotto voce*): "I
don't think we are being very responsible here. No matter
what we do, we are portraying lesbians in a bad light.
There are students here." Lois: "Well, look at me. I have to
die in order to play a tragic heroine. . . ." Photo by Phil
Wyatt.

three of them onstage there was no company member outside to serve as director for the scene. As Lois pointed out, the scene was essentially directed by the writing process. Since it was an edited re-creation of a real-life rehearsal, their primary task on stage was to present a selected view of themselves. Deb appeared as the one who wanted to make sense of the language, while Lois was the one who wanted to keep things going smoothly, and Peggy, ever the moral barometer, resisted, saying "I'm not going to do this!" and "This isn't right!" The scene was so tightly and simply scored that the audience soon caught on to the idea that it was a dramatization rather than a spontaneous breakdown of the piece. It was an example, however, of a device that I use often in my work. If one invokes the "liveness" of theater, where the unexpected and unplanned can easily happen, and scores in a "mistake," the audience is riveted. The stakes are raised, and, when the show is resumed, the audience is present with a renewed attention.

The rest of the play was structured so that Alcestis died fairly early in the evening. One of the first premises of the project was that Alcestis would be rescued from the world of the dead to speak her piece, but the script developed such that the Alcestis who returned was not the Alcestis played by Lois but, instead, the spirit of Alcestis as embodied by women whose deaths were the result of male abuse. This dramaturgical decision had the fringe benefit of allowing Lois to direct more of the production from the outside, which was a decided advantage in working with a large group of fledgling performers.

Split Britches left most of the scoring of their own performances until last. In working on their sections they used the student assistant director as an outside eye. They appreciated her feedback, even if it was advice that they frequently chose not to take. The rejected ideas served as a catalyst by provoking a reaction of "Oh no, we won't do that; we'll do this." This kind of outside eye can galvanize the group and help it take the next step.

In their own work, when not serving as outside eyes for each other, the women of Split Britches have developed what Peggy calls a "muscle" that allows them to sense how they look to the audience. They are adept at gauging the audience's reactions and adjusting the show accordingly. This is something I think most performers do, but they are frequently told that it shows their lack of concentration.

This is particularly true in schools of naturalistic acting in which the director is deemed to be the only person allowed to say how anyone looks onstage. I think this disempowers the performers and requires that they deny their own perception of their work. Split Britches also relies selectively on comments from friends. In self-created and performed work it can be crucial to have an outside "eye" who does not have the final word on a piece, as distinct from the way the traditional director functions. This is a role that I have often played, and it seems especially prevalent among women. The authority and ownership lie with the initiator of the piece, who has the final word in all matters, but the piece still benefits from having an outsider as an early audience and feedback device.[4]

When I asked Peggy to describe the difference between male and female directors she remarked on what she calls the male tendency to "get psychological, especially in Freudian terms." In this model, after having taken the trouble to discover what lies under the text, the actors, with the help of the director, rebury it as "subtext." But with Split Britches one has a sense of everything being turned inside out. In standard theatrical terms I find it akin to making the subtext the text, something that can only happen if one is both writer and performer. The text always makes emotional sense, though not necessarily logical sense. It is a product of an inclusive, horizontal process, open to the irrational, allowed to remain personal. The permission to include personal imagery that may feel somewhat obscure to the audience gives the piece a very particular aesthetic, unpolished by some dramatic standards but brimming with authenticity. Thus, the audience is trained to think associatively, while the creators maintain a sense of nonobjectification, of privacy and control.

When asked to compare their work with the work usually produced by men Peggy described the latter as "not trusting the relationship between the women, so they do what I call 'cocaine editing': Wham! Wham! Wham! I'm not saying that there's anything wrong with exciting the audience or moving a play along, but it's a question of trusting that a woman or a personal thing is important enough to hold an audience's attention." Split Britches believes that in feminist theater you choose and develop your own roles. Further, Lois speaks of bringing out the best in performers by not applying her ideas of what she thinks the character should be in order to "serve the play." She defines feminist directing as a system that pulls the best out of a person, rather than "slapping something onto them to transform them into something that they're not." And, if a manifestation of internal beauty is far preferable to achieving some external aesthetic ideal, suddenly it is possible to rethink standards of beauty.

This often results not just in nontraditional casting (i.e., reversed gender, different standards of beauty and professional levels of skills like singing and dancing) but in nontraditional role formation. Split Britches, for example, takes images and archetypes from popular culture. The group may add to the image or combine it with a conflicting image: Deb playing a diva playing Death, Lois playing Marilyn Monroe playing Donna Reed of television sit-com fame playing the role of Alcestis, and Peggy playing the Doctor/Dad in "Father Knows Best" playing the role of Admetus. During improvisational sessions they helped the students find archetypes that related to their performance fantasies. Once these were finalized, the actors felt more at ease in their work of trying to develop material for the script instead of from the script.

And what of the women directors trying to work in the commercial world? Peggy likens the situation of the woman director to that of Margaret Thatcher:

> Working in the traditional world you don't even realize how steeped you are in those values; so unless you have contact with alternative ways of working I don't see how you can know anything else. Thatcher was in a world where she was not given any alternative and neither did she search out any alternative. To get where she was, she became used to living in a man's political world. And unless they're exceptional, it's the same thing for women directors.

Peggy's words had special resonance for me when I was in Berlin. I was working with a company that was used to male directors who tended to be extremely autocratic. Like many women who have directed under such circumstances, I found that the company wanted me to replicate that model. My encouraging them to make it *our* piece, not just *my* piece, was initially met with great distrust and anxiety. The fact that we were having fun in rehearsals made them suspect that the work was not good. They believed that a state of angst is necessary to create good work. I suspected that they wanted me to yell or break things, because it's often easier when there's a big bad Daddy director to absolve everyone of the responsibility for their work. It takes more time to develop work along the feminist model, and there was a fear that the work in Berlin wasn't happening quickly enough and that the extensive improvisations and discussions were not leading directly to material that could be performed for an audience. They deeply distrusted their own ability to write and perform text. But, because I have little command of German, they quickly saw the need to take responsibility in this area. The process transformed them from actors waiting passively to be directed into co-composers of the work and may have been the most successful part of our collaboration.

My intuition led me to try something I had never tried before. I assigned the entire production team to write what we called "haikus," or little three-line pieces of text. These were then typed up on strips of paper, which were placed in a hat. A company member would draw a strip and then stage it, developing a scenario in which the text could be used, casting it as she or he saw fit. The lines "Where?" "There." "Already gone." for instance, were tried out in rehearsal as lines for Lilith speaking about some magic she was weaving but ended up in the final script as the opening dialogue between Ikarus and Eve as they watched sea gulls on the beach. Each haiku was staged twice in rehearsal with two different company members serving as "directors," so that it was clear that they were simple linguistic frameworks on which a variety of scenes could rest. But, more important, the company saw that they were all capable of writing the text for a scene. We created more material in this manner than we could have possibly used, but generally I find it far easier to trim or cut portions of a show than to add or create new material.

In the process of making *Honey, I'm Home* Split Britches could have chosen to work from the anger that the play evoked, but Lois comments: "It sounds real corny to say this, but in order to do this kind of work, you have to go to a place that's a lot about love. I mean it's about that openness." They describe their work as coming from a "prepolitical" place in which unconditional trust must be established before one can build the politics. Ultimately, this kind of subversion seems to be generated from a sense of spirituality and a sense of humor.

Honey, I'm Home was hilarious in its examination of the way "maleness" gets constructed, and male students certainly joined in the fun. In one scene Peggy, as Admetus, led the three male students who played Heracles, Admetus's father, and Admetus's best friend in a rollicking version of the Muddy Waters's song "I'm a Man." This song includes lyrics such as

> All you pretty women
> Standing in line
> I can make love to you, baby
> In an hour's time
> 'Cause I'm a man
> Spelled M-A-N . . .

The audience roared at the hyper-butch choreography as they spelled out the letters with their bodies, but perhaps the funniest thing was that, because of their youth and relative inexperience in performing, Peggy was certainly the most successful "male" performer of the four. The "real man" in the scene was actually a woman.

Both Split Britches and I came to *Honey, I'm Home* from working in a New York theater scene that had left us burnt out, betrayed, and jaded in many ways. Working on the show resulted in a renewal of energy and commitment. For Lois it "wasn't just one of those bonding experiences you get in a workshop. There was something beyond that." Peggy thinks that the renewal has to do with her worry about the future and the sense that "these kids are not just kids that are gonna be in the audience, they're gonna be doing it." There was a sense of preparing the future generation, as Deb said, "of making a difference in someone's life with no strings attached." It was, as Lois put it, "a creative fitness program," a sort of artistic aerobics that left them feeling "muscled." Their confidence in their process was enhanced, and their unexpected pleasure in using Euripides's structure led Lois to discover that she is interested in working on another Greek classic. The salient effect, however, was one of regeneration.

From my perspective another important aspect of Split Britches' work with students was that it provided them with a model of how gay and straight feminists can work together. Though always referring to lesbian culture, the work of Split Britches is not about coming out as lesbians but, rather, as Lois puts it, "about taking it for granted that lesbians exist in the world." Their shows are built from their lives, and, as lesbianism is an essential part of Lois and Peggy's identities, it is inevitably represented and explored in their work without their needing to point to it. Peggy says: "We don't come from a political point of view per se. We do come from our personal experiences; that's how we're able to do this." Lois reflects: "This leaves us marginal in both worlds. We're marginal in the straight world because we're not straight, and we feel marginal in the lesbian world because we're not straight (laughs) in our presentation. . . . We do another kind of theatre that the gay community often doesn't understand."

Prior to the arrival of Split Britches the class had been reading and discussing the different strains of feminism and had gotten stuck on two words used by Sue-Ellen Case in her book *Feminism and Theatre:* "separatism" and "man-hating." At certain moments it seemed as if those were the only two words in the book. They became synonymous with "feminism." By the time the women of Split Britches arrived, all of the students' fears were quite close to the surface. Deb remembers: "We had come to symbolize some kind of nine-headed monster, and it seemed to me that when we walked in and were reasonably pleasant and accessible, it was like preparing to meet a monster and in comes a little kitty." And then we watched a class fall in love. The effect has been lasting. What the students took away from the project was a sense that gays and straights can work together without either side being erased and that individuality need not be obliterated by politics. New types of shows are being produced as part of the school's theater season, and they are being created and rehearsed in new ways. Even students who were not a part of the process are feeling its effects. What would be considered a deviation from the norm in most of the commercial theater world has become the preferred model, if not the norm, in our program.

I asked Split Britches what advice the group had for young feminist directors. The members gave me a combination of general and specific recommendations. Peggy stressed the importance of traditional training, saying, "The only reason we can do what we do is that Lois had all that training," referring to the university and post-academic acting and directing classes Lois took in standard theatrical craft. For directors working to develop original material Peggy thinks it is important not to be overawed by the process of "getting the words on the paper." She regards the ability to write as a gift but emphasizes that there are techniques that can be used to bring out these gifts. She also recommends visual training in the form of art and design courses. As she puts it: "Learn where people look good on the stage and where they don't. Learn those balances." For Peggy this is related to choreography, another skill she finds important for directors. A full repertoire of exercises and workshop techniques is also necessary, since picking the right exercise can sometimes lead a group out of a scripting or staging impasse. And all this needs to be balanced with an ability to recognize what is interesting, especially those fortunate rehearsal accidents that lead to a leap in the piece's growth. It takes faith in your instincts to know when to drop the preconceived idea and go with what emerges during a rehearsal.

Lois seconds Peggy in her appreciation of her own training because it taught her the rules: what works onstage and what doesn't work. Sometimes she remembers the rules concretely, but by now much of her process is intuitive. She also defines her training very widely. "My yoga classes have been as instructional to me in terms of acting as any Stanislavski class I ever took. You have to think of anything you do as training for the theater." Not that Split Britches plays by the rules. In fact, much of the fun in their work comes from flouting theatrical convention. My own experience has led me to concur with Split Britches: that you need a full knowledge of conventions and rules in order to subvert them. Only then can you achieve the type of camp sensibility central to their work.

Deb, on the other hand, does not particularly recommend playwriting classes. She says she has "spoken to so many people, particularly women, who have found playwriting classes unconstructive to their efforts to write plays, scenes, or monologues." She attributes this to a formulaic approach that results in scripts with car chases, rapes, murder, and conflict-and-resolution. For Deb reading plays, including the works of Brecht and Shakespeare, is all well and good as long as it is balanced by the knowledge that one need not imitate them. It was important for her in working with the students on *Honey, I'm Home* that they learn that their own thoughts and personal images were theatrically viable and presentable. She believes that this comes from not being intimidated by the process of writing but by acknowledging that everyone writes and that everyone needs to recognize the writer in her- or himself. She says:

There is a stream of consciousness and, either alone or collectively, you just drop the line. You get the line down there, you reel it in, and you acknowledge that what you've got there is a real fish from a real stream, and that's all it is. That's not all it is, there's the intellect, but that comes much later—the "editor." . . . I encourage people to let it come later, not to have to have it make sense, not to have to have it be beautiful, not to have it be anything other than what it is. Later you learn to fine-tune it.

For me writing is an oral crafting of words, rather than a process involving paper and typewriters from the outset. Just as Lois believes that while directing a scene she will *hear* what to do if she listens and that actors can figure out what to do by listening to their impulses, I believe that writers, too, can listen to find out what comes next.

Another important suggestion Lois has for the feminist director is to find a group of people to work with on a regular, though not necessarily exclusive, basis. Although the work of Split Britches is stimulated by work they do outside the group, it is profoundly shaped by their familiarity with each other. Lois urgently recommends becoming as independent as possible from the commercial theater system. The amount of work available for people is limited in theater, especially for women, and even more so for feminists. But by setting up your own producing networks and mechanisms you can maximize the opportunities to generate work, especially feminist work.

In every production there are the dark days when the way is unclear, tension is in the air, and opening night looms. I was in just such a period when I was transcribing the following part of the interview with Split Britches:

> *Peggy:* I watch people, and I really don't know why they do theater when I watch the traumas that people go through. They think they have to kill each other to put on a show. They think that's normal. It's just awful.
> *Deb:* Well, it's awful enough without all that stuff . . .
> *Peggy:* Well, maybe that other stuff is just to keep you away from the self-doubt . . .

In her first attempt at professional directing Lois recalls being terrified during the whole process and having to constantly tell herself to listen to her impulses, her own inner thoughts. She formulates her advice to directors with the words: "Listen carefully and you will hear what the next step is. You don't need to follow a formula necessarily or to follow anyone else's method." In Berlin I also came to share her belief that sometimes directing is about not knowing what to do. If no solution presents itself, it may be better to walk into a rehearsal or meeting and admit that. That then turns the problem back over to the group. It may cause some initial unease, as the model of omniscient director is subverted, but it gives the piece back to the group, where more cooks and richer soup may again be the order of the day. In order to say "trust me" to a group, you have to have set a tone during the rehearsal process that permits the group to allow you to say "I don't know" when that is the truth of the situation. The company needs to see that as a strength, not as a failure.

There is one final image I want to leave with you. During those dark Berlin days, especially during the times when I felt unequal to the task and far from home, I recalled something Peggy had said to the students early on in the process of making *Honey, I'm Home.* "Think of your fears as a big black dog next to you breathing uncertainty into your ear. What you must do is acknowledge its presence and tell that dog, in no uncertain terms, to 'Sit!' " In addition, I would recommend developing another voice that whispers in your other ear. For me it was the voices of the women of Split Britches as I transcribed their interview. My hope is that each of you will develop your own interior voices of solace, encouragement, and advice.

NOTES

1. The show I developed in Berlin was entitled *Wenn Vögel Flügel Hatten, Der Fall Ikarus.* I have retained the German spelling of Ikarus in this essay.

2. Split Britches was founded in New York in 1980.

3. The residency was at Hampshire College in Amherst, Massachusetts, and was funded by the Massachusetts Council on the Arts and Humanities.

4. Though much of their work comes from the interior impulse work that Joe Chaikin and others have developed, there is no feeling that they are stifling or constricting their work by looking at it with their own outside eyes. When it works best they seem to be oscillating very rapidly between being inside the

moment, or impulse, and looking at it from an audience's or director's point of view. This allows them to take full advantage of their live and lively art form to shape each particular performance for *that* audience, *that* night, in *that* theater.

PART 3

Constructing the Text

Constructing the text is what you do when you can't bear to direct one more play by Shakespeare, Ibsen, Pinter, or Shaw, or when the forces of production around you afford you the precious time and space to create your own. Where, then, do you go for materials? Who does the scripting? Is there a script? *Is* there a playwright? Interestingly, there are only two playwrights to be found in this section, George Ella Lyon and Gertrude Stein, and neither of them writes anything resembling a traditional play script. Glenda Dickerson borrows the writings of Alexis De Veaux in order to construct her piece, and Marianne Goldberg's piece evolves out of a complex interaction between her own body and feminist theory.

Left to their own devices, feminist directors working to develop new material tend to gravitate away from realism and away from Aristotle, as if in some deeply intuitive way they recognized a hostile environment. We wonder if traditional dramatic structure doesn't routinely impose certain distortions on women's lives and women's experience. There has been a lot of speculation about climaxes and male sexuality as they are inscribed in Aristotelian dramatic action, but perhaps the real issue is control, the impulse to shape human action into something predictable and manageable, and to name oneself as the author of that shapeliness. This is exactly the kind of male narrative that has systematically excluded women from the beginning of recorded literature, so it is hardly surprising that the dramatic forms of that narrative hold no particular appeal for women developing their own work and their own voices. As Glenda Dickerson puts it so succinctly, "You can't wear your scarlet dress in Big Daddy's house."

It is worth recalling Sabrina Hamilton's essay here and the way Split Britches produces new work: that the jobs of playwright, director, designer, and performer routinely intersect and overlap. The same thing appears to hold true in this section. There is Marianne Goldberg's delicate and deliberate overlapping of her roles as performer, director, and theorist, and the way the role of director seemed to dissolve when we were working on Stein. There is Ann Kilkelly's account of how her role as director and her work in theory got woven into script development. And if we happened in on Glenda's rehearsal, wouldn't *everyone* have been up on the stage dancing? So which one is the director?

GLENDA DICKERSON

Wearing Red: When a Rowdy Band of Charismatics Learned to Say *"NO!"*

When Susanna Jones wears red
Her face is like an ancient cameo
Turned brown by the ages.

Come with a blast of trumpets, Jesus!

When Susanna Jones wears red
A queen from some time-dead Egyptian night
Walks once again.

Blow trumpets, Jesus!

And the beauty of Susanna Jones in red
Burns in my heart a love-fire sharp like pain.

Sweet silver trumpets, Jesus!
—Langston Hughes

Red, bitch-red, blood-red, true red, crimson, blush, flush, glower, lost cherry, scarlet, rose, smolder, flame—these are the colors of our shame. I can still hear my grandmother say to me, "Don't be afraid to wear red; you can carry it." I did not know then that those words from her would guide me as I guided a rowdy band of Charismatics toward self-revelation.

My grandmother, Ada Taminia, was born out of springtime in Somerville, Texas, in 1897. She was the color of a summer day with soft skin and hands she was vain about; when she went to Iowa as a young teacher she would not protect herself from the bit-

153

ter winters by putting coal into the potbellied stove until she first protected her hands with gloves. She had a large mind and a flair for imagining infinite possibilities. She was feisty with a tongue like the red wasp's sting. She had a clear, precise way of speaking, with a cadence like a Gatling gun. She had a hot temper and was quick to offer to "shoot you and pay for it." She could sometimes be found doing a merry Mexican hat dance, which she learned during Mexican summers. She played the piano beautifully. She had a poem published in W. E. B. DuBois's *Crisis* magazine when she was twelve and was a consummate race woman, active in the Daughters of the Eastern Star. Like all her siblings, the five Kilpatrick sisters, she had beautiful feet and well-turned ankles, upon which she walked to church on Sundays in a dignified rush, her hat in her hand, smelling of Estée Lauder's "Youth Dew." She was elegant in the way of antique rose gold.

My grandmother lived in a house surrounded by old trees and spectacular plants and a bed of four-leaf clovers. Her dining room was papered with beautiful silver and gold leaf upon which Japanese girls twirled their umbrellas. All her rooms were filled with stacks of books and magazines. If I asked to borrow one on my annual visit, I had to promise to bring it back, because, as she put it, "I am saving them to read when I retire." The books were never read. Not long after she retired from Jack Yates High School, where she taught Spanish to Debbie and Phylicia Allen and scores of others, her voice receded to childish chatter. Soon it descended into silence. For the final years of her life her fine mind was held prisoner in a body that had betrayed her. Johnny Nash sang at her funeral.

My grandmother was the first director I knew. She played the piano for her Spanish classes and clubs and orchestrated and choreographed little plays for them. Her voice was the first one I remember hearing that could move groups of people around, telling them what to do and where to go and bringing order out of chaos. When I went to Houston to join the caravan that would take her back to Somerville for the last time, I realized how long it had been since I heard her scolding, her stories, her charges, her directions. Because she had been unable to use her voice for so long I had forgotten it.

Now I am going to exalt my grandmother's incantatory voice, which could move groups of people; now I am going to speak of the day I moved a band of Charismatics to wear red and be willing to "pay for it"; now I am going to speak of creating a neoliterary mastaba for the stage, built on the words of Alexis De Veaux, which came to be called *"NO!" A Parlor Reading*. But first I am going to speak of reclaiming the colors of shame.

As the peacock feather is anathema to the American theater artist, red things were forbidden fruits to me and my girlfriends growing up. They conjured up images of slinky satin stretched tight over big butts that wiggled and hinted at tales too steamy to be uttered aloud. They conjured up images of blood mysteries, dirty and secret. They conjured up images of loud lips laughing too long and too lustily. "And dey makes me tired. Always laughin'! Dey laughs too much and dey laughs too loud. Always singin' ol' nigger songs! . . . Who wants to be mixed up wid . . . uh black woman goin' down de street in all dem loud colors, and whoopin' and hollerin' and laughin' over nothin'!"[1]

Alice Childress knew about it:

Once a lady took care-a me when I was a child . . .
Woman wouldn't let me wear a red hair-ribbon.
She say . . . "You too black to wear red.
Dark people oughta wear dark clothes."[2]

Reclaiming the colors of shame is lifelong work. There is more to it than just taking out a scarlet dress and putting it on. It has to do with my grandmother's words, her charge not to be afraid—her "cultural transmission."[3] Culture is a people's own vision of themselves in relation to the world, created by themselves through a blood continuity of time and space. This "self-vision" is reflected for African peoples in Kujichagulia, the second principle of the Nguso Saba. Kujichagulia is translated as self-determination and means "to define ourselves, name ourselves, create for ourselves and speak for ourselves instead of being defined, named, created for and spoken for by others."[4]

It is in this context of self-vision, or self-determination, that my tale is here told. The courage to "wear red," to redefine, rediscover, reclaim that which has been misdefined for us, starts in the heart and is then reflected in the work we do.

My reclamation began, as often happens, with a journey. The journey started in a magic place of "miracle plays"[5] and kindred spirits and stalled in a truck on the Manhattan Bridge. I had set out on New Year's Eve in a giant U-Haul truck between my real brother and my play brother to conquer New York. I would soon be joined by a sweet, dusty rose–colored little girl with long thick ropes of hair and the sweetest smile and brightest eye. *I* was *her* mother. This time. It was the Easter Sunday morning of my life, but my bonnet was not red. We got the truck unstalled and moved into a mansion set in a park where the winter trees looked like angels. From there it was a winding road to Alexis De Veaux's kitchen table.

For an African-American woman director trying to make a living in New York City a scarlet dress might as well be a scarlet letter. My vision as a creative artist was firmly rooted in the oral traditions of African slaves, of the masking miming ritual spied on the plantations, in the knowledge that in African art the audience is chorus. My vision could not be contained in a bedroom, a kitchen. I wanted to lead the choral dance of misplaced people—the flying Africans— and thus experience ecstasy. To inspire the dance of the serpent as she becomes the luminous flying bird. To turn Sojourner Truth's world right side up again.

Having offered to sell my life as dearly as possible in the 1960s, I longed to become a competent and complete personality in the 1980s, capable of reflecting a whole and holy vision in the works I brought to the stage, particularly from nondramatic sources. But the vision I saw so clearly, inspired subliminally by my grandmother's example, was not of value to the happy male producers. I took to wearing browns and beiges, all quiet earth colors because I felt too LOUD. I found myself unable to ANNOUNCE like Fannie Lou Hamer, the big, fine woman from Ruleville, who knew that she was good.[6] Somehow along the way I had learned that I was bad. As a black woman, I was saddled with two misconceptions. The first was that I was to serve black men: "The major concern of the Negro woman is the status of the Negro man and his need for feeling himself an important person."[7] And the second was that I was to look like someone else's vision of me: "the present cultural ideal for slenderness in women leads us away from an older, frightening imagery of female abundance . . . and so we invent woman in the image of man's image of woman."[8] At what cost! The cost is a blood price, draining our energy like the vampire colonialism drains the lifeblood of the Third

World. These drained energies are not only of the present and future but also of the past, of memory itself.[9]

Lost memory, submerged charges, silenced voices, forgotten dreams. These were the colors I wore. How weary I was of personifying in true color "the other." How I longed not to have to explain myself. What would I not give to announce and not apologize. Where was the language that spoke of the kind of liberation I had in mind—a way of living or operating that is not solely defined by what we are transgressing, resisting, or deconstructing? Perceiving one's self as seen by others leads to self-consciousness, not self-awareness. Where was the eye that turned inward and was pleased? How do we define ourselves when we are living someone else's vision, women living on the edge of time? How could we learn to exalt the culture of the African-American woman from Africa to America, to trumpet our grandmothers' voices?

bell hooks had not yet defined for us decentering—subjectivity free from the norms of a dominant heterosexual ideology—so I hearkened back to our Women in Black:

Too long have others spoken for us . . .
We wish to plead our own cause.
Too long has the public been deceived by misrepresentations, in things which concern
us deeply . . . [10]

Like Amanda Wingfield, I cried, "deception, deception." With Valerie I sang, "Give me something real." I wanted to deliver an act of resistance. "To speak as an act of resistance is quite different than ordinary talk, or the personal confession that has no relation to coming into political awareness, to developing critical consciousness. This is a difference we must talk about in the United States, for here the idea of finding a voice risks being trivialized or romanticized in the rhetoric of those who advocate a shallow feminist politic which privileges acts of speaking over the content of speech. Such rhetoric often turns the voices and beings of non-white women into commodity, spectacle."[11] Don't deceive me. Don't deceive me. Give me something real. My voice was silent, stifled, enraged, strangled. I had something to say and couldn't get it out. I did not wish to simply privilege the act of speaking but also to employ direct speech without being mistaken for Sapphire. Yes, I was angry, but I had no desire to spew forth bile. I didn't know it, but what I wanted was to come to voice. I was like the heart of Georgia Douglas Johnson's woman embodied:

> The heart of a woman falls back with the night,
> And enters some alien cage in its plight,
> And tries to forget it has dreamed of the stars,
> While it breaks, breaks, breaks on the sheltering bars.[12]

But soon I would enter a cage of crystal in the sun. Soon I would become a lionhearted gal, a brave African huntress. Soon I would wear red and learn to say "NO!"

"NO!" was created within the global context of subversive theater worldwide, emerging Third World feminism, and the demystification of the notion of transgression. There is a danger in transgression, of seeing that which exceeds human comprehension. All the warriors flirting around in the Terrible Mothers' gardens always came to no good: Adam, Oedipus, Theseus, Orestes, Gilgamesh. But when our children are at risk there is danger in silence . . . and when our mothers' rapes are the things unspoken, snuffed out like Dorothy Dandridge, recycled like Ruth Brown, plasticized like Diana Ross, little-remembered like Diana Sands, then there is an anguished cry for light, light, light, the light of truth. Yet we are punished for speaking out. bell hooks calls it "disclosure, revealing personal stuff." And she is asked, "Do we have to go that deep?"[13]

When I directed *"NO!"* I found for myself bell hooks's "liberatory voice," that of the uppity black woman. I came to voice by shining the clean light of day on the things unspoken, the taboos, the personal stuff. I reclaimed the colors of shame. "What glorious red and purples light has taught me."[14]

The seeds from which *"NO!"* flowered were planted, like much great woman's work, at a kitchen table. I wanted to find a way to bring to the stage the nonpareil voice of Alexis De Veaux as it was reflected in the varying forms she used to express herself: her poetry, her short stories, her political statements, her plays, her sexuality. I took the idea to Alexis, and she was willing. We began by sifting through all of the unpublished work Alexis had at that time. She was generous in allowing me to peruse the mass of material and extremely trusting in letting me make choices. We spent afternoons over Miso soup and evenings over fine wine ("For the Negro was famous then, as now, for spending his [sic] money for fine clothes, furniture and jewelry and pianos and other musical instruments, to say nothing of good things to eat")[15] discussing how we would piece this piece together.

Alexis suggested we produce it ourselves. This also was a step toward liberation. I was so used to thinking I had to sit and wait for someone to come along and offer me a play to do (and too often having to accept it because the rent was due) that the idea of taking the reins in our own hands and just doing it ourselves was as titillating as jumping off the Brooklyn Bridge and sprouting wings. There was some fancy footwork surrounding the question of how to bill the director: Should it be "conceived and directed" or "adapted and directed for the stage"? After much anguish we settled on "adapted for the stage and directed by," but I must emphasize that there was no play before we started.

As I lived with the material, reading it over and over, so many thoughts went through my mind. I found that I was scared to reveal the things she wrote about, things that should be kept "under the rose" and not bandied about in the light of day. So different a praise-song from the *Iliad*. I talked myself into having courage, into being a lionhearted gal, because the other thing that was happening, along with the fear, was excitement. I began to see a company of women who were unafraid, swishing and swaying and swimming through these gutsy words. I began to hear the chorus of voices affirming ourselves. I began to feel the choral dance itching in my toes. I was winded as though from a long run. My head was spinning all the time. It started to feel like something that had to be done. Alexis was adamant that we have represented the spectrum of Africamerican women, thereby defining Africamerican beauty for ourselves through our choices.[16] We wanted to say something about ourselves that had never been said before, and we wanted to say it in our own voices, in our own way. We wanted to include male actors if they were needed to honestly portray the text. We talked about performers, number of performers, houses, musicians. Soon we started to name names and shapes and colors. Suddenly I got hold of a style.

I suggested we call it a Parlor Reading to denote the elegance of bygone days and to distinguish it from the more usual staged reading. I wanted to communicate a sense of opulence, sensuality, self-awareness, consciousness, longing, anger, laughter, big butts, big mouths, gap teeth, unruly hair, mystical beasts, our dreams. I wanted to salute the satin of Sarah Vaughn's voice, the sass of Judith Jamison's hips, the red of Dorothy Dandridge's mouth. I wanted to include the silky feathers of our Native American forebears; the intricately kinky locks of our African ancestors; the henna, Shalimar, and Evening in Paris our mothers wore and the royal blood-colored heart of Winnie Mandela. I wanted to be sure to have in it the swish and sway of Senegalese djalaba, the erect carriage of basket-toting Nigerians, the graceful glide of the Dance Theatre of Harlem, the urgent beat of the calabash, the sexy exasperated sigh of sisters filled to the brim with having to react to misogyny, bigotry, and capitalism, being disrespected, misconstrued, misunderstood, and miscalculated. When I looked in the mirror I didn't want to see those monsters anymore. I wanted to hold up the mirror and see ourselves. I knew I had to create the mirror. I knew I had to craft the megaphone. I suggested we call it *"NO!"* because of a story Alexis told me from her childhood about refusing a request from her stepmother.

The official title was *"NO!": a new, experimental work of neoliterary events, political messages and innovative stories for the stage.* The production was woven from the following threads of Alexis De Veaux's writings: *EROTIC FOLKTALE #7;* a short story, "THE RIDDLES OF EGYPT BROWNSTONE"; excerpts from a new play, *WHEN THE NEGRO WAS IN VOGUE;* and poetry. It was first performed at the WOW. (Women's One World) Festival at 25 St. Mark's Place on 1 March 1981. It was billed as "A Flamboyant Ladies Theatre Company–Pilate International Artists Production of *'NO!' A Parlor Reading.*" The performers were as follows: Ms. Cheryl Lynn Bruce, Ms. Risë Collins, Ms. Yvette Erwin, Ms. Yvonne Erwin, Ms. Gwendolen Hardwick, Ms. Judith Alexa Jackson, Mr. André Liguori (Robinson), and Ms. Marilyn Nicole Worrell. The musicians were Ms. Madeleine Yayodele Nelson and Ms. Lorna Warden. All performers were given the title "Diva," with the exception of Mr. Liguori, who was entitled "Count."

The Parlor Reading was rehearsed in our apartments. I gathered together the material I had chosen into a loosely structured format. I began with Alexis's poem, "THE ALTAR OF LIBERATION." The poem was used (during performance) to build an altar that sanctified and liberated the performance space. The sound and sensibility of each Diva's voice dictated the material I assigned to her. There was lots of trial and error. I blocked the play on the women, not from a prompt book of preconceived notions. There was no separation between us. I never sat down. I was right up onstage with them as I told them where to go. Turned on by their laughter and their juices, I swished and swayed with the best of them, getting in the middle of the fun—being outrageous, sexy, bitchy, right along with the other Charismatics. I whirled on arched feet, grown merry like a hat dance. I played, with fingers grown beautiful, on the instruments of their voices. Gone was the pompous director's gaze, absent the royal director's chair. Left was the transcendent voice of an uppity black woman. I gloried in the voice that was telling them to wear red, reclaim the colors of shame, to be not other than themselves but, instead, larger than themselves; that was moving the Divas and the Count; that was bringing order out of the primeval chaos of the mastaba coming to the stage. As we read and talked and walked through the material, visions came to me like ideas emanating from the Female Soul of the world.

For example, for the *EROTIC FOLKTALE #7*, which begins:

ONCE: between a time in the land of FA (which was somewhere on the skirts of Brooklyn) lived a woman named Usawa who was dizzy for a sculptress named Blackberrie who sold mushrooms in the afternoon at the gourmet vegetable stand near the park near Usawa's house.

Usawa was a woman with skin blacker than earth in Senegal with eyes when one looked into eyes that sucked in continents and lakes and rivers in her lips so thirsty for this woman Blackberrie she was lips spread in whispers from the Upper Volta.[17]

Once Usawa and Blackberrie were cast (Risë Collins and Judith Jackson) it became evident that the rest of the cast had to participate in this erotic marketplace. Searching around my living room, I picked up three Senegalese baskets and asked the women to put them on their heads, as they sashayed around following Usawa and commenting on the action. There was a lot of tumbling to the

ground of baskets as we rehearsed, but on 1 March all baskets
stayed firmly in place, because we called on our cotton-picking
ancestor, "who drops the seed which she carries in a bag hung
around her neck. This was done in the month of March."[18] We had
less than half a dozen rehearsals. All of the clothes the Divas and the
Count wore came from our closets but were mostly Risë Collins's.
They were all dressed in rich reds, accented with opulent purples. I
gave no thought to Langston Hughes's "Sue Jones." I didn't remember
my grandmother's charge. It seemed the only proper color to reflect
our intentions.

A description of the rowdy band of Charismatics who built the
mastaba for the stage that came to be called *"NO!"* may help to serve
as a potpourri of necessary ingredients for those who would reclaim
the colors of shame.

Alexis de Veaux. Author.

Central voice and creator of the poems, short stories, play scraps,
found poems, and new myths from which *"NO!"* was woven. An
ebony woman with dreads and gap teeth—learned in tai chi, vegetar-
ian home cooking, holistic healing, Third World politics; she writes
her life and in her writing mirrors all of us. Llama, sphinx, and other
paradisical beasts roam through her mind along with blue suede
shoes, sarcophagi, and fragrant pussies. She lives in giant, incensed,
Africa'd rooms, where she roams like Hathor, ruminating over the
bejeweled, bedazzled, bewitched universe she inhabits. Soon she goes
to her writing room and hammers out her lush tales. As I write, my
mind is flooded with images of Alexis across continents: standing
sun-drenched in Nairobi, her hair a glowing henna-red, enrobed in
bright African colors, her eyes shielded with amber glasses; patiently
breathing out tai chi postures in a jumbled brownstone in Harlem;
shrugged into a flame-color shantung suit in a concrete jungle in
Buffalo, consorting with women of color from all over the world;
standing, standing and grinning, grinning, grinning between Nelson
and Winnie Mandela in their backyard on the day of his liberation.
Today she is two steps shy of a doctorate in American Studies. Dr.
Charismatic, the bird of paradise—her blackness is the beauty of this
land.

Konda Mason. Coproducer
(Pilate International Artists).

A small, slight woman the color of pecans. With skin as smooth as Sarah Vaughn's voice. A cascade of unruly dreads, growing every which way and one long beaver tail hanging down her back because she didn't want to "tear my hair." She didn't want to spear her food either, so she traveled everywhere with chopsticks and pulled them out at a minute's notice. She didn't want her food just cooked anykinda way in anyoldthing, so when she went a-courtin' or on visitations she carried her personal wok and spices. Alexis and the adaptor/director met Konda in a loft in Greenwich Village to discuss her participation as coproducer of the Parlor Reading. She came gliding around the corner, irradiant like a dolphin, hesitant, a hint of scandal in her wake. Konda Mason is a mercurial mermaid with a feisty business sense and a gynocentric worldview. She was in the process of carving out a self-defined producing career for herself, focusing on the music industry. She was dirt-poor (as we all were), dressed like a waif, and had gardening earth under her fingernails. She was as soft-spoken as a whispering tree and as fervent as a handball slamming against a city wall. There was nothing she would not do to make *"NO!"* a reality, "so thirsty . . . she was" to reclaim the colors of shame (DeVeaux 1979). She assisted the director, gathered props, counted the money, and swept the floor. Today she lives in London, where she manages the singer Caron Wheeler. Her hair is in twists of new dreads, streaked with threads of silver. It shines, as do her nails, her eyes, her rich home-girl clothes, her fine mind, her irradiant spirit, and her singularly sensitive, shimmering, seaborn soul.

Risë Collins. Diva.

Six feet tall, and that's not all. Girlfriends' hair and thoroughbred nose. From her we learned about "bitch-red" nail polish and many other bitcheries of the most delicious colors. Risë was a woman who knew herself and liked her knowledge. She took Manhattan by storm. The buildings rocked and the sidewalks rolled when she walked by. The grass bowed in obeisance, and the clouds parted to make way. The sun put a big grin on his face, and Sister Moon hummed "My Lord, He Calls Me by the Thunder." Big as it is, fine as it is, Manhattan couldn't hold Risë Collins. She fell in love with a Japanese man and took her big fine self to Japan, where the Ancient Goddess sits atop Mount Fuji, her namesake. Mountain Mother is gently colored like an oriental watercolor. Her hues are those of twilight; she wears a white crown of snow. In this land Risë was a giant. I see Risë now, standing tall, painted in fire colors, flaring her magnificent nostrils facing Mount Fujiyama, her grandmother. Mountain Mother recognized her, seeing that she had supped at Kali's breast; had her dandruff scratched out by Oya; learned to cook in Aunt Jemima's kitchen. Risë played the role of Usawa in *EROTIC FOLKTALE #7*, the "woman with skin blacker than earth in Senegal with eyes . . . that sucked in continents and lakes and rivers. . . ." After *"NO!"* was finished I heard she had moved back to the Texas prairie from which she came. I don't know where she is or what she is doing, but I like to imagine her, sitting regally among the Mountains of the Moon, mystic source of the Nile, serenely picking out her hair with the opalescent teeth of a mother-of-pearl comb, humming a windsong of fearsome tenderness, sipping the waters of Lethe from a Baccarat-stemmed glass. Pearls float out of her mouth as she sings and strums her hair and sips.

Yvette-Yvonne Erwin. Divas.

Identical twins. One dances, the other poets. These girls are gazelles. They are the colors of buttermilk, dripping from the Mother's breasts. They are long and willowy, and they high-step like deer. They have voices that rattle around in their rib cages and sound like sirens' songs. They have a baby sister, Andrea, who christened them "Yvette-Yvonne." ("You have no idea what it is like to live with Yvette-Yvonne.") They were the babies among the Divas and brought shiny enthusiasm that was like a new penny. When they did The Sisters, seated on a bench twirling a Chinese umbrella, facing each other, it looked like my grandmother's wallpaper; it looked like a mirror; it looked like looking into a mirror of ourselves; it looked like looking into the mirror we had finally crafted ourselves. Today Yvette chants and writes and mothers two children. She is sometimes seen on "The Cosby Show." After the parlor reading Yvonne twirled away to dance with Alvin Ailey. I imagine her now pirouetting on the head of a pin, raising a shout from Alvin the Angel.

Marilyn Worrell. Diva.

A pristine peacock, with nothing whatsoever in common with the dour peahen. She struts her iridescent colors when she walks. When she walks she walks on rose petals. A disciplined, contained, ginger-colored woman of uncommon beauty, she seems to be dusted all over with the fine gold mist of an Egyptian papyrus. She is elegant in the way of antique gold. She is mature and brought the fine steady hand of Isis to the *sorosis*. I saw her recently in Saks Fifth Avenue. Such a steamy rush of memories flooded my brain, it was like being in a greenhouse where brown orchids grow. There she stood in the very midst of the crowd of Mother's Day shoppers, calm as a summer day, lustrous as the Harvest Moon, telling me tales of magical queens and metaphysical shenanigans that absorbed her and flowed from her golden pen onto ivory parchment paper and demanded a life of their own. She seems timeless, still calm and contained, like the eye of the storm. She is luminous like moonlight on the water. She taught us how to moonwalk ten years ago. When she made suggestions for sinewy movements she swept us away to the primal garden, where brown orchids flourish, where blackberries bloom, where bitten plums stained our lips red, red, red.

Gwendolen Hardwick. Diva.

A small woman with a big life, she smolders like the coals in my grandmother's Iowa potbellied stove. Husky voice heavy with responsibility, she is cofounder, with Alexis De Veaux, of Flamboyant Ladies Theatre Company. All-around athlete in school, "so fit so fine, so girl so full," she eats from Xikum, the divine fig tree.[19] Matches her acting with her social consciousness. Does not just accept roles but, instead, creates roles, other possibilities for theater. She tries to represent a heightened sense of ourselves, so that we can glean more about ourselves. Called from the icy winter of Wisconsin by the author to come and say *"NO!"*. The poem "NO MORE PROPHETS" was written for her. While staging "THE RIDDLES OF EGYPT BROWNSTONE," the adaptor/director asked her to

Gwendolen Hardwick and André Robinson in "*NO!*" by Alexis De Veaux, directed by Glenda Dickerson. Photo by Sharon Farmer.

take off her top, to bare her breasts, in order to codify the shameful crime (revealed in the above-named short story by Alexis) of child molestation by a family friend. She remembers being called to the side and asked, "Do you mind taking off your top?" She remembers experiencing "a sense of excitement, knowing something special was going to happen; something beautiful and terrible and dangerous."[20] It was at this moment that she learned to represent a heightened sense of herself and continues to do so today. At the Parlor Reading her little baby dreads stood up fiercely as her blouse came over her head and somehow spoke of her vulnerability. The audience was dead quiet, participating with a silent gasp, as we talked our lives, disclosed, told personal stuff. They knew by Gwendolen's defiant disclosure that we believed in what we were doing, that Alexis's words spoke for all of us, that, though we were rowdy, this was not about acting up. This was about digging up. Digging up our mothers' voices, our babies' cries, our trampled-on dreams, our bright colors turned drab and grey. Today her dreads are cut in a fiercely smart style. She lifts weights and has a strong, full body. She goes into the schools, the prisons, drinks from the wise cup of the elders, creating other possibilities for theater; stays abreast and alert like Electra, watching for evil, calling it out, wrestling it to the floor and pinning it down. Also she is uppity. Also, unlike Electra, she smiles. She seems to me to be a child of Pelé, a deity who embodies the possibilities of female self-development. Pelé, the volcano goddess, whose fire was said to regenerate the soul.

Judith Jackson. Diva.

Gliding along like a stately ship's figurehead, red sails in the sunset. Studied mime in Europe with Marcel Marceau, always liked silence, what's happening when you're not talking. She performed "FOUND POEM #6" and dramatized through her mimed improvisation Alexis's discovery that *hysterectomy/hysteria* were from the same Latin root and how one can lead to the other; how women are misjudged from the very root of things. When she was called to say *"NO!"* she felt we returned to an ancient manifestation of rite, like tribes that take their grounding from the cycles of the moon. The people danced for the first menstrual cycle. In *"NO!"* she feels, we were doing that dance. *"NO!"* was old, ancient, not new, returning to ourselves.[21] Today she is rich in thoughts and good ideas. She creates performance pieces that are bigger than life, reflecting life, using media like old masks, leaping out of trees. She wants to take them to Zaire, to the source, and talk about them (the people) to themselves in her voice like the red wasp's sting. She hopes in ten years to be as happy as Cheryl Lynn Bruce.

Cheryl Lynn Bruce. Diva.

Seemed happy to us because she seemed whole-hearted. She seemed together. Her hair reflected a constantly changing array of home-girl styles. Her dress was an elegant mixture of fine cloth and homeland.

Her creative soul was deep and exciting. Her coal-black eyes gleamed with mischief and mayhem. Cheryl Lynn Bruce had blown in from Chicago and swirled into the company of Charismatics. We did not know her, although we knew her well. Cheryl Lynn was Cadette in *WHEN THE NEGRO WAS IN VOGUE.* In that role she danced the dance of separation from her mother and acceptance on her own terms from her man. To Cadette she brought a rambunctious, revolutionary fervor that was a mixture of Angela Davis and Brer Rabbit. Her supple body was all a-quiver with excitement. She sidled her way through "I AM A THRIFT SHOP JUNKIE" and spoke for all of us who search out "the thrifts" in every city we visit, at every opportunity we can find. She seemed altogether the together woman of color for the 1980s. Today she tramps the grapes of wrath on Broadway. I hope that she is happy.

André Liguori (Robinson). Count.

Triple Cancer, moves nothing like a crab; rather, he moves with the delicate, measured gait of fine Arabian steeds. "Limpid pools" sounds trite but describes his eyes. The lone male among the divas, he was comfortable in the company of women. His relationship to the rest of the company never had the feeling of a harem or a barnyard, or man-on-horseback. Alexis described him best in her poem "the oracle of the zebra":

> he/was what his momma called
> ivoryblack
> women gathered on carolina porches
> then/to peek at nellie gin's boy
> nickname him pear tree
> drop nickels or hurry inside
> to make cold sage tea/because he was
> thunder pretty . . . [22]

He says today about that time that the Divas gave him lots of benefits of the doubt and empowered him for life in ways only Charismatics can imagine. The powerful impact of the company of women continues to inform his attempt to convey his ideas without compromise.[23] I always used to associate him with fine shoes, because the first time

I saw him in a television studio in the District of Columbia he came rushing in, thunderpretty, late for rehearsal, with a shoe box under his arm, which he put down carefully before issuing his genteel apologies. This is the image that informs his life: conscientious, beautifully mannered, coming to dance, to fly, but with his shoes planted firmly on the ground. His presence among the bevy of beauties was a strong cold current. Smooth like the current, he was a calm, quiet rod at the center of the flower storm. I remember him as Orestes in another production that I directed. He was all gold—gold skin, gold loincloth, gold raffia armor; his arms upraised as though to fly, proclaiming "Your brother lives and I am he." Today he is the general manager of the Crossroads Theatre Company in New Brunswick. He is still all gold, solid, good. Whenever I see him a gold aura surrounds him. He stands poised to fly like Pegasus to places magical and faraway. Because he is conscientious and to the manner born, his feet stay planted on the carpet of the Crossroads, but when he takes flight I know he will take the other Charismatics with him, proclaiming "your brother lives. . . ."

Madeleine Yayodele Nelson. Diva.

Madeleine supported the other Charismatics on the calabash:

> When Madeleine plays the calabash
> she carries OPEC in her hair
> she carries the PLO in her hair
> she carries the Peoples Republic of Nicaragua
> in her hair
> on her shoulders
> Madeleine's dreads
> are full of uprisings in Haiti
> and Mississippi
> and Brooklyn.[24]

and sultry Lorna:

Lorna Warden. Diva.

crooned like sassy Sarah, like saucy Chaka: "Bring baby down the Nile."[25]

On 1 May the Parlor Reading was fully staged and costumed, the scripts incorporated into the action. Now imagine this: a cavernous space in the East Village. Dark and cold. Transformed in a day to a place to say *"NO!"*—into a womb from which we emerged newborn with blood and disdain smeared on our thick red lips. Peacock feathers and fresh flowers, candles, fringed scarves in hot colors formed the backdrop for the Charismatics to work their show. They performed such provocative titles as:

I Am a Thrift Shop Junkie
Cuntery
The Sisters
Cold Hands/Warm Pussy
The Diver
The Riddles of Egypt Brownstone
But: Who Got the Wings in Atlanta
Found Poem #6

The large circular space was peppered with pillows of opulent fabrics and sassy colors. The dense, lush overgrowth of the poetry was accented with saucy fans. When Usawa strutted to the market a chorus of Charismatics trailed her, commenting on her beauty, toting baskets on their heads. From the marketplace we took off in hurried dignity, smelling of Alexis De Veaux's handmade version of "Youth Dew," pellmell, pummeling, getting to the end. Along the way we stopped our fun to lament Egypt Brownstone's rape and mourn for the dead children in Atlanta and honor the ancestral prophets. Such a strolling, strutting, sashaying the audience had never witnessed. Smooth, chile! Such a festival of hip shaking, dread tossing, breast heaving, and lips talking back, you never saw. Only Isis, arrayed in red, could have been more splendid.[26] The audience sat at café tables and talked back to the Charismatics. They stomped and hollered, stood and clapped. The Charismatics glowed. The evening began when Alexis walked in with birds-of-paradise for all the Charismatics. We surprised her by ending the evening with a line of tai chi postured Charismatics who whispered *"NO!"* and bowed to her on the last exhalation. The audience went wild. We saw red. We were in seventh heaven: the foundation of the earth, the meeting of the mighty waters.[27]

The Charismatics line up for a curtain call for "*NO!*" Center, wearing hat, is the author, Alexis De Veaux. The director, Glenda Dickerson, stands second from right. Photo by Sharon Farmer.

Now enter King Woody, who took the magic "*NO!*" and moved it to his New Federal Theatre, located at the Henry Street Settlement House. For a while it seemed that we had moved upstairs. The loyal audience followed and rooted us on every night. But the rowdy "*NO!*" had sprung up from our own soil, from our own hands, and should never have left home. Some big mistakes, some bad decisions, and "*NO!*" died. A lot more people saw it because of the run at Henry Street, but "*NO!*" reached its zenith at the WOW Festival. *The lesson we learned is that you can't wear your scarlet dress in Big Daddy's house.*

The Charismatics are scattered. They have never all been in the same room at the same time again. Perhaps they never will. Perhaps ten years ago they were assembled together for the last time on earth. But I say, like Sojourner Truth's mother, "I look up at the stars and they look up at the stars."[28]

The ride from Paradise to Brooklyn seems long ago and far

away. My brother is married to Makeda, the Queen of Sheba, and they have a girl and a boy, both with ancient Ethiopian eyes. My play brother is frying chicken for Alvin and the other angels, knocked off this planet in a ball of fire but surely laughing in the Mountains of the Moon. The U-Haul truck had lots of successors, but they all are retired now. The dusty rose–Dorothy Dandridge-colored little girl is almost-a-woman and acts every day more like the mother of mine that she was in a former life. She is heir to the fine, rowdy legacies of the Charismatics who got together in gilded space, wearing red, and told the world "We say *NO!*" The halcyon days seem misted now, as though by delicate clouds. But the memory of that night in a transformed space when sisters and brothers came to witness the Charismatics whip up a storm warmed by Oya's breath—their blood-red hearts beating in tune, their poppy lips singing in unison, their sorrel souls swimming abreast, their bitch-red nails scratching down the blackboard; subversive women, enemies of the state, Bad Girls talking back, being loud, being rowdy, ANNOUNCING! Well, that memory alchemizes my life. It will not tarnish. It is guaranteed, like my daughter's nearly life-size rocking horse, purchased when she was six months old and guaranteed for her lifetime and beyond. Guaranteed.

There is one Charismatic not yet mentioned but not overlooked. It is

The Adaptor/Director, Glenda Dickerson,
The Praisesinger.

After *"NO!"* the adaptor/director was often pursued by Kali, who pulled her hair and made her behave. She fell from grace. She renewed her determination. Sometimes the Earth Goddess cried out in the night; the adaptor/director heard her well and wailed along. She spent years wandering in and out of caves; breasting the waves of the mighty waters; searching for the shibboleth to put her back on track; gazing at the moon; seeking out seashells for secrets and apples, figs, pomegranates, peaches—emblems of the Great Mother—for sustenance. She scaled mountains, discovering throne after empty throne waiting for the Goddess to take her seat.[29] She lives now in a labyrinth of rooms strung together with rosemary for remembrance, striving to become whole-hearted, to put the bits and pieces of the heart back together again. What she has not seen cannot be:

> Sunsets and rainbows, green forests and
> restive blue seas, all naturally colored things are my siblings.
> We have played together on the floor of the world
> Since the first stone looked up at the stars.[30]

"*NO!*" was done in "the hour that began her wanderings."[31] In that hour, ten years ago, she learned to sing in her mothers' voices. The ancestral prophets taught her how—when she was hungry with an unnamed desire, thirsty with an ineffable longing, languishing from a self-imposed ennui—to bite the forbidden apple, symbol of possibility, bite it, chew it lustily, let the juice run down her chin, relish it, love its bright red color, and never never fear the consequences of her appetite. In that hour she uncovered and reclaimed the mysterious thing that would be silenced, the mysterious thing the oppressors would stifle, the mysterious thing that will make us free. It is that thing in our mothers that straightened their backs when they walked down the church aisle Sunday morning dressed to kill. It is the gleam in their hot-combed hair and their patent leather shoes. It is the nerve to shoot and pay the price. It is the nerve to don the colors of shame—as the peacock, as the zebra, as the mermaid, as the serpent, as the sphinx, as the big fine woman from Ruleville, as the Women in Black, as bad girls, as True Women—and proudly pay the price.

Red, bitch-red, blood-red, true red, crimson, blush, flush, glower, lost cherry, scarlet, rose, smolder, flame—these are the colors of our shame.

Now my tale is ended. The moral of my story is this: because my grandmother was silenced, "she looked at me to speak for her. She depended on me for a voice."[32] In that hour, ten years ago, my voice flew out of my body like a cork flying out of a champagne bottle. In that hour I believe I spoke for her. In that hour I came to voice.

My grandmother's body lies in a sandy champagne-colored grave in Somerville, Texas, between her mother and her father, "wearing red."

But her soul looks back in wonder how I got over.

NOTES

The epigraph is the poem "When Sue Wears Red," printed in *The Book of American Negro Poetry*, edited by James Weldon Johnson (New York: Harcourt, Brace and World, 1958), 242.

1. Zora Neale Hurston, *Their Eyes Were Watching God* (New York: Harper and Row, 1990), 135.

2. Alice Childress, *Mojo* (New York: Samuel French, 1969), 17.

3. Eleanor Traylor first called the words *Grandma say* a cultural transmission.

4. The Nguso Saba (The Seven Principles) were created by Dr. Maulana Karenga in 1965 for use in the African-American seasonal celebration, Kwanzaa.

5. The author coined this term to characterize certain adaptations for the stage mounted in Washington, D.C., from 1969 to 1973 as modern miracle plays. See Glenda Dickerson, "The Cult of True Womanhood: Towards A Womanist Attitude in African American Theatre," *Theatre Journal* 32 (1988): 50. Also see Vera Katz, "Solitary Sojourner," *New Directions* 17, no. 2 (April 1990): 32.

6. See Paula Giddings, *When and Where I Enter* (Toronto: Bantam Books, 1985), 301.

7. Giddings, *When and Where*, 329.

8. See Kim Chernin, *Reinventing Eve* (New York: Random House, 1987), 179–81.

9. See Monica Sjoo and Barbara Mor, *The Great Cosmic Mother* (San Francisco: Harper and Row, 1987), 26–27.

10. These quotes are from "Freedom's Journal," March 16, 1827, and can be found in *In Their Own Words*, edited by Martin Meltzer (New York: Thomas Y. Crowell, 1964), 18.

11. See bell hooks, *Talking Back* (Boston: South End Press, 1989), 14.

12. Qtd. in J. W. Johnson, *American Negro Poetry*, 181.

13. hooks, *Talking Back*, 1.

14. The poem "For a Godchild . . ." by Toi Derricotte is printed in *Home Girls*, edited by Barbara Smith (New York: Kitchen Table, Women of Color Press, 1983), 3.

15. Giddings, *When and Where*, 20.

16. *Africamerican* is James Weldon Johnson's term and is quoted by Eleanor W. Traylor in her essay "Two Afro-American Contributions to Dramatic Form," in *The Theatre of Black Americans*, edited by Errol Hill (New York: Applause Theatre Books, 1980), 47.

17. All work by Alexis De Veaux mentioned is copyrighted in her name. The "Erotic Folktale" is copyrighted in 1979. Her short story "The Sisters" is printed in Smith, *Home Girls*.

18. Meltzer, *In Their Own Words*, 36.

19. See De Veaux 1979, and Barbara G. Walker, *The Woman's Encyclopedia of Myths and Secrets* (San Francisco: Harper and Row, 1983), 1093.

20. Interview with Gwendolen Hardwick.

21. The ideas characterized here are Judith Jackson's, from an interview with her.

22. Copyright 1974, Alexis De Veaux.

23. Interview with André Robinson.

24. This is an excerpt from Alexis De Veaux's poem, "When Madeleine Plays the Calabash," copyright 1980. Madeleine is founder of Women of the Calabash and made the instruments that she played for the production.

25. These lines and many others from Alexis De Veaux's writings were improvised upon with felicitous results by Ms. Lorna Warden. In addition, she used her voice as an instrument to complement the words, actions, and calabash. She substituted herself for piano, bass, and drums.

26. Egyptian scriptures said: "In the beginning there was Isis, Oldest of the Old. . . ." Hermetic texts said Isis revealed the mysteries of the stars to God, who was her son. Egyptians addressed her as "Mistress of the gods, thou bearer of wings, thou lady of the red apparel . . ." (Walker, 453–54).

27. Walker, *Woman's Encyclopedia,* 800.

28. See Harold Courlander, *A Treasury of Afro-American Folklore* (New York: Crown Publishers, 1976), 255.

29. Walker, *Woman's Encyclopedia,* 695.

30. See Maya Angelou, *Now Sheba Sings the Song* (New York: E. P. Dutton, 1987), 40.

31. See Zora Neale Hurston, *Dust Tracks on the Road* (Urbana and Chicago: University of Illinois Press, 1984), 89.

32. Hurston, *Dust Tracks,* 87.

Marianne Goldberg

Straddling Discourses

A ballerina straddles a bicycle, wearing a silver tutu, a cyclist's helmet, and cycling shoes and gloves. Lit only by an array of lights strapped to her bicycle, she is raucously riding at top speed to high-volume, prerecorded music from *The Sleeping Beauty*. A cameraman is instructed to follow her, but he cannot contain her image as she whizzes in and out of his frame. This ballerina has been charged with setting mind and body on a collision course. She has been charged with presenting a piece of choreography rather than a keynote address. Pedaling, pedaling, flying—she charges across the space like a wild typewriter. (SIDESHOW, live gallery performance from THE BODY WORD SERIES, Northampton, Massachusetts, January 1989[1])

In 1986 I began a project called THE BODY WORD SERIES. Several works in this series were created specifically for audiences at conferences on women and theater. I considered these specialized audiences, composed of a mix of theater practitioners and theorists, as incubators inside which a new kind of performance might be born. Female performers could take risks, bolstered and creatively challenged by the spectatorial warmth of those committed to change in women's roles onstage. Spectators could push forward to new perceptions about women, gender, and performance. At times I created opportunities for them to enter stage space and codetermine the action. During conference discussions there was often tremendous friction between practitioners who focused on experiential process and theorists who argued for an overriding cultural analysis. I found this friction generative—it ignited further work in which I linked experience and theory, with the goal of opening new possibilities for women in theater.

Performances can be instants of intervention in which something unknown can happen, in which women can come into being and into interaction in tender and courageous ways. This can happen through simple acts of breathing or of sensing mobility inside the body. I give these acts time and space onstage. Both audience and performers can shift direction midstream in my work, with a sixth sense that emerges in the theatrical situation. They can move, talk, draw, or shape gestures that do not necessarily express identity but, rather, press beyond a known identity. I put means of theatrical representation, and thereby of self-construction, into female hands, literally, via cameras, tripods, cable cords, paper, pens, or typeset text.

To date THE BODY WORD SERIES has included live performances, videos, gallery installations, and pieces created for magazines—crossing the genres of performance, writing, and visual arts. I question divisions between nature and culture, body and word, practice and theory. I suspend myself and the audience within multiple discourses—those of the camera, the printed page, and the theatrical space as well as those of body and language. If the activity of theorizing is linked to the written word, while that of staging performance to the live body, I set out to disturb that polarity. I make theory physical, or, alternately, intellectualize gesture. I am on the one hand a performer and choreographer-director and on the other a writer and performance theorist. I want to link the body and the word, to explore the process of translation between verbal and nonverbal discourses. I want to bring scholars and performers together to brainstorm, improvisationally, during live performance.

Debates at conferences on women and theater have polarized body and mind, being and culture—and practice and theory. If the nonverbal realm is marked as precultural and the linguistic as cultural, then the body is cast as a wild zone, offering only a kind of regression to childhood or nature, and the word is divested of its imaginary and ecstatic potential. In this polarization only talking cures or theoretical treatises seem to offer possibilities for social change, while the pleasures of the body are considered uncoded eruptions. With THE BODY WORD SERIES I suggest that there is a greater flow possible between body-based perceptions and cultural analysis.

When I began THE BODY WORD SERIES I was in the process of editing an issue of the journal *Women & Performance* on the body

The body accumulates and sheds meanings through social practice:
It can lie as easily as the word.

Body	Body
Woman	*Man and Woman*
Nature	Culture
Unconscious	*Conscious*
Outside History	Within History
Outside Discourse	*Constituted by Discourse*
Primitive	Civilized
Organic	*Arbitrary*

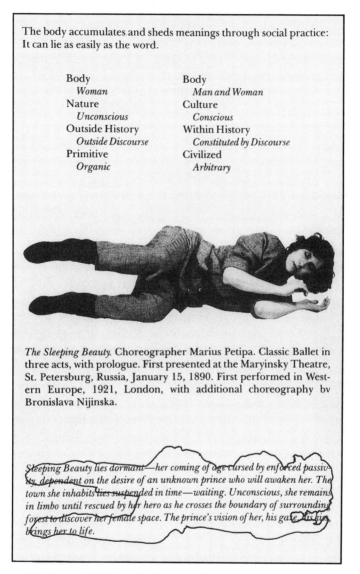

The Sleeping Beauty. Choreographer Marius Petipa. Classic Ballet in
three acts, with prologue. First presented at the Maryinsky Theatre,
St. Petersburg, Russia, January 15, 1890. First performed in Western Europe, 1921, London, with additional choreography bv
Bronislava Nijinska.

*Sleeping Beauty lies dormant—her coming of age cursed by enforced passiv-
ity, dependent on the desire of an unknown prince who will awaken her. The
town she inhabits lies suspended in time—waiting. Unconscious, she remains
in limbo until rescued by her hero as he crosses the boundary of surrounding
forest to discover her female space. The prince's vision of her, his gaze, his kiss,
brings her to life.*

Marianne Goldberg in the printed version of
BALLERINAS & BALL PASSING published in *Women
& Performance 6.* Photo by Babette Mangolte.

as discourse.[2] As part of the issue, I created a theoretical montage on the theme of the gendered body and its cultural construction. In that piece, BALLERINAS & BALL PASSING, I mixed the codes of reading with those of the stage. I created a text in which images of my body appeared alongside theoretical statements—at times colliding with words. I choreographed movement explicitly for the two-dimensional format of the page, then had it photographed and arranged its layout in juxtaposition with the typographic text. I called BALLERINAS a "performance piece for print."[3] Playing with possible relations of body and word, I began to explore how gestural language is as symbolically imprinted as the written word.

For BALLERINAS I dressed as a lecturer. I wore a belted, gray checked suit that seemed to me ambiguously masculine and feminine. As this persona, I quoted from gestures from the ballet classics, estranging them by performing them in odd relationships to gravity. In some moves I appear to be standing, whereas I was actually simulating verticality while I lay on the floor, as photographer Babette Mangolte took pictures from overhead. Some of the poses were taken from *Swan Lake* and *The Sleeping Beauty,* performed by such greats as Margot Fonteyn. I questioned the gender meanings of these gestures by placing them next to passages of text in which I analyzed the naturalness of masculine and feminine stereotypes in dance. In BALLERINAS I looked at the way the body is shaped by choreographic training systems and dance canon formation, hoping to stake out a new cultural space for the female performer as a subject with agency. I began to search for female predecessors to "inhabit." Across one page I printed classic gestures by Bronislava Nijinska, Isadora Duncan, Martha Graham, and Yvonne Rainer—artists who responded to their times with courage and insight.

Social, economic, and theatrical forces shape the body. The symbolic and the imaginary coexist in the body, as they do in language. Gender meanings are enmeshed within our tissues, within our bones. The body speaks a language as intricate and layered as verbal language, and as contradictory. Like language, the body is malleable. It constantly accumulates and sheds meanings. (BALLERINAS & BALL PASSING, live performance version, San Diego, California, July 1988)

Marianne Goldberg in the live performance version of
BALLERINAS & BALL PASSING, with mechanicals of the
printed piece behind her. Photo by Robert Tobey.

The printed version of BALLERINAS was based on a theoretical lecture I had delivered at a theater conference in 1986.[4] In 1987 I took portions of that lecture and inserted choreographed gestures into the usual theorist's behavior as I stood behind a lectern while speaking at Duke University's "Symposium on Women and the Arts."[5] In spring of 1988 I published the printed version of BALLERINAS in *Women & Performance,* then immediately proceeded to rework the piece as a live performance with greater theatricalization of voice and gesture. By treating the crossovers between lecture, theoretical treatise, and performance as crossovers in media, I thought that the female body might slip between the representational modes of theory and theater, thereby evading known meanings to create new ones.

There is no one original format to BALLERINAS of which the others are "adaptations." The crossover between media challenges the identity of the work and the representation of the female body, the original essence of which cannot be easily located. In both live and printed versions body and word are constantly at play, shadowing, interrupting, or overlaying one another. Whether theoretical or theatrical, all of the materials of the work are available as one surface text. In the process of exploring what can happen when body and word are juxtaposed in print I found that an unpredictable blur, called a moiré, can blemish the coherence of the image. I strove to create images of the female body that were like moirés between media, accidental blurs of communication in which the apparatus of representation, which codes the way the female body is to be perceived, might be jarred.

Feminist film theory has been particularly influential for me in its focus on dismantling oppressive representations of the female body. In 1975 filmmaker and theorist Laura Mulvey had concisely described the way the female body is viewed in cinema—the eye of the male film director linked with the male cameraman, the eye of the male spectator outside the film linked with that of the male protagonist inside the narrative.[6] In the early 1980s Mulvey reconsidered this theory of the male gaze, pointing to its "negative aesthetics"—the ways in which it trapped women in the position of object.[7] She and others began to consider the possibility of spectators who might create alternate possibilities. I wanted to find ways for the female body to thrive while inhabiting theatrical space. In 1989, when I performed COMING INTO PARTS, I had hopes that together with an audience I might initiate an open-ended performance text that could spawn new meanings for the female body. On an event called "Reading the Signs" at a conference on feminism and theater I invited dancer Eva Karczag, my Alexander technique teacher, to perform a duet with me, COMING INTO PARTS.[8] In it Karczag and I performed on top of tables behind which academic panelists usually speak.

In studies with Eva Karczag and others over the years, I have been developing a greater capacity to listen to my body's needs and intelligence. As we moved together on top of the panel tables, Eva Karczag and I supported one another physically and verbally, allowing incremental changes to occur within our bodies at each changing instant. The quiet tones of our voices, as well as the sounds of our breath, were projected out to the audience via microphones. As in our individual sessions, I remained intently aware of the mobility I sensed in various parts of my body. Karczag, through touch and verbal encouragement, helped me to open rather than constrict those parts, expanding the space inside my bones, joints, and organs.

I want to move my leg toward my midline—it's scary to have my hip socket a little more open—maybe my body's getting used to the idea How does it feel to you through my hips? My coccyx feels a little squashed like it used to yeah earlier I felt I was withholding my arm from space I haven't been writing I'm overcoming some image of like a car crash in my pelvis Keep going? That was good Hhhhh wow it was like a wave of air, you know? I mean I must be preventing my body from getting air . . . Hhhhhh Keep going? Whhhhh oh that feels like it's changing so pleasantly Hhhhh I want to go this way . . . let's see Hhhh . . . My pelvis feels like two sides of a riverbank Yes, my pelvis feels like two sides two banks of a river the two sides of my pelvis are like riverbanks (COMING INTO PARTS, New York City, August 1989)

One of the images that emerged from my study with Karczag was of my body splitting into independent parts—my thigh stretching out from my pelvis, separating in pleasurable expansion. Yet, as I approached this expansion, I confronted distorted body images in which my legs felt impossibly small in relation to my torso. I had to fight off intensely disturbing images in order to wedge a space for another perception—that of my pelvis free to choose between going its own way or joining in motion with my legs. This potential for separation was not about coming apart but about coming *into* parts— the unsuturing of the body.

In feminist film theory suturing is that process through which one shot becomes "glued" to the next in the audience's eyes: a sequence of shots assures that a consistent set of narrative and gaze systems cohere around the female body.[9] How different is this coming into parts of the body from the training techniques of ballet or codified strains of modern dance, in which the student is asked to articulate positions in a geometrized space that is already predetermined. By creating potential openings in the way parts of the body join together, both the inner gaze of the performer (the way she images her own body while performing) and the external gaze of the audience might be freed from the scopic process in which the female body is habitually objectified for a viewer. In both Eva Karczag's own evolution of the Alexander technique as well as in my training in Kinetic Awareness with choreographer/filmmaker Elaine Summers, I have spent years "undoing" the impact of conventional dance training on my body—including unraveling gender profiles that often position the male as the jumper, the one who covers space, and the female as the one with flexibility and delicacy, who is manipulated by the male and displayed to the spectator.

The various forms of movement reeducation, such as the Alexander technique or Kinetic Awareness, address issues of repression and censorship at the cellular level. Constricted muscles hold traumatic memories of the socialization process of becoming "feminine"—of learning to restrain arms from moving through space with power or to keep legs tightly closed in public. Releasing can carry with it intense physical sensations, emotional crises, or psychological and social insights. It can also give rise to flights of imagination, as the body opens with surprise to new possibilities for motion. The performer can become aware of ways in which her most primary patterns of breath, muscular contraction, or body image have been habitually patterned in identification with cultural images. Movement education techniques can also allow the performer to reconnect to physiological needs and drives that may regenerate the body.

At a 1982 Barnard College conference on the politics of sexuality

Carole S. Vance insisted that "feminism must put forth a politics that resists deprivation and supports pleasure."[10] In COMING INTO PARTS Karczag and I were not focusing on the kind of debilitating visual pleasure analyzed by Mulvey; we were exploring an unrestrained sense of well-being in the performance of fluid, energized movement. We were focusing on the experiencing body, not on an objectifying gaze.

In the desire to bring theory and practice into collaboration, preceding the performance of COMING INTO PARTS, I had approached two conference theorists and invited them to come onstage while Karczag and I performed. I suggested they respond to what they saw by speaking into microphones set up at lecterns. To further open the boundary between spectators and performers I asked playwright/actor Anna Deavere Smith to speak from her seat in the audience. I gave her a text to read that I had transcribed from a session with Karczag. As she spoke, it became unclear to the audience whether she had spontaneously decided to interrupt the performance or whether her speech was staged. Another conference participant took Smith's participation as an invitation, and she spoke up from the opposite side of the hall. She was a bodywork practitioner, and she wanted to come onstage and work with me.

At this moment the performance's structure was fractured more than I had expected. COMING INTO PARTS began to degenerate into a realm of unknown meanings—a degeneration that I consider extremely fertile. Meanwhile, the theorists who I had previously invited to respond to the performance—Rebecca Schneider and Elin Diamond—entered the performance, along with Smith and Ann Gavere Kilkelly, who was to "moderate" the session. I had anticipated that the audience might begin to speak and hoped that the content of the performance itself might become the negotiation of meaning between performers and spectators. The audience broke out into debate about whether or not the conference spectator should enter the stage space. The discussion that ensued was partly about the right of the female spectator to directly affect what happens onstage, partly about the right of female performers to touch one another in healing ways.

With this negotiation of the boundaries of the performance there developed a problem of even being able to know what the performed image was. Instead of images of female bodies, what came to the foreground was a blur of communication—a kind of live moiré—that threatened the illusory coherence of the stage picture. Ironically, the event turned out not to fulfill the promise of "Reading the Signs" at all but, instead, to present the *unreadable*. The group became focused on what might be at stake in this attenuated instant of confrontation between performers and spectators, between those who were performing bodies and those who were performing theorists, and between one spontaneously formed audience cluster and another. The "meaning" of COMING INTO PARTS lay between all the participants in the room, and the space felt very large to me, the air thick, the performance stalled in a fascinating moment of not-knowing.

In Chicago in August 1990 I continued to structure avenues for spectators to enter the performance.[11] My piece, LIVE BODY/ SCREEN BODY, was part of a panel I chaired with theorist Jeanie Forte, titled "The Body as Constructed by Various Gazes." In my own mind I reversed the panel title to read: "Various Gazes as Constructed by the Body." As part of a theoretical introduction I gave at the opening of the piece, I proposed that together we might create a scopic field that not only did not oppress women but that encouraged new relationships between vision, the body, and the camera.

LIVE BODY/SCREEN BODY included a showing of HEAD HEART HIPS, a videodance I shot at the Atlantic Center for the Arts in Florida in April 1990. The idea for the videodance evolved out of my second performance piece for print, HUDSON ROVER, which had been published in *Artforum International* in December of 1988.[12] To create the stills for HUDSON ROVER I had asked photographer Robert Tobey to rig a camera on the ceiling that could be triggered at my initiation rather than at his. There was actually no one behind the camera, and I called out when I wanted images of my body to register across the emulsion.

To further pursue this strategy of absenting the cameraperson, for HEAD HEART HIPS, I had installed a video camera on the ceiling and rolled out a huge sheet of charcoal-gray photographic backdrop paper ten feet below it. I spread a layer of fine sand across the paper. Rather than focus on the visual design of my body for the camera, I paid attention to the friction between paper floor, sand, skin, and the silk of the blue jumpsuit I wore. The trace of my motion registered doubly—across the sand and across the videotape. I re-

Marianne Goldberg in HUDSON ROVER. Photo by Robert Tobey.

mained pointedly unaware of the exact boundaries of the aperture's frame.

In the videodance that resulted, parts of my body appear then disappear at the edges of the monitor. An ametric rhythm emerges in the play between my shape and the edge of the frame. The rhythm has as much to do with what happens in the implied "space off" as with what is visible within the boundaries of the frame. To further skew issues of visibility the viewer sees my body as if from above—an unlikely location that, far from the perspective of the king's box in a proscenium theater, seems like a floating view from nowhere in particular. The body takes its own space and time, unrestricted by familiar geometric points of origin or metric pulses.

When I played HEAD HEART HIPS during LIVE BODY/ SCREEN BODY I stood beside the monitor, wearing the same jumpsuit I had on in the video. The contrast between my live and screen bodies was accentuated by the text I spoke, which I had culled from a tape recording of a photographic session I had staged in a New York University lecture hall in November of 1989. During the staged session Karczag and I danced while we spoke an associative stream of words in conversation with Elin Diamond, two photographers, and the institutional lecture hall space. Our images were split between the photographers, Tobey and Paula Court. The usually invisible photographer behind the camera became visible in the lens of the mirroring photographer. Court, who had trained in Kinetic Awareness, splintered the images further by offering Karczag, Diamond, and me her extra camera, resulting in an interplay of shot-reverse shot . . . shot-reverse shot, . . . the multiple cameras dispersing and deflecting the origin of the gaze throughout the room.

She doesn't want to pose her foot The camera makes it a pose No cameras for a minute—ok—no pictures for a minute I just need a time without any . . . I didn't get a chance to connect with my . . . shoulders Did you bring the close-up attachment? Come close that's what I feel now I think I'd like more support Shoulder Elbow Neck Chin I'm thinking of putting my chin on the camera Bodies can change because Because of their presence I'm displacing space . . . just by moving I'm changing the space The freest object in the room seems to be the camera because it has an apparatus that hides it Disarm The camera is

touching you Cameras are weapons Do we become still and wait until the camera is turned on? There's a visual rhythm and a sensual rhythm and they don't have anything to do with one another Go ahead with what you're doing Can I take a picture? I'm so unphotogenic Can you get closer? Let's go on . . . Can people get as absolutely close as they want to—way inside the motion? Can you hear me? Can you hear me? Yes! (COMING INTO PARTS, photographic session, taped conversation between Goldberg, Karczag, Diamond, Tobey, and Court, included as text in LIVE BODY/SCREEN BODY, Chicago, Illinois, August 1990)

As I excerpted lines from the photo session in the live performance in Chicago, I stood next to the video monitor, directing the text toward my "screen" body as she danced HEAD HEART HIPS. In front of me spectators faced one another in two banks of chairs I had set out in rows on either side of a five-foot-wide strip of photographic backdrop paper. The paper, unrolled, extended about twenty-five feet. At one end of it, to my side, was the video monitor, at the other a third bank of spectators facing in. The unwritten surface of the paper created a fissure in the audience space, across which glances were exchanged between viewer and viewer, viewer and performer.

On a previous panel conference participant Betty Bernhard had spoken of her trip to one of the old Italian proscenium opera houses, noting that spectators' views were not securely sutured to the king's view, as usually suggested by historians. It seemed to her that spectators could also catch the gazes of other spectators via mirrors installed in their opera boxes. When the HEAD HEART HIPS video had completed I picked up a disposable flash camera, read label directions aloud on "how to shoot flash pictures," and handed the camera to Bernhard. She began taking photos of the performance, as did other spectators, who picked up flash cameras that lined the edge of the photographic paper.

Rebecca Schneider, who I had again invited to be a "performing theorist," stepped onto the photographic backdrop paper with me and handed me a video camera. She wrote a question across the paper, and I pointed the camera at her emerging text, which flashed across the monitor for the rest of the spectators to read: "What is the space between my live body and my screen body?" I gave the camera back to Schneider and lay down to begin a floor dance, sliding across the surface of the paper. She videotaped me, then handed the camera to other spectators, and the gaze was dispersed around the roomful of women, from video camera to monitor to flash cameras to spectator's or performer's eye.

As I danced amid those ricocheting gazes, my "stage directions" were to let myself fall back into the sensation level of my body—into three "hearts" I imagined in the interior geography of my body: the first, deep inside my head at the pineal gland; the second, my actual heart; and the third, my pelvis, womb, or heart-shaped sacrum.[13] I began to let motion generate between the impulses I experienced in these three hearts. My body responded with a flash flood of gestures. Schneider and I proceeded down the runway of photographic paper, which spectators later described as a fashion show ramp or parade route. The long, umbilical-like video cord uncoiled as we progressed. Spectators continued to photograph the event or to use the video camera when Schneider handed it to them or wrote and drew all over the paper with pens we offered them as we passed by.

What is the relationship between the movement of the line in writing and the movement of the body in dance? Is there a picture outside our frame? Is it outer space that is our frontier or rather the inner space or maybe the body? Is she inscribing herself or her image on the screen of my mind/memory self? (Spectators' writings, LIVE BODY/SCREEN BODY)

Schneider and I had planned that the image on the monitor would black out when we had traveled three-quarters of the way down the paper. As Schneider pushed the off button on her remote control, she began to dismantle the viewing apparatus. She took the camera off the tripod and approached me, her legs and arms multiplied by the three tripod limbs that she splayed outward as far as they could go. The video apparatus was now eye to eye with me—low to the ground, down at the level where I squatted and lumbered. I asked the audience to hand me the video camera, and I aimed it directly at Schneider. She entwined her body in the tripod, focused the now empty mounting surface for the camera directly on me, eyeing me through its hole. When she attempted to turn the monitor back on via remote control nothing happened.

As the audience caught wind of this power failure, the room became charged. I faltered momentarily, sensing that viewers had become more fascinated with my screen image than with my live presence. Now they were left with an actual rather than electronic body—and there seemed to be a sense of loss, as if the infatuation of the performance were suddenly over. I rallied and accelerated into motion, letting the three hearts clang together energetically and disperse their racket into the surrounding space, calling out to the audience as I rose to vertical, "Can you still see me when the camera is off?" The moment of the failed apparatus established a sudden and unforeseen opportunity for the actual bodies of the people in the room to emerge and become visible. In a postperformance discussion spectators told me that this moment was for them the death of the performance parade, a moment of great possibility in its opportunities for agency and choice.

NOTES

1. SIDESHOW was performed live by Sara Hostetler, a teacher of Body Mind Centering (a movement reeducation technique), a cyclist extraordinaire, and a student of ballet. The video of the piece has been included in subsequent performances of THE BODY WORD SERIES.

2. *Women & Performance: A Journal of Feminist Theory* 6 (1987–88). As a member of the editorial board of *Women & Performance,* I have found a home base in the journal.

3. Marianne Goldberg, "BALLERINAS & BALL PASSING," *Women & Performance* 6 (1987–88): 7–31.

4. I delivered that lecture at the American Theater Association (ATA) conference in New York City. ATA was a precursor of the Association of Theater in Higher Education (ATHE).

5. This first performance version of the lecture took place in Durham, North Carolina, in January 1987.

6. Laura Mulvey, "Visual Pleasure and Narrative Cinema," *Screen* 16, no. 3 (Autumn 1975): 6–18.

7. Laura Mulvey, *Visual and Other Pleasures* (Bloomington: Indiana University Press, 1989), 161–66.

8. This conference, which took place in New York City, was sponsored by the Women & Theater Program (WTP), a division of ATHE. I had performed

BALLERINAS for the group the previous year in San Diego. The WTP has been a fertile context in which to create work that bridges theory and practice. It provides a place to perform for feminist spectators who actively participate in propelling my work toward new questions. I have enjoyed wonderful exchanges with performers and scholars.

9. See Kaja Silverman's chapter, "Suture," *The Subject of Semiotics* (New York and Oxford: Oxford University Press, 1983).

10. Carole S. Vance, "Pleasure and Danger: Toward a Politics of Sexuality," in *Pleasure and Danger: Exploring Female Sexuality,* edited by Carole S. Vance (Boston: Routledge and Kegan Paul, 1984).

11. This performance took place at De Paul University, as part of the WTP annual conference.

12. Marianne Goldberg, "HUDSON ROVER," *Artforum International,* December 1988, 11–13.

13. These images had emerged during one of my Alexander lessons with Eva Karczag.

ANN KILKELLY

"Broads" Too Tight to Sing

The original title of Kentucky playwright George Ella Lyon's *Braids* was *Braids Too Tight to Sing.*[1] During the preshow ticket sales a man called and asked to buy a ticket to "that show he heard about on the radio, 'Broads' Too Tight to Sing." When corrected he hung up without buying a ticket. In the context of the University of Kentucky Women Writers' Conference, which sponsored the first production of the play, it was awful and funny, and the remark remains in our production history to remind us that "broads" wear "braids," that "tight" serves the male gaze, and that singing does not. Produced outside the male stream of playwriting, *Braids,* more than any piece I have directed, incorporated my readings in feminist theory.

Braids conflates the onset of menstruation with the foreclosure of subjectivity. Although the play concerns the impact of community, family, and other social structures on a young woman, Emma, it avoids any implication of a stable identity for her. Rather, it creates a sense of Emma's constant struggle as she positions and repositions herself. Built in a series of intersecting monologues, the play engages the spectator in the manner of traditional storytelling, but the stories are multirelational and nonlinear. I directed the monologues to the audience, purposefully stressing lines of communication from actor to spectator; I developed parallel sound and movement texts that often disrupted the spoken text; I chose a minimal set that could be read in several simultaneous time frames. Because the play suggests that Emma has no identity separate from the character voices and their stories that surround her, I kept them and her onstage and visible at all times. I wanted my directing to support and serve the whole collaborative process and to have a texture with as rich and complex a life as the text.

The first script developed from a collection of monologues George Ella began over Sunday morning conversations at my kitchen table. She read "Housekeeping," a monologue written, she claims, to "capture my grandmother's voice because I knew she was dying." Hence Lou Buckner, Emma's grandmother on her father's side:

> I don't want another soul in my house tracking up my rugs and that's that. I have to go over them every morning of this world with a broom and I don't intend to do it of an evening too. Help. Some help they'd be. Glenna—she's my daughter-in-law—she drug two of them women in here. Said they were from the Home Health. Huh, I said. I need them like a hog needs a saddle. I am 87 years old and I tell you, I'll not have it. I told Glenna if they came back I'd get a big stick and run them off. I'll run her off too. It's true I don't get around too good and most days I only wear my house-coat, but that's because I can't find my clothes. There's a body around here that takes things, I tell you, and that's awful to say when you live alone. It's the truth though, honey. Even my bras.

Lou is old, fiercely independent, and a growing problem for her family, who want to help her. She rejects the women from Home Health and her panic and paranoia grow as she moves in and out of "reality."

As George Ella describes it, no sooner did Lou's monologue emerge than the others in the family started clamoring to speak. The next voice was Glenna's, and she was furious: "You can't marry just one person, oh, I expect you know that. Choose a man, you choose his mother. This has been my lesson, bitter as a lemon seed, and I've bitten down on it again and again." Then Luther, Glenna's husband, Lou's son, spoke: "I've dealt with a lot of problems in my life, and I can take them as long as there's a solution or even a hint of a solution. But the thing with mother—this has got me stumped. . . ."

Papa Clayton Buckner, Lou's husband, Luther's father, talked obsessively about "a man's work":

> What's the world going to be like with everything off a quarter of an inch? How are folks going to feel when their new floors buckle and their walls crack and their gadgets overload their sorry wiring? I'll tell you one thing: it'll be dark and they won't

have a candle, and if they do, it'll be in some cabinet that's stuck shut, rolled to the back of somebody's tilted shelf.

In rapid succession came May and Earl Perkins, Glenna's parents, and finally Emma, the young daughter who struggles to say anything at all: "Do you know how hard it is to tell the truth about your kinfolks? Almost as hard as telling your kinfolks about the truth. But I am going to try. I tell myself I am only Emma, but these people are me, too—The Buckners and the Perkins—their voices and their memories."

In the rapid emergence of the pieces no pattern was clear, but an important turning point was the revelation that Emma had double vision and in her adolescence quite literally had struggled to see like everyone else. The monologue "Parking Meter" humorously described her headlong encounter with a parking meter, which she hit trying to go between it and its double, "slightly higher and tilted to the right." All the characters immediately chimed in with opinions about "the trouble with Emma," but it was finally Glenna, Emma's mother, who gave us the breakthrough. In the fall of 1984 George Ella and I drove together to a conference in Atlanta, and it was speeding down I-75 that she read "Leafpile" to me. In it Glenna reveals that Emma had "cut up her wrists" in an attempt to commit suicide before school one day and, "having survived, went to school in long sleeves to hide the bandages." Glenna says, "she lies around like a leafpile, and then one day you find out she's on fire."

The whole thing was cooking, whatever it was. George Ella said it was "a level of mess or revelation" and asked, "is this profound or just profuse?" Eighteen monologues from seven characters. I tentatively offered the notion that, when lots of characters speak out loud, it tends to be a play, though George Ella kept saying she didn't know how to write a play. And I knew what she meant. This text had no central action that was logically prepared for, no single topic or organizing theme. We had seven clamoring voices, none of them even talking to each other. As George Ella later wrote, "We are pulled toward one character and then another, our loyalties parted, our certainties twisted and crossed. There is no single truth, no minor character, no villain. These are the Buckners and the Perkinses—braided tight for life."

I said it really didn't matter if it fit anybody's notion of what a play was. I heard it, I could see it, and I thought she should continue. The voices were so alive, so immediate, and I heard writer/actor Jo Carson's voice as Lou.

During the months that George Ella wrote, she and I and Martha Gehringer, a friend and colleague, met on Sundays over my kitchen table; Jo came to Lexington to do a reading. As she was a long-time colleague and friend, we invited her to read Lou's monologue. She did, and together we planned the grant and the event that would culminate in the first production.[2]

What I didn't say to George Ella was that if she doubted that *Braids* was a play, I was equally unconvinced I was a director. I had years of experience producing and staging multimedia events to showcase new work by women; I took many classes in theater as a graduate student, and I had been in lots of plays, but I had no formal training as a director. I still don't. Somehow the term *director,* with its guru images of Grotowski, Serban, or Brook, the people I most admired in my graduate school years, existed in another realm. When I had worked with women playwrights before, I had avoided anything like mainstream venues, preferring a kind of salon, or closed community, where work could be supported and produced cheaply, with everyone involved getting paid, however little. I worried that somehow this meant that it wasn't real work. It's an interesting phenomenon that both George Ella and I continued to work on this project despite the fact that we were always aware of the larger theater world's potential critique. It was the guys, the "big dogs," as Jo Carson describes them, that sat on our shoulders, demanding roast beef sandwiches and beer and sending our muses off in wrong directions and chiding them about reading the map wrong. And here theory became somehow the source of inspiration, or, in less mystified terms, began to suggest a kind of call and response with new work, echoing back and developing names for the kinds of perspectives we needed to keep going.

Like so many academic feminists, my work in the early 1980s tended to be about the reclamation of women's lives and stories. My sense of feminism was shaped by literary discourse: Virginia Woolf, Sandra Gilbert and Susan Gubar, Annette Kolodny, and others demonstrated that literary production was hopelessly skewed. I had also consumed large doses of Artaud, Brecht, Derrida, and Barthes, and

I had begun to be aware of French feminists, particularly Kristeva, and British feminists working in class analysis. I had seen the relationship of deconstruction and the postmodern style to playwrights like Beckett, Pinter, and even Shepard. But how, I wondered, could my own feminist analysis, then heavily literary and tending toward cultural activism, incorporate theoretical positions that seemed hostile to it? It felt like two different and alien worlds—one with its complex, male, and sometimes bloated linguistic complexity, and the other with its radically important but, I felt, sometimes oversimplified social program. And, most important, where was the clear application of feminist theory to the kinds of plays I wanted to direct? I stuck to an activist position, refusing to direct plays by men and working with women playwrights to find venues for new work and to help them tell their stories. *Braids* came in some sense from this position, but we very quickly were drawn into issues about the play and authorship that required analysis beyond the thematic and social concerns of the play, which were obvious and relevant.

It was exactly those analyses by Sue-Ellen Case, Jill Dolan, Elin Diamond, and others[3]—the heated debates about feminism itself, about the male gaze, about the limitations of cultural feminism and the application of film theory to theater practice—that suggested to me the links I needed. Apropos of those same debates, I worried about authorship, about stories; I saw the complicity of master narratives in patriarchy. But how could I inform the production with theory and not undermine George Ella's process? How could I direct a play whose voices came from Appalachia without employing reductive and offensive stereotypes? I do think that without the tacit encouragement supplied by theory I could not have directed the play at all; however, the theoretical issues I struggled with also excited me so much that I wanted them to be the play. I nearly paralyzed my own ability to work because of my need to negotiate and theorize every moment, every word. My sense of being an outsider to the region, the fact that I was an academic and middle class despite my own working-class roots, even my love of language, created a political complexity I both welcomed and feared.

I was terrified of communicating my theory-induced paralysis to George Ella. But then I reminded myself that theory and discourse about theory are porous and flexible, teasing out previously nebulous ideas. Theory is experimental and creative, not rigid and rule bound.

And I believed that in the context of a supportive community it was all right for me to join these new ideas to a text I loved. And so I shared these thoughts and speculations, in the language of theory. And so began a conversation of such complexity, range, and pleasure that I suspect the play became the secondary text, or even the pretext for those conversations with George Ella and others. I took the position that the play could, even should, be developed in monologue, letting its multiple strands remain intact. I resolved that we would keep talking and find our way to the text by letting it develop with the actors.

I gave George Ella *Still Life* by Emily Mann, because that play's presentational, monologic form suited my sense of a text that made the political personal and vice versa. It was a play in which multiple monologues worked very well, suggesting in the lack of dramatic dialogue the profound sense of isolation that was part of the Vietnam War's impact on the people in the play. George Ella read it and began weaving the monologues together, and a whole shape began to emerge.

For some time I had been interested in what seemed to me a very important phenomenon: widespread use of monologue by women playwrights.[4] The monologue in performance, especially from a female speaker, potentially subverts the public (male) domain of stage representation by suggesting the presence of interiority, of private space. Monologue can be an "other" space where women can insert themselves, a site which comments on the presence of a realm traditionally characterized as "feminine." Playwriting handbooks, mercifully few and mostly published in the United States since 1900, are united over the need to eliminate the unnecessary, or "contaminating," monologue. The prohibitive language employed by these texts to describe monologue is reminiscent of sexist suspicions about the female body and voice. The monologue, like the female body, needs to be contained or eliminated lest it grow out of control and "pollute" the dialogue.

George Ella began to weave, braid, or "emplot" the stories, developing multiple parallel strands of monologue that built until they would erupt into dialogue, but only rarely and only under pressure. She describes the monologue as "an equal opportunity employer; everybody gets to talk." In the public arena of dialogue power relations determine who speaks and how. Drama is social in this way.

The monologue suggests nonpublic speech, existing within, and framed by, dialogue.

The play developed over several months of readings and conversations with actors, most of whom were also in the subsequent productions. It finally settled into two acts, the first centered around the Buckners (paternal grandparents) and Lou, and the second around the Perkinses (maternal grandparents) and Emma. Over the course of the play multiple stories are told, spanning the lifetimes and memories of all three generations. In particular, Lou and Emma appear at several ages, Lou from seventeen to eighty-seven, Emma from nine to twenty-seven. The shifts in age are signaled by memory and association rather than linear development, so that at any given time a character may speak out of any historical moment of her life without using the past tense.

Emma does not narrate; rather, her memory and her listening create a space in which others speak. Ironically, this position of Emma's, as receiver of these lives and texts, as a listener who speaks about not speaking, becomes the focal "problem" of the play, and other characters often give advice or directions to or about her:

> *Lou:* Of course she can't sing with her hair braided tight like that. Pulls her skin back so all she can do is cry. Besides, fat-faced girls shouldn't wear braids. Makes them look like shoats.
>
> *May:* If she'd been my child, I'd have cured her with a keen switch.
>
> *Grandpa Earl:* Talk before you walk and your tongue will be your ruin.

As more stories from the past begin to open the seams of the present, they reveal the incongruence and disappointment that lie just under the surface. The text converges on the mother-daughter, Glenna-Emma, relationship and Emma's "double vision," a literal condition, for which she has surgery, and also a metaphorical expression of her place. Emma says, "and it wasn't just in church that I saw too much. I saw two of everything until I was thirteen years old."

As the writing began to merge with the rehearsing and producing, my understanding of feminist theory kept suggesting that, as director, like Emma, I had to listen, not impose notions of shape but, instead, find ways to echo the culture the stories came out of without sounding sentimental or stereotypical. I wanted to foreground the gender issues that are George Ella's main concern. Ongoing discussions about the relationship of feminism to deconstruction and post-modernism gave me the strong sense that, theoretically at least, the hegemony of a plot could be undermined by juxtaposing stories, by underlining the presence of the actor, by forcing constant destabilization of point of view. Though I distrusted narration in theater (how easily this could be directed as a kind of *Our Town,* given the ease with which the personal story invites empathy and the voices of the mountain region invoke stereotypes), I saw the possibilities of multiple, simultaneous narration as viable for feminist exploration. Simultaneous and overlapping monologues could suggest the isolation of this young woman and create the cacophonous community around her.

None of this could have happened within the usual four-week rehearsal structure. *Braids* took nine months in the writing, producing, and directing. I raised money to produce the play because I wanted George Ella's work to be recognized. I wanted to be part of its development. I wanted the actors to be part of the development. I wanted to wait and listen until the next choice was clear. I wanted to work in my community, not in the semiprofessional theater community, which sought to emulate Actor's Theater of Louisville emulating the Circle Rep but, rather, the community that exists in the geography of Kentucky.

Though I was an outsider in Kentucky, I worked to hear the poetry and music of the mountains, of Harlan, George Ella's home. No sooner did I hear them than I began to be aware of the stereotypes and bigotry that the world brings to bear on writing from Appalachia. A university colleague of mine calls any text from Appalachia "that voice." I heard jokes about outhouses and flush toilets. One of the actors, prior to a performance at Appalshop, gave directions to Harlan by saying, "you know, just drive to the asshole of the world and you'll be there." He is from Idaho. He passed this remark off, in George Ella's presence, as a joke. Regional stereotyping was painfully clear: all mountain people have broken-down cars in their yards. They smoke corncob pipes. They wear raggedy clothes, and all talk the same funny way. They are all poor and barefoot. "Acting" them often meant adding a constructed concept, voice, or accent, usually having less reference to the southern Appalachians than to stereotypical, media-generated images. Voices became "that voice," one voice, as false as L'il Abner or the Beverly Hillbillies.

At great length we discussed the issue of regional accents, what they were, whether to use them or not. Ultimately, because I believed that the geography and "voices" of the region were already part of George Ella's written language, and because I was theoretically interested in underscoring rather than minimizing the presence of the actor as distinct from the character, I coached actors to drop any "acted" regionalisms. I felt that "voice" training and diction in themselves encoded powerful class distinctions that privilege the supposedly educated over others.

I asked the actors to speak in their own voices and listen actively, responding to what the other characters said, even though direct response almost never occurs in the play itself, and characters speak out of different time frames or represented spaces. In this way the actors would carry on multiple imagined conversations that were never spoken but nonetheless made themselves felt in the text. I asked the actors to listen "vertically" to the sounds and meanings they produced within their shaft of isolation; I asked them also to listen "horizontally" to and think about the sounds and meanings produced by others onstage. This "listening" was a technique I learned as a rhythm tap dancer, from Brenda Bufalino. When many voices were speaking I thought of them as polyrhythmic and that the actor's task was not unlike a drummer's in a rhythm ensemble. But when one speaker was in monologue the others also had to maintain and understand the connections that sometimes merged pieces together. They also had to simultaneously respond to and analyze the words of others. What resulted was a kind of alienation effect that suited my sense of the importance of multiple listening and pried apart the boxes of realism that constantly tried to enclose the text.

This acoustic acting became increasingly important to my directing process, as I understood more and more how representation tends to mold voices into voice and that the effect of this on Emma is silence.[5] We struggled with Emma's relative silence amid the profusion of voices around her. Later George Ella said:

It's Emma's listening that allows them to speak. But in order to find her voice, or a braiding of voices—those things that have formed her but that she'd never been able to hear—have to be heard. Because there are not many things in *Braids* that those characters have said before. It's what I was saying before, about monologue being an equal opportunity employer. That they do get to say those things, and that the subtext, or the underside, the inside, is turned around and shown.

Braids presents Emma's particular dilemma as the struggle for voice in her movement toward the onset of female maturity. Glenna explains it as menstruation, but it is also the articulation of absence, loss, otherness. In several passages George Ella associates surgery for double vision with this onset of menstruation, the suicide attempt, loss of faith, and death:

> *Glenna:* But these weren't the hard parts. I'm getting to the hard part. Of course, Emma had to mature before anyone was ready, least of all her. Eleven years old. She was too young to know what all that blood meant and I couldn't tell her. My mother never mentioned such things. I said she was growing up and not to worry. But I could see that she did.
>
> *Emma:* You know how you see two of everything, but only half of it is real, and if there's a lot going on you get confused . . .
>
> *Luther:* It's not like that for everybody. Most people only see one.
>
> *Emma:* Mother took me to doctors over at Scoville. I saw too little, too much, the wrong thing. Finally they did surgery—pried my eyes out like a doll's and tightened the strings. For two weeks my eyes were bandaged shut.
>
> *Emma:* It was Mother that took the bandages off. We were at home in the study. She peeled back the gauze and there she was, my concentrated mother, in a room with only half its windows and books. Then she gave me a mirror. I looked in and saw my one face, skin red and swollen, eyes wary. (*to Glenna*) It's much better. . . .
>
> *Glenna:* Emma would probably say now it was hormones. Society. Or my fault. I don't know. We only talked about it that one day. The principal called me to come to school. It was

lunchtime. Emma had cut up her wrists. Done it at home the night before. And having survived set out for school the next day with long sleeves to hide the bandages. I didn't notice; mornings were hurried. But the blood came back. So there we were, driving around the playground and then the whole school.

"What in the world were you thinking of Emma? Tell me everything. I have to know."

Emma: I have to know, you said. But how could I tell you? How could I talk to you if you wouldn't talk to me? I had to know too, but you wouldn't tell me.

Glenna: I could have slapped Emma. Held her tight and slapped her again. But I was driving. I bit my cheek until I tasted salt and iron. "I want you to stop all this right now. I want you to hold up your head and smile and not say another word about it. Do you know what this would do to your father if he found out? It would kill him. And how can I keep him from knowing? Tonight you'll start that dancing class, like it or not, and you'll PERK UP, Emma. Next year you'll go to the city school. This is bad, but you can put it behind you if you really try. If you turn your back on it right now."

Emma: Yes.

Glenna: She said "yes," cool as you please. Not a tear on her face and my heart pounding. I knew she needed toughness, so I didn't hug her when the lunch hour was over. "Get out. And come home ready to shape up."

When Emma had surgery they "pried her eyes out like a doll's and tightened the strings," a violent but "naturalized" way of correcting her vision. This operation, literal on the level of story, signifies the constant functioning of patriarchy on the woman/child who sees too much. This section of the play articulates the accession to female maturity as the loss of double vision and the acquisition of adult discourse, succinctly contained in Emma's "yes." Although the section approaches the linear logic of standard realism, the monologic structure is broken only once, at the moment of this "yes." The play, at this moment, sutures Emma to the world her mother provides, at the sacrifice of multiple vision and desire. Yet because the voices of the play have been established already as having multiple functions, because the monologic structure has now given the spectator access to double vision, or vision times seven, there is slippage.

I tried to support this textual complexity with aural multiplicity. I designed the music for the production with the help of a composer. We gave her popular songs from the time period, hymns and folk songs to incorporate into an acoustic piano score. Pieces of songs occur—"Red Wing," "The Tennessee Waltz," "Animal Crackers in My Soup," "The Girl That I Marry," "Just as I Am," "I Come to the Garden Alone," and "Barbara Allen." Never was a whole song sung through to the end; usually, songs and dialogue overlapped, and the score itself was a pastiche of the pieces, usually in minor keys or modulating from majors to minors, as in the case of "The Tennessee Waltz." My intention was to invite pleasurable response to familiar and much loved popular songs that encoded idealized heterosexual romance, appropriate spirituality, or correct female behavior. "The Girl That I Marry," for instance, written for a male voice, suggests that "the girl that I marry will have to be / as soft and as sweet as a nursery." This song, like others, is used partially and becomes ironic when sung by Emma and juxtaposed with characters' commentaries, thus driving a wedge between pleasurable response and the text's signification.

For the opening of the play I gave each character a tag line and asked the actors to improvise overlapping their lines. It was Emma's job to travel the stage space, using her tag line "Listen. I am only Emma" to express her need to be heard. They moved from their tag lines into a song, each different. Lou sang "The Tennessee Waltz," Papa Clayton sang "Amazing Grace," and so on until they were all singing full out in complete disharmony. One by one Emma moved to them, and they joined her in "His Eye Is on the Sparrow." Lou held out over everyone until the last line, when she reluctantly joined in.

At various points throughout the performance, particularly in moments of stress, I brought back this cacophony, so that the character Emma struggled to be "heard" in one sense, while the actor playing Emma struggled literally to be heard over the other six voices. A particularly important scene in this regard is a passage in which Emma describes coming to understand the hypocrisies of religious practice:

After I was baptized with water, I waited for the baptism of the spirit. I was a little worried though. The only people who speak in tongues around here are the Holy Rollers. That wouldn't do. It was their kids who got run out of Sunday school. But I thought when the spirit came I would understand. The scales would fall from my eyes and I'd see that all around me people were living the Gospel. I waited, as intensely as I used to wait for Santa Claus, but that baptism never came.

The family, having become a congregation, preceded this speech by singing the hymn, "Just as I Am," and now, behind these words, they sang, "I Come to the Garden Alone," whose chorus ends:

And He walks with me
And He talks with me
And He tells me I am His own.
And the joy we share
As we tarry there
None other has ever known.

The melody of the song is achingly beautiful, but in a feminist context, here suggested by Emma's failure to receive traditional grace and her inability to believe because the myth failed her, the words become a chilling reminder that when "she" comes to "Him," "He" gives her the text and takes her for "His own." This taking and being taken is supposed to be her source of joy. In one of the verses I asked the actor playing Emma to sing over the others and make sure she was audible. I asked them to escalate their volume at the end of her speech so that she is finally drowned out and joins them, singing harmony for the final chorus. Had we only the harmony and the spiritual closure of the hymn's text, it could be a moment of religious community. But, given Emma's words and the context we were in, it reflected the complicity of the church in the oppression of women. She was "His own." I was very nervous that this moment might be read as endorsing Christian forgiveness and comfort. Feminist theory gave me the tools to analyze the ideology at work and, I hope, effectively subvert it while still allowing direct emotional impact.

Metaphors of vision and visual aspects of the production needed theoretical underpinning as well. I suggested earlier that I kept all actors visible at all times to imply the presence of them in Emma, as she says, "These people are me too; their voices, their memories." They are materially present to the spectator, even if we understand the moment to exclude them in the time or space that one "scene" represents. I directed actors who were not "playing" a scene to frankly acknowledge their own presence onstage and to be cognizant of the action around them. They are, variously, chorus, spectators, witnesses, and congregation; at points some are alive in the story being told, and some are "dead," but they are always present for the spectator. This directorial idea creates discontinuity with the offstage space; actors *are* only at the moment of incorporating the characters or themselves onstage.

I used minimal properties, only those that had a specific, material function: chairs, a door frame, a change of shoes and a sweater for Lou, a piano bench for Emma. All age changes, and there are many in the text, had to be simply created by the actor, with no realistic techniques of artificial aging or gestures that read age or youth. Jo Carson, as Lou, changed the pace of her movement, took off her glasses, and sat down on the edge of her platform when she became the younger version of herself. Again it was important to me, given my interest in disrupting the conventions of realism, to maintain the separation of the actor from the role, thus making it possible for Emma's double vision to have resonance for the spectator. It was my hope that the audience would sense that identity is always unstable and socially constructed, especially female identity.

Moreover, throughout most of the play I positioned Emma, when she was listening, at the periphery, or margins, of a scene. Spatially, she traveled the cracks where one represented scene shifted into another, whereas the others stayed somewhat stable except in specific scenes from the past. I used the proscenium stage by choice, as it suited the presentational character of the monologues but maintained the separation of actors and spectators. Any reaching across the proscenium arch was framed in reference to realism. The compositional shape of the playing area was triangular, with Emma at its off-center and changing apex, as she was pulled from one side or one character to another. Her movement patterns and gestures frequently mirrored or shadowed that of the character she was listening to, though her own lines were spoken mostly from a far downstage position, sometimes even from the edge of the stage, where she sat as a child. In the vertical upstage, horizontal downstage composition, the oldest characters, the grandparents, were the furthest upstage, the parents center, and Emma down. They were free not only to direct their stories to the audience but to look at them and at Emma. At the same time she was closest to the audience and often took visual, if not aural, focus. I hoped that in this way Emma would appear as the object of their scrutiny but that she and the others would look at themselves being looked at, at least multiplying and commenting on, if not subverting, the direction of the gaze.

Reception has been problematic: people insisted on seeing the play as about the mountains, not of the mountains. Often its personal stories, flavored with the music and the idiom of the region, were called "trivial" by academics. Conservative administrators liked it, they told me, because it was "sweet" and had only "clean language" and that what they liked about me was that I was a feminist, but I wasn't "strident." They were, in fact, something like "Daddy" in Lou's anecdote near the end of the play:

> Lordy mercy, if my Daddy knew I'd chopped my hair off like this, he wouldn't let me in this house. He don't know how country it looks to have all them years piled on your head. But I fixed it for him. I had my hair cut—braided, like he liked it, and I kept the braid. So all I have to do is wrap that braid around my head, pin on my hat, and off I go. He never looks that close and we both rest easy.[6]

Lou's braids function as the adopted mask of femininity, which allows her a measure of double-dealing in her world: "off I go." The unresolved but complex and revealing nature of the play can be read in Lou's final line to Emma: "whoever you are, you are a sight for sore eyes."

The contradictions of Emma's position in the stage representation had no resolution. Our attempt to suggest the multiplicity and instability of Emma's identity was always in some sense contradicted by her focal position. Yet the fact that she speaks less than she is spoken about and yet remains visible *and* focal, for me suggests an honest and complex moment for a female character and for women in theatrical representation.

The process of braiding ourselves and this text together was difficult yet deeply pleasurable, and this, I imagine, will allow the call and response of theory and practice to continue.

NOTES

1. The life of the various productions spanned four years, from 1984 to 1988. The first performance was produced for the University of Kentucky Women Writers' Conference 4, 5, and 6 April 1985. The second was at Appalshop in Whitesburg, Kentucky, during November 1985. In 1987 Marie Mitchell at WEKU FM radio in Richmond, Kentucky, produced a one-hour tape, which aired on Public Broadcasting Service (PBS) affiliates in the region. Quoted passages in this essay come from the manuscript of the radio production. The play remains unpublished.

2. Lately George Ella has reminded me that a layer of all this was our mutual longtime participation in the Women Writers' Conference at the University of Kentucky. I mention this because the existence of that conference and the Kentucky Foundation for Women were two very empowering agencies and, more important, gave us a sense of working already within a feminist community, who turned out in wildly enthusiastic droves for the opening, to our surprise and delight.

3. Although it is difficult for me to isolate specific texts of these three writers that influenced me then, I heard and participated in many discussions of these issues at American Theater in Higher Education meetings, especially during the Women and Theater Preconference programs. The nature of those theoretical arguments has been amply laid out by E. B. Sullivan in the first chapter of this volume, and both Sue-Ellen Case's *Feminism and Theatre* (New York: Methuen, 1988) and Jill Dolan's *The Feminist Spectator as Critic* (1988; reprint, Ann Arbor: University of Michigan Press, 1991) have fully articulated the variety of feminist positions within evolving performance theory. Elin Diamond's discussions of Brechtian historicization, such as her essay "(In)Visible Bodies in Churchill's Theater" (in *Making a Spectacle: Feminist Essays on Contemporary Women's Theatre,* edited by Lynda Hart [Ann Arbor: University of Michigan Press, 1989]) have helped me find ways to apply new theoretical frameworks to my directing practice.

4. I developed this idea in "Contextualizing the Monologue," a paper presented at the New Languages for the Stage Conference at the University of Kansas, November 1988.

5. In *The Acoustic Mirror: The Female Voice in Psychoanalysis and Cinema* (Bloomington and Indianapolis: Indiana University Press, 1988) Kaja Silverman investigates the issue of voice in cinema and psychoanalysis, and further investi-

gation might explore the application of those ideas to the stage, where the body and the voice in the body have material presence.

6. According to George Ella, this story refers to the old-fashioned practice of having one's hair braided and *then* cut, still in the braid.

REFERENCES

Case, Sue-Ellen. 1988. *Feminism and Theatre*. New York: Methuen.

Diamond, Elin. 1989. In *Making a Spectacle: Feminist Essays on Contemporary Women's Theatre*, edited by Lynda Hart. Ann Arbor: University of Michigan Press.

Dolan, Jill. 1991 [1988]. *The Feminist Spectator as Critic*. Ann Arbor: University of Michigan Press.

Lyon, George Ella. 1984a. *Braids*. Unpublished MS. Lexington, Ky.

———. 1984b. *Braids*. Performance in Carrick Theatre, Lexington, Ky., 4, 5, and 6 April.

———. 1985. *Braids*. Performance at Appalshop, Whitesburg, Ky., November.

———. 1987. *Braids*. Audiotape. Richmond, Ky., WEKU FM, March through April.

———. 1991. Interview with Ann Kilkelly, 8 August.

Mann, Emily. 1982. *Still Life*. New York: Dramatists Play Service.

Silverman, Kaja. 1988. *The Acoustic Mirror: The Female Voice in Psychoanalysis and Cinema*. Bloomington and Indianapolis: Indiana University Press.

ELLEN DONKIN AND SUSAN CLEMENT

Directing Stein

This essay is about directing plays by Gertrude Stein. The two plays we chose, For the Country Entirely, A Play in Letters, *and* A Play in Circles, A Circular Play, *are first and foremost without characters or character assignments of lines and so unlike most of Stein's operas, or some of her plays (*Yes Is for a Very Young Man, *for example), there is not even an implicit scenario. We both have relatively traditional training in directing, and so the problem we set for ourselves was this: How does one direct a play that gives none of the usual directorial information? How does one respect the language and still find a coherence without imposing ideas on the text that compete with or devalue it?*

We worked separately on these productions. We were in phone contact periodically but only to commiserate; we actually developed our working processes independent of each other, as will become clear from the accounts that follow. Two very different approaches to these texts resulted. What they shared is what we will call "contextualization." In each case we found it necessary to drop Stein's language into a dramatically conceived context of the director's own invention, creating a resonating structure in which Stein's language seemed to magically acquire coherence, multiple levels of meaning, characterizations, and tremendous humor. When we compared notes later we were interested to discover that Stein herself had emerged as a character in each scenario.

In the accounts of our respective productions that follow, we will try to clarify how we used contextualization in the directing process and how we brought contextualization into balance with a respect for Stein's language so that the context chosen was not an arbitrary manipulation of her language. We both were in agreement that there are dangers if her texts are treated as nothing but meaningless sound. We felt that there was a crucial distinction to

*be made between word play and meaninglessness and that this difference had
to be addressed if the plays were going to become truly performable.*

*As a general introductory observation, it should also be noted that there
are probably a myriad of ways in which Stein's play scripts can be contextualized. Susan's created a context through the use of physical space and properties; Ellen's invented a relationship between two characters to create context.
One of the most historically successful efforts to contextualize has been Virgil
Thomson's setting of Stein operas to music. In a letter to Ellen he said: "As
a bit of general advice with regard to the obscure texts, I have always found
it embarrassing when directors attempt to illustrate any meanings that they
may find in the words.* These plays need a structure added. There must
be invented for each one a scenario, which the actors can mime while
reciting the text. This does not need to have any connection whatsoever with the text; often this method works best when there is no
obvious connection" *(our emphasis).*[1] *The importance and complexity of
Thomson's statement were not clear to us until our projects were already well
underway.*

*There is one preliminary point that needs to be underscored, which is
that our solutions of problems in these two Stein play texts are not to be
understood either as prescriptive or definitive for the plays; they are descrip-
tive of a process that, except for the work of Leon Katz, Virgil Thomson,
Larry Kornfeld, and a few others, has gone remarkably undocumented.*[2]
Rather, they are to suggest the multitude of solutions available to any director.

Ellen Donkin: *For the Country Entirely, A Play in Letters*

The first thing I discovered, as Susan did, was that these plays by
Gertrude Stein completely upend the traditional hierarchy of the di-
rector-actor relationship. The dislocation and anxiety that such a re-
orientation produces in both actors and director are not to be interpreted as an early sign of failure. It was my experience that working
on *For the Country Entirely*[3] made it completely impossible to direct
in traditional ways, since the traditional hierarchical structuring in
directing presupposes, by its very pyramidal nature, that the director
holds the answers to what the text means. Meaning in Stein's work
is so elusive, so mobile, and sometimes so fleeting from one rehearsal
to the next, that this positioning of the director and the directed
rapidly becomes untenable. Her language, for example, has to be

spoken and felt through the body before *even line assignments to character can be made*. As director, I found these assignments impossible without first hearing my actors, Jill Lewis and Rhonda Blair, speak the lines.[4] We debated over each assignment as a threesome. My job as director was to legitimize the exploratory process rather than to provide dazzling insights into the text.

My second major job as director was to cast the piece, which was done simply on the basis of who was willing to give time to the project (if three people had volunteered, I would have worked with three; had there been a mixed group of men and women, or just men, there would have been a different product). My third job as director was to invent a scenario, based in good part on the people who had volunteered. But my "authority" was limited to these three areas. All the rest was worked on collectively.

The rehearsals tended to be "talking" rehearsals, rather than improvisational or exercise-oriented. The problems of meaning posed by the text were so massive that we stayed heavily verbal throughout the rehearsal process. Perhaps I should not be surprised; the play is subtitled "A Play in Letters." For the first two weeks I fought a deep sinking feeling that Stein was having me on, and that underneath it all there really was no meaning and no shape to be had. It felt like the emperor's new clothes. It is difficult to describe the kind of panic that this induces in a director. Theoretical discussions of multiplicity and the refusal to shape a theatrical piece in traditional ways are only just now starting to get translated into directorial procedure. There was no map. Even the notion of "auteur" directing was no help. Although the scenario is left up to the invention of the director, there is implied in auteur directing an even heavier concentration of authority on the director, because the concept rests so completely on one person's vision. Working on Stein is different: the text is a fluid but incontrovertible material object that insists on collaboration—among actors, directors, and, most important, Stein herself. It's not that there is a Meaning there to be found; it's that, between and among the group of you, meaning is *made*.

Another lesson I learned from the work was that Stein's plays have dramatic action and shape, although neither of them were initially recognizable, nor did they emerge through the usual analytical procedures. They were not "packaged" in readily accessible ways; the ultimate shape of the play seemed to us to willfully and impudently cheat narrative expectations. I have already stated that in *Country*, as with many others, Stein assigns the lines to no characters; on paper the play looks like a poem. Also there were pragmatic issues to be considered: Jill and Rhonda found it virtually impossible to memorize lines and scenes—twenty-two pages worth—which had no shape. It didn't matter if the shape were repetitive or completely lacking in climax, or circular. There was just an urgent need for a shape of some kind. This seemed to me a matter of actor's process that was not negotiable. I couldn't ask them to wade through a formless sea of words without some sense of the direction they were headed in. If to be an actor meant having an action (as distinct from being a reader, for example), then it became necessary to see if the language yielded up to us an action.

The process that followed was partly one in which we approached the text and asked for an action but also one in which we consciously *imposed* a scenario upon the text, within which those answers about action might happen. The scenario was my suggestion, and after some discussion Rhonda and Jill agreed to it. We were by mutual consent deliberately limiting the range of acceptable actions by creating a context.

That context was a lesbian relationship; the resulting scenario was a bed—Jill and Rhonda in bed together. The choice came out of my earlier readings of works like "Pink Melon Joy," *Tender Buttons,* and "Miss Furr and Miss Skeene." These pieces had seemed to me wickedly funny and very personal investigations into female sexuality and especially lesbian sexuality, although the lesbian sexuality never felt rigid or exclusive of heterosexuality. This scenario grounded the language of the play in the experience of sex, of a relationship between women. By using this scenario we deliberately sought to make the text more concrete rather than less so.

The scenario in place, our next step was to read the play aloud and listen for voices, for beats, for anything resembling dialogic structure. It was at this point that we made an initial assignment of voices to Jill and Rhonda, on the basis of what sounded to us like a question/answer formation, or a statement/counterstatement or a statement/comment. What follows is the first few lines of the play as they appear in print; the second version shows our character assignments for those lines:

Version 1:
Almond trees in the hill. We saw them to-day.
Dear Mrs. Steele.
I like to ask you questions. Do you believe that it is necessary
to worship individuality. We do.
   Mrs. Henry Watterson
Of course I have heard.
Dear Sir. Of course I have heard.
They didn't leave the book.
Dear Sir.
   They didn't leave the book.
Yes Yes.

                                        (Brinnin 1970, 11)

Version 2:
Jill: Almond trees in the hill. We saw them to-day.
Rhonda: Dear Mrs. Steele. I like to ask you questions. Do you
   believe that it is necessary to worship individuality? We do.
   Mrs. Henry Watterson.
Jill: Of course I have heard. (*pause—Rhonda looks as if she is
   about to correct Jill in some way.*) DEAR SIR. Of course I have
   heard. (*Rhonda nods enthusiastic approval.*) They didn't leave
   the book. (*Rhonda glares; Jill resignedly:*) DEAR SIR. THEY
   DIDN'T LEAVE THE BOOK.
Rhonda: (*with restored good humor*) Yes, yes.

Later on, when we felt more secure about the text, it was aston-
ishing how few changes were necessary from these initial assignments. This may have been because very early—almost within the
first page—a certain consistency began to emerge out of the "character" assignments. Jill's character consistently had a much easier time
dealing with blurred boundaries; her sexuality was relaxed and receptive, her pace leisurely. By contrast, Rhonda's character tended to
want to name things, to categorize and define, to clarify limits, to
structure situations. For example, in the very opening lines, we ran-
domly assigned the first lines to Jill: "Almond trees in the hill. . . . We
saw them today." We were flagged by something peculiar in the
syntax of "in" the hill and not "on" the hill, but all in all there was a

ruminative, reflective quality, a repleteness. To which we had
Rhonda reply with the next line: "Dear Mrs. Steele: I like to ask you
questions. Do you believe that it is necessary to worship individuality? We do. Mrs. Henry Watterson." There was a world of difference
here. First, Rhonda was speaking in the form of a *letter,* a highly
conventionalized way to communicate, and particularly so in the context of a bed. We felt that any prop that actualized her writing letters
(like paper and pen) would be not nearly as interesting as if she were
simply speaking to Jill in letter form. Without the props her need for
a formal structuring *of their relationship* got *foregrounded* in a much
more explicit way. In this context the choice of "Mrs. Steele" was a
pointed way to get Jill's attention and created a marked contrast to
the softer and more natural imagery of almond trees and hills. Also
the use of "Mrs. Henry Watterson" to sign off the letter seemed to
us a sly reappropriation of the symbols and forms of polite social
address, which is itself completely appropriated by male forms and
structures. "Do you believe that it is necessary to worship individuality? We do," says Rhonda. What is she saying here?

We set about the task of finding a subtext; it was to be the first
in a long series of such tasks. In fact, searching for subtext was the
bulk of our work as it developed over the next several weeks, but it
was searching for subtext in a new and specific way that was unfamiliar to us from previous theater work. It was a process much more
akin to unpacking densely imagistic poetry than, for example, tracing
the erratic rhythms of Varya in Chekhov's *Cherry Orchard* in order
to discover why she is in tears about a pair of galoshes at the end of
the fourth act.

The subtext we invented for Rhonda's character was as follows:
Rhonda and Jill have just made love. Hence, Jill's observations about
almond trees *in* the hill and not *on* the hill. Like all the other natural
imagery in the play (including "country"), this phrase gets forced into
such peculiar grammatical constructions that one is forced to examine
the language for something other than literal meaning. Almond trees
and hills in the context of the bed all become new ways of exploring
and describing the geography of a woman's body. In fact, this play
was originally published in a collection entitled *Geography and Plays*
(1922). I thought about other images for women's bodies and remembered a song from grade school with the line "she's got hips like
battleships" and also the term *bullet breasts* and *torpedoes* to describe

the bras of the 1950s. Stein's renaming of this territory was for us an act of reclaiming it, from a battle zone to a territory for play.

Why, then, does Rhonda counter this pastoral peace with a letter to Mrs. Steele about the need for individuality? *Worshipping* individuality, no less. Something about the dissolving boundaries of lovemaking has Rhonda's character rearing back in an anxious effort to reestablish clear boundaries.

The line after this is "Of course I have heard." This we assigned to Jill because we sensed a natural break after the sign-off "Mrs. Henry Watterson." But then the next lines didn't make any sense. "Dear Sir, Of course I have heard." We solved it as follows: if Rhonda's anxious assertions about individuality are a way of insisting that Jill acknowledge her separateness, her otherness, then Jill responds to the letter with a weary, resigned "Of course I have heard." Rhonda makes a squeal of protest, and Jill quickly corrects herself and plays the letter game by saying "DEAR SIR: Of course I have heard." The subtext is suddenly rich: Jill's good-humored acquiescence to Rhonda's querulous demand for correct format suggests a long relationship between the two women. This ritual of reestablishing boundaries is a pattern that Jill has learned to cope with, although only with conscious effort. This effort, the coping, the sense of humor, suggest a love of the mundane and believable sort, not the grand passion of the epics.

Next line: "They didn't leave the book. Dear Sir: They didn't leave the book." We chose to do a replay of the earlier lines: Jill again, this time I suspect on purpose, wanders into the same trap, by forgetting to communicate through the formal structuring of letters. Again she is caught; again she corrects herself with pointedly labored effort, to which Rhonda responds with gleeful approval, like a child who has just won a game of cards, "Yes, yes."

What is important about this little opening section is the *nature* of the subtext. I have said that looking for a subtext in a play by Stein is not the same as looking for subtext in *The Cherry Orchard*. In Stein all the concrete objects are missing. The material reality of letters or almond trees is not a certainty, whereas in *The Cherry Orchard* we can depend upon the galoshes being a material presence. When Varya finds them and weeps over them and flings them away from her, we are to understand that they signify her broken romance with Lopahin. The galoshes, and her actions with them, cover a thing that lies unspoken in the play, although it is nonetheless clearly articulated in other ways subtextually. In Stein we are at sea; there may or may not be real letters, a real book, real almond trees. These may or may not collectively articulate a relationship between what may or may not be one or more characters. Because decisions about the scenario, the characters, and the speeches have all been left up to us, the subtext becomes not an illuminating parallel to the spoken text but, paradoxically, the text itself. Without the invented relationship between Rhonda and Jill the spoken words are meaningless. In other words, in Stein the subtext generates the text, whereas in Chekhov and other more traditional playwrights, the text generates the subtext.[5] The process of uncovering subtext in Stein is not one of authoritatively imposing meaning on the language but, instead, undertaking the delicately dialectical process of setting up a probationary structure and allowing the language to resonate inside that structure.

Where the use of subtext can go wrong in Stein is when the subtextual exchange between characters becomes so richly articulated and so believable that it creates emotional impulses that begin to overdetermine the language. When I suggested that taking a Stein play apart is like unpacking poetry what I also hoped to suggest is that Stein's language is as rich and precise and distilled as the language I expect from good poetry. Her lines are rhythmically immaculate: I remember one day paraphrasing one of Jill's lines in an effort to illustrate something, and she winced visibly because I had accidentally substituted "can't" for "cannot" and had done violence to the meter of the line. When the subtextual emotional impulses become very strong and very rooted the actors may inadvertently begin to deform the language by imposing naturalistic rhythms on it, by requiring of it a colloquial ease of speech. The result is that the language is forced to stretch itself over a realistic surge of emotion in ways that obscure other meanings and the play of words. Actors have to be brought back to center and required to come to terms with the form and rhythms and rigor of Stein's language and with how the language shapes the emotion and the gesture, instead of the other way around. In this instance one does function as a director in the traditional sense. Ironically, Jill's relative lack of theater training and her British enunciation stood her in good stead; Rhonda's extensive training and experience had to be unlearned. She solved this herself with little help from me and later described the process as one that paralleled working on an aria in a foreign language, that the emotional colors and the sounds of the words became bonded in a way that transcended literal translation. In one of her character's especially manic efforts at exercising control through language, for example, I asked her to slow down and speak with a kind of careful deliberateness that allowed the words to be heard. Then the frenzied anxiety of the language built to its own crescendo:

> This was the way to reason. Did he leave after the other came. Was he a sea captain. Was the other one of the same profession although a citizen of another nation. Now as to the word citizen. The use of it differs. Some are inclined to ratify the use of it others prefer to ask what is a citizen. A citizen is one who employing all the uses of his nature cleans the world of adjoining relations. In this way we cannot conquer. (*Shouting and obsessed*) We do conquer and I ask how, how do you do. (Brinnin 1970, 17)

To which Jill replied with a mischievous smile: "Dear Sir: When it is necessary to come you will come." Rhonda deflated and then said sheepishly, "Yes, Sir."

The text will absolutely resist all efforts to be naturalized into more familiar kinds of dialogue. If the actors persist, the results will be embarrassing. When Stein subtitles this "A play in letters" she means business. In our production we deliberately counterpointed the formality and elegance of the language against the intimacy of the relationship. It was our feeling from the beginning that at least one of the messages of the play was that this formality and witty word play was what facilitated that intimacy, or, as Jill once put it, that a lot of erotic effort went into word play.

In general, we found the same thing to hold true for gesture in Stein. We discovered, as Thomson's letter had warned, that gestures that attempted to "act out" the words also created embarrassment, that a certain formality and size and gestural punctuation were necessary. On two occasions Rhonda and Jill made love in our production; after some abortive attempts to act out the movements under the sheets, I had them hold up the sheet like a great screen over them and let the language do the work. "This is *so pleasing*," said Rhonda from behind the screen. My journal reads: "All the traditional devices of realistic acting are foiled. These characters operate through letters, language. . . . They communicate most effectively in a kind of game format. A heart to heart, a direct appeal, would be mawkish. This has a formality that allows for a different kind of intimacy, one of total support but not of total openness. The acting has to reflect that."

A word on transitions: as with any other play, there will be a tendency in the actors to collapse transitions or to conflate separate beats into one long flat one. Here again you may find yourself functioning like a traditional director: the oscillation from the traditional to the nontraditional place of the director seemed to us a healthy one. In this instance it will help the actors to clarify subtext when this begins to happen. I also sometimes found it helpful to ask them to play a certain scene as an argument, even though no such thing was indicated in the language. Often where there had been flatness and no shape suddenly beats and subtext began to clarify. Later we would discard the argument as such, but the beats would stay clear. I called this "grammatizing the text."

We came finally to the issue of dramatic action. This emerged only in the last week of rehearsal, and it came to us like an epiphany. Rhonda's action throughout the play was to insist that Jill play by her rules, engage in public discourse (by playing the letter game), and honor her demands for separateness, for individuality. Jill's action throughout emerged as a kind of antidote: she repeatedly tried to introduce private discourse, to talk about the body and landscapes and not about the city or about reason and numbers. She also tried to encourage Rhonda to *express her wishes,* and this too had to do with the body. In scene 6 Jill finally exploded with frustration: "Dear Sir. Remember that when you have no further requests to make you must not blame me" (Brinnin 1970, 21). One page before the end of the play, however, Rhonda was able finally to ask, a little tentatively: "Dear Mrs. English. Do you like a different country?" We noted that this letter in the text was not signed and completed but, rather, open-ended. Jill responded: "Do you mean higher up in the hills?" And Rhonda said shyly with a grin, "Not so very much higher" (Brinnin 1970, 21). And this ended as the second of the two lovemaking scenes. At the very end Rhonda and Jill spoke simultaneously, directly out to the audience. First Rhonda: "We all have wishes." To which Jill responded like an approving teacher, "*Expressed* wishes." And then Rhonda began her last letter, this time turning to Jill: "Dear

Jill watches resignedly as Rhonda begins to lecture to midair: "A citizen is the one who employing all the uses of his nature cleans the world of adjoining relations. In this way we cannot conquer. (*Shouting and obsessed*). We do conquer and I ask how, how do you do!" To which Jill replies with a sly smile: "Dear Sir: When it is necessary to come you will come." Photo by David Daigle.

Sir. Will you come again and eat ham?" And both women turned directly to the audience and said wickedly, "Not in this country." "Fish?" asked Rhonda innocently. And the two turned back out to the audience again and grinned: "Not in this country" (Brinnin 1970, 22). Here they embraced and fell back on the pillows, and the play came to an end amid explosive laughter in the audience.

The action of the play as it evolved through to the end became an invitation into private discourse, not only from Jill to Rhonda but also from Stein to the audience and to us. Rhonda learns to relinquish the mastery of discourse, of public discourse, in favor of expressing her wishes, so that she and Jill are not caught recreating bad heterosexual models in which the wishes of one of the two parties are suppressed and the old subject/object formation emerges. On the other hand, in this new country in which we both can speak, can we not also maintain difference and not allow homosexuality to collapse into homogeneity?

In this new country. Cunt-ry. The images for female sexuality are abundant: pinks, peas in a pod, the point of Inca, asphodels, olive trees and almond trees, embroidered handkerchiefs, houses with interesting entrances, country roads where electricity is easily had. This was new country for us as well: this was a play with shapes but no shape, with language that refused to be directive, with offerings of texture and rhythm rather than literal meaning. As a group of three, we felt that we had ventured into new country, that Stein had given us permission to play inside her own private discourses. To our amazement and delight, in the actual performing of these private discourses, there was a response from the audience that suggests that they were perhaps not so private after all.

Susan Clement: *A Circular Play, A Play in Circles*

A Circular Play redefines what it means to run around in circles.[6] For Stein running around in circles has none of the usual connotations of futility and frustration. Rather, it is the delightful process of discovering how to play. Playing is the means and the end in this text.

Like many of Stein's play texts, *A Circular Play* has no defined characters and therefore no assignment of lines. Consequently, in casting the show I looked for actors with strong personalities that I could utilize in lieu of dramatic characters. I also wanted a group of actors with a wide spectrum of ages and physical types. My final cast consisted of three women and two men ranging in age from nineteen to sixty-seven. One of the men sprained his ankle and showed up for rehearsal with a cast and a crutch, and these too were incorporated into the show.

A Circular Play is made up of forty-five sections, each of which is titled as if a separate act. The titles begin by numbering: "First in a Circle," "Second in Circles," "The third circle." From that point on the simple logic of numbering ends. The titles vary; some are descriptions of circular objects: "Circle hats," "Round Circles," "Circular watches." Others make reference to relationships in Stein's life: "A Mildred Circle," "Encircle Alice." Still others explore the concept of circles: "A Circle Higher," "The idea of a circle," "Beauty in a circle" (Van Vechten 1949).

As in For the Country Entirely, the play contains lines that, spoken aloud, sound like dialogue but which have no character names attached:

Can you believe that Mary Ethel has plans.
Indeed I do and I respect her husband.

                              (Van Vechten 1949, 147)

Stop being thundering.
I meant wondering.
He meant blundering.
I have been mistaken.
No one is so certain.
She is certain.
Certainly right.

                                                   (140)

Other sections consist of lists of objects:

Canned fruit and sugar.
Plates at toys.
Coal and wood.
Hat blocked.

                                                   (140)

There are references to people or places familiar to Stein:

> Miss Mildred Aldrich is isolated. Is isolated with the president.
> (140)

Another significant element was the way Stein appears and reappears as a character within her own drama. She finds ways to insert her voice, her thought processes, her mistakes, and her comments about the audience.

> It is not necessary to run around in a circle to get ready
> to write a circular play.
> I used to be able to do this very nicely.
> Once more I think about conversations.
> Do I sound like Alice.
> Any voice is resembling.
> By this I mean when I am accustomed to them their voices
> sound in my ears.
> (145–50)

The play starts, it stops, and then playfully circles back on itself reminding us of earlier sections: "First in a Circle" becomes "Circle One," "Second in Circles" becomes "Circle Two." Then Stein refuses any closure with her final lines:

> Fourteen circles.
> Fifteen circles.
> I wonder if I have heard about those circles.
> (151)

I found this text completely opaque. It defied all traditional notions of plot, character, and theme. It was a risk not to take a strong hand and try to develop a directorial concept, but I decided to trust that everything Stein had written had some sort of logic, even if it was not immediately apparent. I went on the assumption that the words were not simply nonsense, but that in order to give them life something was needed, some sort of context within which the actors could create and the words could resonate. The difficulty was doing this without imposing a narrative structure, since I still felt sure that any coherent form like narrative would work against the grain of the text.

Although no one element tied the piece together in the usual sense of theme, I found that certain words, images, and thoughts created a field of associations from which I could work. What emerged was a range of categories, all related to circles: circular objects, time moving in circles, circles of friends, inclusion or exclusion from a circle, words and sounds that circle around one another, and objects with parts that move in circles. These categories served as my primary tools in taking the text apart and for creating a context out of which the designer and actors could work. They also provided me with a way to work that released me from narrative structure, coherent thematic statement, or consistency of character, place, or time. As soon as I felt freed of those restrictions, I began to feel freed of trying to impose some sense on Stein's words. Instead, the words were allowed to take on meaning as the scene evolved, in the context suggested by one of the categories.

Once I made this initial decision about the play's structure it became apparent that the entire ensemble—actors, director, and designers—were equally engaged in the production of images. We all became cocreators of the performance text. The text was so difficult to comprehend that each one of us actively (and, at times, desperately) searched for a point of personal connection with the material. I saw the production as a conversation between the written text and everyone involved. It was by no means the product of a single directorial vision.

The other major decisions I made in the traditional directorial sense were to delete some sections of the play, repeat some, and rearrange others, although I did decide to leave Stein's own titles intact as ways to demarcate individual scenes. Our rehearsal process, which was three weeks, was not nearly enough time for the kind of exploration the full script would have needed. The amount of time needed to develop and rehearse a Stein production can be easily underestimated. Rehearsals take about twice as long as those for a more traditional script.

Probably the most important decision I made was that improvisation would form the basis for the actors' work but that, rather than building scenes from characters or situation, I would see whether we could build scenes using *props*. I thought about umbrellas and other circular objects as possible source material. My collaboration with my set designer, Lynn Graves, suddenly became central.

As I worked with Lynn to develop a space in which the work could grow, we began looking for objects that might exist in this new world. We chose many of the props based on images and associations from the text. We looked for circular objects: parasols, hats, a wheelchair, a tricycle, balls, a child's wagon, a ship's lifesaver, a bullhorn. Also, because the play itself involved playing with language, we brought in newspapers and computer paper. Finally, we decided we wanted to visually represent Stein on stage, so we chose a typewriter and created an area in which Stein might entertain.

As Lynn and I began to gather props, we noticed that many of the circular objects were either things that facilitated transportation (the wheelchair, baby carriage, bicycles), or they were parts of machines that were used to communicate (record players, film projectors, tape recorders). We were struck by how these were machines whose purpose was to produce meaning.

Somewhere between our search for circular objects and our reading of the text we arrived at the idea of a machine as the central set piece. The machine was a way to theatricalize how Stein's text functioned. Each component of the machine (and, by extension, of the play) made sense when taken individually (a clothesline, a crank handle from a washing machine, bicycle wheels). The overall effect, however, was surprising and somewhat mysterious, as if we were asking the audience to look a second time and to reexamine familiar objects.

Once we had our chosen objects we worked on a ground plan. Again we looked for a way to represent *how* Stein's text operated, rather than *what* it meant. We decided we wanted to disrupt the stage space in a way that paralleled Stein's disruption of language. This opened up the possibility of staging multiple simultaneous scenes, or of scenes that the audience could hear but not see. My directing training had taught me how to guide an audience's eye, tell them where to look, point to different characters, establish focus in a scene. But all this seemed wrong for Stein, because it made decisions for the audience that I felt Stein would have preferred the audience make for themselves. Consequently, the ground plan was designed to allow the audience to experience the show in a number of different ways. They could choose to watch one part of a multiple scene and not another or experience certain scenes aurally but not visually, and so on.

We decided on arena staging. The show was staged in a black box, and, in addition to the arena itself, it utilized three wide audience aisles as acting areas. The first of these areas contained the machine, the second was Stein's study with desk and typewriter, and the third was a conversation corner with chairs and table. What prevented the sitting area from looking realistic in this world of nonrealistic images was the presence of an antique metal gynecological table (which transformed during the show from a piece of furniture to a percussive instrument and eventually back to its intended function).

In my work with the actors my first concern was that they begin to enjoy the language and play with it in the same way that Stein played with it as a writer. We first worked vocally. The actors would go through a number of repetitions, until the meaning of the individual words began to slip away. I found that this was an effective means for acclimating my cast to the text. Once they stopped worrying about what the words meant they could begin to play with the consonants and vowels and find delight in the pure sound of the language. The more we worked in this vein, the more adept they became at playing with the language. Some sections were explored through song, such as duets, trios, chants, or sound compositions. We found a life and sensuality in the language that we had not yet experienced.

The next step seemed to be finding ways for the actors to get the language into their bodies, to find a physical rather than psychological connection to the language. A sound and movement exercise formed the basis of our work in this area. We would begin with a line or a phrase, and one actor would experiment with the sounds until a gesture began to emanate from the sounds themselves. This gesture would grow into a walk and finally into some kind of character. The ensemble would then take this original impulse and do their version of it, making it larger or smaller. The strength of this process was that it gave us a way to create characters and situations and relationships that did not rely on narrative but, rather, on the sounds and rhythms of the language. An unexpected side effect was that it also made Stein less mystifying to the actors. Once this exercise was familiar they were able to work from it on their own. That allowed me to step back and watch them work and to shape the scenes by selecting from their work.

What follows is how we solved some of the play's problems using improvisation around props and word games. In the opening scene of the play, which is entitled "First in a Circle," for example, the first line reads:

Papa dozes. Mama blows her noses. We cannot say this
the other way. Exactly. Passably.

(Van Vechten 1949, 139)

I found in preparing to work on this scene that I needed to go through a series of questions before I discovered a fruitful direction. My logical thinking never cracked a line open. I operated on the assumption that it didn't matter what the words meant at all and that it was better to ask oneself *how they were intended to function.* It seemed to me that in this case the line needed to introduce the idea that this text plays with language. Now I began looking for ways to theatricalize the way Stein breaks words away from their meanings and to show that this process of destruction is a playful one. We tried a game of charades, but ultimately something about this context trivialized her words by tying them to a specific action. The scene slipped into being about charades instead of being about language.

Finally, we staged the scene in a blackout with the actors surrounding the audience so that the audience's first encounter with the piece was through sound. We retained part of the charades game by breaking the words apart so that the audience first heard the sound of a breathy *P.* This would grow into the syllable *Pa,* which would be repeated to form the word *Papa.* One actor would gleefully repeat the word, then another would pounce on the sound of it, and then someone else would play with it by stretching out the sounds. This process continued through the entire line until a sentence was formed. In this way the first line of the play became an introduction to playing itself.

The context for this first section of the show was determined primarily by the fact that it introduced the piece. Later in the show the contexts shifted. Some grew from a word or an image that suggested a situation we could improvise on. The section entitled "Beauty in a Circle" is an example of how we created a scene from an image suggested by the text, which reads:

A beauty is not suddenly in a circle. It comes with rapture.
A great deal of beauty is rapture. A circle is a necessity.
Otherwise you would see no one. We each have our circle.
How old is America? Very old.

(Van Vechten 1949, 141)

I began work by using the last two lines as an impulse for movement. These lines reminded me of a description of America from *The Autobiography of Alice B. Toklas* in which Stein posits that America is the oldest nation in the world since it was the first one to enter the twentieth century (Stein 1933, 78). With this in mind we looked for ways to produce the kind of frantic locomotion that the advent of heavy industrialization introduced. In our production this translated into moving through the space in a wagon or wheelchair, by tricycle, or on foot. A frantic race around the space ensued, with actors throwing out the question "How old is America?" and answering "Very old." Suddenly it all came to a halt, and a sound composition followed. The actors found ways to use different objects (the typewriter, the gynecological table, the tricycle) as musical instruments. One person began with a small sound, like the squeak of moving the stirrup on the table, and this was answered by plucking a spoke on the wheelchair. A word was added, more sound, and then another word or phrase. The actors discovered ways to intertwine the words with the sounds of the machines so that they could explore the inherent rhythms of the lines. These few simple exercises served as a groundwork from which we developed our show.

The final challenge was the ending of the show. Though most of the piece involved a great deal of movement, we decided that the final moments of the show should be still. There was a profound transformation in how we all related to the text; the actors now trusted that the play was about language itself. The reason for ending the piece in stillness was to give full focus to the language. The actors were eager to choose their own speeches. No one voiced any concerns over the meaning of the words or their motivations. We were able to create a scene at the end of the rehearsal period that we could never have created at the beginning. The actors, motionless, spoke simply and directly to the audience.

The audiences were a great testing ground for the piece. They ranged from people who were very familiar with Stein's work to members of a sorority coming to see a "sister" in the cast. The one thing these audiences shared was their response to Stein's humor. Her jokes, puns, and language play reached everyone across the board. Someone commented to me that watching the play was like being inside someone's mind. I was struck by the accuracy of this phrase, as it precisely described my experience of working on the material. By deciding to grapple with this text without imposing my own ideas, I had allowed a context to develop. It felt as if I had unwittingly stumbled into a personal relationship with Stein. By working with her small "acts," I was able to stage the multitude of new beginnings that make up her thoughts. I could see that there was a wisdom in her exploration of circles. We had left the world of linear time and entered into an exploration of beginning again. Beginning again usually has a pejorative connotation, because it can imply previous failure. Stein's play resignifies "beginning again" to mean something that is full of richness and pleasure and has no pejorative connotations at all.

★   ★   ★

Two closing thoughts: the first has to do with Stein's notion of a text being like a landscape (Stein 1935, 122, 128). Plays need not move, for Stein, any more than a landscape moves. Also, no one character should be any more important than any other, or than the landscape itself. The second idea is one that Stein borrowed from her studies with William James at Harvard and which has been termed "the continuous present" (Davy 1978, 108). By this she meant that the internal reality of people's lived responses to daily life is a discontinuous series of thoughts and interior monologues, interrupted periodically by snatches of conversation. It differs from stream of consciousness in the sense that the continuous present is not a series of connected thoughts but, rather, of disconnected thoughts. Stein's drama makes an effort to reflect this perception of internal life as a series of beginnings. What we found in working on her plays is that the directing process must itself address these two issues of landscape and continuous present. For example, the refusal of a hierarchical directorial structure is essential not only to the director's survival but also to the preservation of a special kind of subversive joy. Equally important is the idea of new beginnings: a director must yield up the dramatic build implicit in the rehearsal process itself, *because it is quite literally possible to go on working and rediscovering these texts for months at a time, and your production will be a record only of your collective intersection with the text at a certain moment in time. Also new beginnings / continuous present is an attitude about rehearsing that creates a new and delicate segue between the pleasure of each other's company, the drift of our lives, the events of the day, and the work itself. We made our best and richest discoveries on the days we allowed ourselves to run lines while sunbathing or in between discussions of our love lives. It was at these moments that the complexity and power of a concept like continuous present began to reveal itself and in which we felt, almost palpably, the presence and pleasure of Stein herself.*

NOTES

1. This letter is dated 4 May 1983.

2. Some of the most helpful accounts are Thomson's discussion of "Four Saints in Three Acts," in *Virgil Thomson* by Virgil Thomson (New York: Alfred A. Knopf, 1966); in John McCaffrey's "'Any of Mine without Music to Help Them': The Operas and Plays of Gertrude Stein," *Yale/Theater* 4 (Summer 1973): 27; "From a Director's Notebook" by Lawrence Kornfeld (*Performing Arts Journal* 1 [Spring 1976]): 33; Kate Davy's "Richard Foreman's Ontological-Hysteric Theatre: The Influence of Gertrude Stein" (*Twentieth Century Literature* 24 [Spring 1978]): 108; and in John Houseman's *Run-Through* (New York: Simon and Schuster, 1972), 99–127.

3. This production was staged and videotaped at Hampshire College in May 1986.

4. Both the actors for this production were Hampshire College faculty members. We had no budget, and consequently no designers and no set, and we used the lights left over from a previous hang.

5. When I say text I include all of what the author has given us: character names, character's speeches, plot line, dramatic action, character development, given circumstances, and scenario.

6. This production was staged at the University of Washington, Seattle, February 1986.

REFERENCES

Brinnin, John Malcolm, ed. 1970. *The Selected Operas and Plays of Gertrude Stein.* Pittsburgh: University of Pittsburgh Press.

Davy, Kate. 1978. "Richard Foreman's Ontological-Hysteric Theatre: The Influence of Gertrude Stein." *Twentieth Century Literature* 24 (Spring).

Stein, Gertrude. 1933. *The Autobiography of Alice B. Toklas*. New York: Random House.
————. 1935. *Lectures in America*. New York: Random House.
Van Vechten, Carl, ed. 1949. *Last Operas and Plays*. New York: Rinehart.

PART 4

Rehearsing the Text

This final section raises one of the key issues of the book, something that is addressed in nearly every essay but which now needs some thoughtful formulation. The issue is this: If we imagine that the feminist director is invested in changing representations of women, whether by directing feminist drama, by subverting a male dramatic narrative, or by helping to construct a new piece, must not this same director also be rethinking the way she casts and rehearses? In other words, how can the product be subversive if the process stays the same? Isn't the directing process itself part of how meaning gets created or suppressed?

The contributors to this section have each worked to rethink some aspect of process, and some interesting themes recur. One of the most important is the issue of directorial identity and authority: new ways to rethink that job include collaborative directing and codirecting. Amy Gonzalez and John Lutterbie in particular reflect on their sense of the director's job as provisional. John argues that the historical authority of the male director, *or even its imagined presence,* can nullify the kind of exploration that allows women's experience of life to emerge. Joan Schenkar believes that overlapping jobs, such as director and playwright, can prevent a feminist playwright's work from being neutralized in production.

A second key issue is casting: how not just *who* we cast but the *way* we cast can profoundly affect an actor's sense of investment and discovery. Andrea Hairston and Rhonda Blair offer some important thoughts based on years of directing experience. A third recurring theme in this book is the issue of dramaturgy: how historical research and theory can deeply affect the coherence and authority of a production. Addell Austin Anderson and Andrea Hairston both feel that historical research in particular was essential to their rehearsal processes. And finally, in Joan Lipkin's essay, we read a warning: that for the feminist director, the job of rehearsing isn't over just because the show is up and running. Joan demonstrates how negative reviews can cause both cast and director to submit to the judgments of some imagined external authority and, in effect, abandon the production. At this stage of production, when the normal procedure would be for the director to begin to withdraw from the show, Joan argues that the role of the feminist director is to move forcefully back to the center in order to "take back the show."

We come back now just for a moment to Andrea Hairston's essay because it touches on all of the issues raised in this section: directorial authority ("I detest . . . playing God"), casting ("I hate auditions. They remind me of slave auctions"), and dramaturgy ("They [the cast] had no idea what millions of black people had been doing the last couple of centuries. . . . Everyone contributed what knowledge they did possess."). Her essay also describes students raiding flea markets for racist miscellany, and we would offer this final reflection for ways to rethink the rehearsal process: get out of the rehearsal hall and take a look at how the world looks at you.

ANDREA HAIRSTON

"I Wanna Be Great!": How to Rescue the Spirit in the Wasteland of Fame

Introduction: Meditations on Feminist Theory while Jogging in Germany

Dashing, struggling through foreign woods, along an alien stream, trancing out in someone else's mother tongue, I can't escape the thought that, much to my dismay, I am not at all in search of a "women's aesthetic." Some feminist! Tripping over exposed roots, I have to admit that such august categorizations as women's aesthetic, "black aesthetic," "men's aesthetic," or "Eurocentric, Afrocentric, Asiocentric aesthetic" make me want to puke. The image of dialectical, sacred dualities (Good and Bad, Black and White, Male and Female), of endless holy warring oppositions pushes me over the edge: I dry heave over elegant assessments of art, humanity, and experience that seem downright dangerous to anybody who has the unmitigated gall to reject cosmetic cover-ups and work for profound transformation. Effortless, appealing, time-honored generalizations from the official and/or unconscious canon are anathema to anybody trying to discover, uncover, and recover a spectrum of life-affirming truths. I reject the struggle to bury human diversity and complexity into such simplistic conceptualizations as suicidal, as unworthy of our vast capacity for creative expression and survival.

Cursing weakly, I hug a tree. Of course, women have similar experiences, ideas, reactions, thoughts, feelings born of shared biological and social conditions. Stretching across space, time, and culture, these ways of being a woman profoundly connect each of us to every woman. I would be the last to devalue or expunge (as is often the case) the beautiful developments, delicious insights, and wondrous discoveries of women, of Asians, of children. I don't want to hunt down and exterminate the black or Lesbian characters in the ongoing historical drama that has been made to seem so white and straight, so European and rich. I refuse to uphold the official version of truth and beauty in which the rest of us are nowhere to be seen except as powerless victims of the mighty and magnificent maniacs who've driven us all to a nasty precipice. The truth is, me and mine have also been creating this glorious history of ours. And, as painful as the thought may be, we have also been racing along to the same nasty precipice on our own steam. We have dominated and despised; we have passed our self-hatred onto our children and convinced them it was love. We aren't just the "good guys" who would have done it all better. We aren't to blame, but we are responsible. I squeeze the tree until bark crumbles against my skin. My mind is screaming: if somebody says one more word to me about "subculture-this" or "minority-that." . . . We are the Culture, we are History, and we are the Future.

No, I am not in search of a women's aesthetic. I don't want to take on all of them wild and crazy girls, who got so much to say and do and be, and reduce us all to our common state of gender oppression, to our SUBREALITY of creative respondents to hellish insanity. What I am straining and aching after is a language for the almost unspeakable (in the tongues I know), almost unfathomable, and certainly contradictory diversity that is my experience of the world. A Spectral Aesthetic from a polyrhythmic perspective. I've been sacrificing my body of experience too long to all sorts of abstract and classical rules and regulations, trying to wring an order out of chaos—but whose order? And why is my order a *sub*order? How am I supposed to ignore the enormous range and variety of the billions of women now living all over this nebulous planet, let alone all those countless, priceless ladies from the past and the sisters about to be born anytime now? How am I supposed to squeeze them all, or anybody all, into *an* aesthetic? My society has been trying to hand me *a* women's aesthetic, *an* "African worldview," a "gay and lesbian sensibility" for centuries: a tidy, narrow gender box with severe race and class specifications into which I was to squeeze my rambunctious, voluminous self; a torture chamber for my diverse spirit opposed to the universal other. In the bounty and beauty of my experiences as a black woman loving women and men I seek a Spectral Aesthetic from a polyrhythmic perspective—in which *universal* means "of the universe" and not "of some garbage can reality" where the rest of us get thrown away and The Man or Miss Thing stand alone for us all. As Gerda Lerner writes in *The Creation of Patriarchy:*

> To step outside of patriarchal thought means: Being skeptical toward every known system of thought; being critical of all assumptions, ordering values and definitions. Testing one's statement by trusting our own, the female experience. Since such experience has usually been trivialized or ignored, it means overcoming the deep-seated resistance within ourselves toward accepting ourselves and our knowledge as valid. It means getting rid of the great men in our heads and substituting for them ourselves, our sisters, our anonymous foremothers. Being critical toward our own thought, which is, after all, thought trained in the patriarchal tradition. Finally, it means developing intellectual courage, the courage to stand alone, the courage to reach farther than our grasp, the courage to risk failure. (1986, 228)

Wonderful wise words that echo in my mind as I meander through preproduction anxiety. Here I am, an educator, out of the woods, home—teaching theater at an "elite" women's college in New England, a "feminist" with principles, ideals, and a thousand theater exercises to get at thinking with the body and acting our way out of the patriarchy. A director on the eve of production, I am all fired up. This is the theater, a rehearsal for the possible! I can give the future a trial run! But who will come to auditions; what will they say?

Actress: I'm not here to be political, revolutionary, or avant-garde artsy-fartsy. That earthy-crunchy, change-the-world, feel-my-natural-self, muck-around-in-my-psyche theater game slop is not my idea of art. I wanna be great, I want the folks to sit up and take notice, 'cause nothing so fine, so outrageous has ever sashayed through there. I want to be the best time in a long time. If I have to be a little raunchy or even ridiculous, I can handle that—just spare me the *heavy shit!* I am not into giving the audience indigestion, a headache, or sleeping sickness while supposedly trying to cure some social disease. If I'm going to bust my ass, I wanna be great!

Of course, my community of performers might have different ideas of theater, art, and success. What if *feminist* is a dirty word? What if politics is an anathema? What if aggressive, hostile applause and laughter—at someone's, anyone's, expense—are considered valid, desired measures of success? What if black women are to be confined to their skin color or transformed to universal colorlessness?

> Perhaps the greatest challenge to thinking women is the challenge to move from the desire for safety and approval to the most "unfeminine" quality of all—that of intellectual arrogance, the supreme hubris of the god-makers, the hubris of the male system-builders. The system of patriarchy is a historic construct; it has a beginning; it will have an end. It seems to have nearly run its course—it no longer serves the needs of men or women and in its inextricable linkage to militarism, hierarchy, and racism it threatens the very existence of life on earth. (Lerner 1986, 228–29)

In the crisis of creation out on the frontiers of change historic constructs, intellectual arrogance, and death-defying hubris are not the comfort and support they seem when shining on the printed page. The threat to the very existence of life on earth is remote, abstract. People are in serious denial; often they've been force-fed rabid denial and self-abuse since they were small children.

> *Actress:* Don't be so nice, beat me up a little with your notes, humiliate me just enough so that I'll strive for your approval. Show me contempt, make me uncertain, and then, when you barely nod at what I do, I'll know how far I've come. For God's sake, don't *gush! Withhold*—all real emotional support, but get angry, get nasty, be a good director, an unpredictable genius, beyond the rest of us. Be a good director, tell me what I'm doing wrong, tell me what I'm doing—I don't really care what I'm doing as long as I'm good, and I know I'm good if you beat me up first. If you're so great that I can't get near you, then I'll trust what you say implicitly. It'll be too painful to think I could be wrong about you. I won't have to think, you'll think, and if you think I'm great—what else do I need? But for God's sake don't gush, because then I'll know I can't trust you.

So in this rather hostile, impossible, wholly typical situation I direct *The Colored Museum* by George Wolfe. I offer performers the authority of their own experiences so that they can meet the great challenge of reenvisioning, recreating their world. I search for my Spectral Aesthetic from a polyrhythmic perspective without really knowing how it's going to look, smell, or feel. I am lost; it's a great feeling.

Auditions

I hate auditions. They remind me of slave auctions. I've got all the power, performers want a part, so they put body and soul up on the auction block. I stopped auditioning in 1983. George Wolfe's *Colored Museum* is a satiric attack on the culturally enslaved image of African Americans. His musical review of "museum exhibits" takes us from the Middle Passage to Ntozake Shange's *For Colored Girls* detailing the history of the "colored" image—bound, gagged, bought, and sold—an exploited, spiritless image on stage and screen, in the streets, and in our minds. In the context of this text slave auction auditions were an obvious threat to the work ahead. Yet I was to direct in a college setting. Auditions were expected: education for the real world. So I decided to take part, to sweat and struggle and scream with everyone who tried out. For three nights, at regular intervals, small groups of hopeful, potential stars and their idealistic director had to develop a common gestural, vocal, and musical language along with minimal ensemble awareness in record time. I sweated profusely, acted silly and profound, pounded drums and a *balaphon,* and abandoned the performers to each other, to themselves.

Auditions were reflective of my intended rehearsal process. The actresses couldn't simply defer to me; we all had to be committed to one another. The body of each individual and the group as a whole, and the music we made, were the common reference points. Listening to a drum and moving from inner impulses while responding to others presented no clear "right and wrong." The performers played with the rhythms, each other, and with their embarrassment, fear, bafflement, and hope. By the time someone was reading from the text all were sweaty, loose, and inspired. I cast practically everybody who showed up, except for the men. The *Colored Museum* could

accommodate a cast of five or twenty-five. I felt free to use every
willing soul.

The few men who auditioned were considerably more inhibited,
definitely less cooperative, and generally more out of touch with their
bodies than the women. None of them were black. After a few hours
of deliberation and a peaceful night's sleep I decided to cast the show
with all women. This had been a possibility for me going into auditions. I had spent too many years in the theater struggling to find all
kinds of men who would be willing to engage in multicultural, feminist, theatrical adventures and explorations. I've pounded miles of
pavement, chasing after men who weren't afraid of themselves or of
lesbians, and who could also act! I have dragged brothers off buses,
snatched innocent victims away from cafeteria lunches and off dingy
disco floors. I have hunted down any scent of progressive manhood,
bagged the dude and thrown him up on stage at the expense of my
sanity for the sake of my vision. I sure hadn't noticed hordes of men
hunting me down so that we could rehearse the possible and dance
toward that better day. Better days had come and gone; therefore, I
vowed to present an opportunity—and, if just women came, I would
work with women. I wouldn't get depressed or feel like my multicultural Spectral Aesthetic vision was a failure; I would rejoice. Look at
all of those talented, hungry women. Better cast as many as could
squeeze in the rehearsal room, 'cause we were going to have a great
time!

The range of female characters in the production was challenging: Miss Pat, our stewardess through Middle Passage; Aunt Ethel,
the singing, dancing culinary genius who cooks up a hot batch of
Negroes right on TV; Janine and Lawanda, two wigs—an angry Afro
and a sultry weave of long tresses—battling to dump their man; and
Lala Lamazing Grace, a tempestuous Diva returning home to America after conquering Europe with her exotic, colored charm. There
were more problematic challenges: Miss Roj, a compelling drag act,
who could snap someone to death; the Soldier, a crazed Vietnam vet
on a murder mission from God; and the Man and the Kid, a corporate
clone determined to be black only on weekends, and the kid he once
was, determined to keep his spirit alive. Definitely challenging—but
I was convinced we could do anything.

Casting is a nightmare, more traumatic than opening night. I
really detest playing God; it goes against my principles. Besides, how

could I offer women the authority of their experience if I started by telling them who they were? Instead, I asked them: Who would you like to be? What roles would you like to play? The question was received with a shocking amount of dismay. In fact, some of the actresses refused to tell me their desires, claiming they would be content with anything, with whatever I wanted. Those who did commit themselves to a slip of paper and stuck it in my mailbox got most of the roles they asked for, except when logistics—rapid costume or character change—made it impossible. There were a few thorny decisions: nobody wanted to play Miss Roj, and practically everybody wanted to be Lala or one of the two wigs. I considered Roj to be one of the best parts; Lala had made me *very* uncomfortable from the beginning. The wig scene was hilarious, so I knew why everybody wanted Janine and Lawanda. Why did they all want Lala? Perhaps playing a powerful gay man dressed up as a woman and defying our notions of gender and power couldn't compare with the opportunity to play a crazy, hysterical woman whose power is frustrated, perverted, and ultimately self-destructive. Or maybe girls just want to play girls. I gave Miss Roj to one of the most experienced actresses. She was initially very disappointed. Most of the performers, however, seemed very happy with their roles. A few who had never performed before were reasonably nervous. Explaining my casting decisions, I emphasized that everyone should have a challenge, a moment to shine, but no one should feel overwhelmed by their roles and our brief (seven and a half–week) rehearsal period. There were no protests.

All the museum exhibit roles were performed by African-American, African, Jamaican-Swiss, and Indian women who looked "colored." Each actress had to create multiple roles. The white actresses would create museum guard roles to watch over the preshow exhibit in the theater foyer and facilitate set and costume changes. The invented roles seemed in keeping with Wolfe's intention of a colored museum yet allowed four more women an opportunity to perform. Three musicians made the cast a total of seventeen women. There was a good feeling in the air. We headed toward rehearsals with no bad blood, no nasty rumors, and no raging cynicism. Only a few whispers of concern: Could a woman act a man impersonating a woman? How were they going to make this all-women-thing work?

Rehearsals

I love rehearsals, even more than performances. Perhaps that's why I direct. Rehearsal strikes me as the very essence of theater—a liminal work space where we practice the skill of transcending ourselves, where hard work is magic. In good rehearsals we find the discipline and control to let go of ourselves and become someone, something else. The text is an inspiration to discover just how many different people and realities we have inside ourselves; it is also encouragement to investigate and experience those people and realities that are beyond ourselves. We can experiment with our actions and learn that the roles we play are historical and cultural constructs, subject to change. In fact, we may discover that the entire social text is subject to massive revision. Lots of folks would skip rehearsals if they could get away with it and just get on to the real thing—the performance, the *audience*. For them rehearsals are or have been a tedious process of ingesting directorial and textual edicts on the road to glory—opening night, when they, the performers, finally do the telling. The critics, however, usually have the last word, and the performers pray it'll be good. I wanted to ensure that with *The Colored Museum* we all felt good about our work, even if the critics didn't. I was determined that we were going to have the authority of our experience.

Rehearsals were physically and vocally rigorous. At each session we warmed up and explored our physical and vocal ranges. Taking on the gestures and movements of others, dialoguing with sound and movement, physicalizing concepts of space and time, we established a full-body common language. I participated in all of the exercises. The performers watched each other work and gave feedback, expressing what they saw, experienced, or felt. The talking, intellectualizing, and theorizing followed active experimentation. After most exercises we would discuss the ideas, feeling states, and images that were evoked by various rhythms, gestures, sounds, and qualities of movement as well as the reverse: what body of sound and movement was evoked by emotions, ideas, or the text. We also offered suggestions for further work. Each person had an opportunity to be audience/critic as well as performer/creator. We not only rehearsed the play; we also rehearsed sharing with one another our perspectives from the inside and outside of performance.

Reading the text became moving, sounding through the text. Questions, criticism, and concerns were verbally expressed only after active attempts had been made to explore, express, or solve a problem. "I don't know what to do, I don't know how, I can't—" were usually interrupted by a firm urge to do anything at all using the confusion or fear as an impulse. Polyrhythmic collaboration was the dynamic principle of organization. During improvisations all the characters from the exhibits interacted with one another whether or not they appeared together in the text. How to perform the play was experienced as a range of possibilities and juxtapositions. The manifestation of one character was dependent on how the other characters were performed. The actresses defined for each other the dramatic dynamics and relational integrity of the museum.

Each performer discovered her character through investigating as fully as possible the diversity and range of her body. Miss Roj turned out to be less of a problem than, for example, the Soldier. This might have had more to do with the differing temperaments of the actresses than with the nature of the roles; however, the Soldier's "belligerent maleness" was more difficult to discover than Miss Roj's.

Finding Wolfe's characters in the body seemed generally less traumatic than discovering oneself physically. In fact, for most of the women, coming into contact with the character of their own bodies was excruciatingly painful. From the perspective of the "civilizing" most of us have endured, living fully in our bodies is an "antisocial" activity. Women know they inhabit objectified bodies. Fat terror and hair terror reign. Style is a question of survival. Whether it's nappy, straight, braided, permed, dyed, bleached, short, frizzy, stringy, or long, hair definitely plays a role in determining the style and shape of life. Wolfe takes a satiric stab at this fact of female existence in the Hairpiece Exhibit, in which Janine and Lawanda battle to be the wig The Woman wears to break up with her man:

> Janine: (Laughing) Just look at the poor thing, trying to paint some life onto that face of hers. You'd think by now she'd realize it's the hair. It's all about the hair.
> Lawanda: What hair! She ain't got no hair! She done fried, dyed, de-chemicalized her shit to death.
>
> (Wolfe 1988, 19)

Wolfe does pay lip service to women's concerns, but the scene is ultimately another cat fight; we laugh at the petty nature of the female realm; we can bust our sides over the kinky, made-in-Taiwan Afro whose naturalness is just as phony as the Barbie doll dipped in chocolate, without fully coming to terms with the agony women endure around such issues. Comedies are capable of such depth. *Colored Museum* doesn't probe deeply, but the scene was provocative enough for the performers to go further with one another.

"White standards" of beauty dominate our visual landscape. All the women, however, were somewhat shocked to discover that each one (black, white, Asian, Hispanic, etc.) was in the midst of body wars. Battles and skirmishes were endless:

> *Actress:* Monster Thighs. All this limp Hair, can't do shit with it. Anyhow my Breasts are really *out of control*. I swear, looking at food, I start to blow up! This Butt is too bony. My entire body is without muscle tone. Wimp material. Built like a stick, with puny bug bites for Breasts. But you can wear anything, I couldn't pull that off. My Mess is so nappy, breaks the goddamned comb. Extensions are the answer. At least you got Lips, all I got is a line in between my Nose and my Chin. Well, I tried starving, but I just couldn't do it.

War. Women confessed much confusion and despair and a strong desire to get out of the body wars. Yet they felt trapped. The entire absurd situation seemed totally out of their control. They hated the landscape of our culture, the glossy, airbrush, music video blown up to three hundred square feet of frozen "glamour," reinforced in miniature 8–1/2 × 11 portable perfection and dispersed all around the world, a perpetual motion assault, flickering in front of billions of glossy eyes. Of course, if we all hated it, who's been buying those magazines and tapes? Who has kept the ratings up? No one doubted that our culture is/was obsessed with the surface, shape, size, and color of the female body—yet many suspected that their own fears, traumas, and desires were excessive, trivial. They believed in the images they hated and were actually relieved that the *Colored Museum* didn't go "too far" and was at least "funny." Our inadequacy in the face of this image barrage is a necessity for so many economic, political, and social structures that our reluctance or failure to question the rightness of the hair skirmishes, body wars, or fat terror on stage, in public, in front of an audience, is certainly understandable. Women have been undone at the core of their being. Transformation is a lifetime of work, of deconstructing and reconstructing. Several life-times. At times seven and a half weeks of rehearsal seemed like a sick joke to me.

Another exhibit in the play, Photo Session, addresses the brutal-ity in the empty images of gorgeous black people opulently grinning and smirking at us from the pages of *Ebony* magazine:

> *Girl:* The world was becoming too much for us.
> *Guy:* We couldn't resolve the contradictions of our existence.
> *Girl:* And we couldn't resolve yesterday's pain.
> *Guy:* So we gave away our life and we now live inside *Ebony* magazine.
> *Girl:* Yes, we live inside a world where everyone is beautiful and wears fabulous clothes.
> *Guy:* And no one says anything profound.
> *Girl:* Or meaningful.
> *Guy:* Or contradictory.
> *Girl:* Because no one talks. Everyone just smiles and shows off their cheekbones.
>
> (Wolfe 1988, 9)

We looked at magazines and mimicked or invented countless poses for this scene. Everyone was fluent in the language of degradation and display; yet no one felt really adequate for its stringent demands. All were acutely aware that to put our bodies on display in front of an audience was to step directly into the line of fire. This periodically hampered our creative progress. Nevertheless, everyone gained confidence through our body work and energetic discussions. The women also shared their confidence, affirming each other honestly, offering insights and perceptions and vigorously challenging negative body images. White, black, and Asian women began tentatively, carefully to discard useless and idiotic preconceptions of each other. They were able to touch one another—physically and emotionally— and appreciate, if only briefly, their miraculous diversity.

Creating the characters for the various exhibits posed several other interesting problems. Hardly any of the women working on the play were familiar with U.S. history. They had no idea what millions of black people had been doing for the last couple of centuries or for the last twenty or thirty years besides suffering and running off at the mouth about it. Stokely Carmichael, Angela Davis, Lorraine Hansberry, Josephine Baker, Nat Turner, Ntozake Shange, Eartha Kitt, and Bert Williams were completely unknown, while TV characters such as George Jefferson and the Huxtables were all too familiar. And world history? Well, Jomo Kenyatta was just hard to pronounce. To remedy this everybody contributed what knowledge they did possess. We spent time looking at minstrel show performers, perusing *Ebony* and *Jet* magazines; we played rhythm and blues, gathered racist knickknacks for our own preshow exhibit: Aunt Jemima–sprouting vases, soapboxes with inkspot workers ready to scour any kitchen whiter than white. Students raided flea markets and specialty shops. Racist potpourri was abundant and often very pricey. The students were amazed by the imagination of racism. They had not really expected bad ideas to take such incredible forms. While discussing the context of a scene or character, we would all scream together, appalled that we didn't know our history or enraged that what mostly white men did before, during, and after their endless warring was called history. The actresses were particularly uneasy about the history of minstrels: blacks putting on blackface and imitating whites—who had put on burnt cork and hit a gold mine by creating caricatures of blacks for racist audiences, a tradition that by no means had died out, a tradition they did not, however, want to join.

> *Actress:* I wanna be great, but I don't wanna go as far as all that Steppin Fetchit stuff—the crap on TV's pretty bad, but not as bad as it used to be anymore, is it? Look what *we're* doing. How are you supposed to tell the good from the bad with how subtle it can get? People don't want to think about all that when they turn on the TV or flop down in the theater. Aren't they there to have a good time? How can you have a good time with a bad conscience? We're doing The Black Show, and everybody is positive it's gonna be one of those heavy things where they get a lecture shoved down their throats. I tell 'em the show's fun, but they already feel guilty—just 'cause it's about black people, that's all, black people, and then they feel guilty.

We weren't in a predominantly black community or a diverse Asian, Hispanic, African-American, etc., community. The audience was perceived as white, and maybe, if we really hustled, some black folks would come too. These black folks were just as "bad" as the white folks though. They were tired of our people singing the racism blues and wanted some "fun" too. This resulted in a desire (sometimes strong, sometimes half-hearted) to play down the "race and politics stuff"—and for God's sake don't mention anything about women or feminists. That would be suicide at the box office. Who wanted to play to empty chairs?

I don't recall mentioning *feminist* too often at rehearsals. The women were very sensitive, some even hostile to the notion of being labeled feminist. This was undeniably connected to the fear of being labeled a lesbian. Nothing could be worse than being caught in the act of loving women—as sisters, friends, or lovers. This was despite the obvious love these women had for each other and other women. These fears posed problems in rehearsal. We had to take care not to play to a "white, racist, misogynist, homophobic" audience or to any audience which had ingested these oppressive values. For the work to succeed we had to risk being difficult and controversial. Smith College was still reeling from racist and homophobic incidents that had received wide public attention. Frustration and anger around these issues were still running high. Students were confused, concerned, and also frightened. Some felt that the Theater Department, by doing a "black show," was privileging Third World performers to the detriment of white performers. Luckily, the strength of authentic body experience gave the actresses much confidence and courage. The characters they had created were in their nerves and muscles. Rumors, innuendo, and vague hostility could not unsettle the truth they had discovered. When they went for the heart of the scene it felt good; when they put the full force of their being behind a word or a gesture they hit an artistic high. They couldn't dilute their performances to trick people into liking the production. Such efforts invariably backfired. As rehearsals progressed, they couldn't help but be true to themselves, to each other. This is what they could offer to the audience. Their body knowledge meant they didn't have to worry so fiercely about being rejected by any audience. We headed confidently to opening night.

Performance: Giving Meaning to Experience

Audiences loved *The Colored Museum*. We packed the house. Some folks just kept coming back, seeing the production two or three times. The performers looked out from the stage and to their delight saw lots of colored folks grinning back at them. Individual scenes were followed by thunderous applause. The racist, women-hating homophobes had stayed home, or they came to the performance but stayed in the closet. It was a heady experience, but the actresses held their own, only occasionally trying to push a quieter group of spectators to the exuberance of previous audiences. Critics wrote warm, glowing reviews, particularly praising the actress who played Miss Roj for her ability to play at being a woman with the "force of a man." And everybody loved the guards. Most people genuinely appreciated the text, the performances, the production. We had a hit on our hands.

Despite our success, I had strong misgivings. I felt thrilled with what we had accomplished, but, having worked with the text, I was more troubled than when I had first read it. The words were flesh and blood, and I felt their impact, implications, and meaning much more deeply. I didn't really know what we, George Wolfe, cast, and crew, were adding to the world of human discourse. I was also troubled by the audience's relief that the play indeed didn't "go too far": it wasn't too political, and it was mercifully humorous. Burning in my mind was another question: Why were so many women (here at Smith College and elsewhere) fearful of being called feminists? Most were aggressively pursuing what had been traditionally granted to men. They wanted equal pay, respect, responsibility, glory, and opportunity. "Housewifery" and other so-called women's work were not their idea of truly living. Although appearing liberated, they shared the general cultural disdain for the work that women do and have done. They feared being women-centered and risking the enormous disapproval that such a position might bring.

George Wolfe finds a measure of approval for being black-centered. Some may see his work as side issue, subculture, minority expression, restricted to the appropriate (limited) concerns of black people (racism and its attendant malignancies). Confidently, however, he writes himself and his blackness at the center of reality and history. He defines himself as the subject of the American drama, as one of the protagonists and not as one of the spear carriers or cleaning ladies for someone else's epic. He speaks to other black people, unapologetically, sending out a sharp challenge: Take care! Even positive images, brilliant ideas (such as those of Lorraine Hansberry and Ntozake Shange) can become dead and negative when reduced to empty formulas or vapid surface, uncritically taken for granted as the truth. The positive truth and power of an idea or image must be a living experience. An Afro doesn't guarantee a positive African political consciousness, nor does straightened hair mean a hated co-opted self.

The Colored Museum does not present women as subjects in their dramas. I may not be looking for a woman's aesthetic, but I definitely want *us* to be at the center of our universe. Wolfe's image of women was disquieting from the first reading to the final performance. His satirical attack against female playwrights Hansberry *(A Raisin in the Sun)* and Shange *(For Colored Girls . . .)* in the Last Mama on the Couch Play Exhibit did not strike me as sharply misogynist; rather, it was his ambivalent presentation of female characters that was sexist. In his satire of black (male and female) theater, he attacks the formula writers who have co-opted and commercialized the inspired work of Hansberry and others. In fact, he attacks all who have taken the creative expressiveness of black people and transformed it into sit-coms and minstrel shows. Ironically, even if his intention is to harshly critique or wreak havoc with the work of Shange and Hansberry, he would fail with audiences (and performers) similar to those at Smith College who are not familiar with the writers or their work. The success of Wolfe's satire ultimately does not rely on knowledge of these specific writers. Everyone seemed to recognize the clichés, the dead images, the minstrelsy, and the danger such cultural reality poses to our society. Without needing to refer back to the original texts we could laugh along with the playwright at ourselves. Humor is a risky enterprise; we suspect it is not serious business. Laughing at oneself is different than being laughed at. Wolfe makes fun of the entire racist social spectacle in which we all play "foolish" roles. At times, however, he simply makes fun of women, of trivial femaleness.

The male characters—such as the Soldier, Walter-Lee-Beau-Willy-Jones, the Man, and Miss Roj—are egotistical and aggressive. They want to stand center stage; they fight to be taken seriously; their sense of self and their struggles are about being, doing, and defining their worlds. They are primarily concerned with power and achievement. Conflicts emerge as they must fight against the outrageous, stultifying limits thrust on their possibilities for self-actualization. The Girls get all bent out of shape over their hair, their men, their children, their appearance, and rarely over themselves. Most are defined by being in relation to others. How they seem, how they are viewed, is the core of their being and conflict. The men fight to be men. The women fight over men or male approval—and that just isn't funny to me.

"Why don't feminists have a sense of humor?" People ask me this question (in various forms) a lot. It irritates me. I hate being an approachable voice for rabid hostile minorities and other oppressed people. I hate stupid, sweeping assessments of large portions of humanity disguised as a reasonable question. The question ought to be: How come people don't like shit dumped on them? Easy answer: it stinks; keep your shit to yourself. Making fun of a man or group of men does not constitute an assault on "maleness" or "male" power. Men are individuals who may or may not share in the power of their group. Women are made fun of in order to diminish their power, to wound their self-confidence, to trivialize their being—in short, to oppress them. This has also been the case for black people (the minstrel shows) and other peoples who knew how to laugh and carry on but had to throw off the vicious sense of humor that ruthlessly attacked them. Because of this, we have often been labeled touchy or oversensitive. The so-called humor directed at women is often more proof that women are trivial, weak, dumb, and hysterical. Each joke reinforces the next joke found on TV, in the streets, in the bosom of our families, and on the stage. George Wolfe's script is very traditional in this sense.

As we started the production, some were afraid that a woman couldn't play a man who imitated women but who transformed "the feminine," the attributes of female weakness and helplessness, into strength and power. Miss Roj ends her(his) monologue in the fullness of her(his) power. Lala seems to be a strong figure who has also gained control of her life by manipulating "feminine attributes." Yet her power proves to be artificial. In the end she loses her mind and her false self and becomes, according to Wolfe's stage directions, her "real" self—a scared little girl. She is saved from her strident willfulness and artificial power by the child she once was, a sweet image who does not speak. The Girl Inside, Lala as a child, comes onstage only to be viewed. Her full significance is found in how she looks and not in what she says or does. Lala does not engage this child in dialogue; her mere appearance is enough to transform the artificial adult into the scared little girl she essentially is. The Kid (the Man's alter ego) in symbiosis has a voice; he argues and struggles with the Man that he has become. The "vision" of his previous innocent self is not enough to convince the Man of the error of his ways; the Kid must argue, threaten, and come back from the dead after the Man has throttled him, in order to have an impact. This active ball of fire is the Man's best self. Lala's best self is a silent, passive image of vulnerability and sweetness, whose essential being is her appearance, not her actions. Once again men do; women just are.

I did not have this clarity about Lala when directing. She just got on my nerves, endlessly raging on and on. I thought cutting down her monologue might help, but practically everything that was supposed to be funny about her set my teeth on edge. I had no respect for Lala. Miss Roj made us respect her; Lala engendered condescending pity: yet another trivial woman, speaking with a fake French accent, freaking out over long hair, fancy clothes, and white dudes. The Soldier goes crazy because he's been in a war. The Man who would only be black on the weekends verges on tragic—as he is an uncluttered metaphor for the dilemma of the black race. Lala's dilemma was confusing, ridiculous. In her scene the reign of terror that women endure is hinted at, laughed at, but not really investigated as significant. Women's dilemmas are exploited for their humor, but gender roles and significance are not satirically challenged. Wolfe does not use the likes of Billy Dee Williams, Michael Jackson, Sammy Davis, Jr., or Rastas and conked heads to fight over which style will best represent black manhood when he tells his woman: "later for you." Why not? Because The Hairpiece scene is about laughing at trivial women.

Wolfe creates typical images of men and women without calling them into question. He does not send a challenge out to the world with a *"Broads and Bitches" Museum,* a send-up of that long-running all-woman minstrel show in which female bodies are exaggerated and grotesque and actresses play out someone else's hateful, degrading text of what it is to be a woman. I should have at least made Lala's

Girl Inside an active ball of fire, vulnerable and forceful. Unfortunately, this inspiration came months after the production, while jogging in foreign woods. I suspect, however, that these insights will illuminate my next production.

These revelations about the text did not disturb my feelings of accomplishment or success with our rehearsal process. The audience had only an hour and forty-five minutes of provocative theater that challenged as well as confirmed prevailing codes of domination. In this brief theatrical encounter audiences were as moved by the capabilities and spirit of the performers as they were struck by the "humor" and liveliness of the text. The actresses had eight and a half weeks of rehearsal and performances. We forged a world beyond the prevailing social texts. I have seen the magic continue to work. They have the spirit to meet the challenges that could lay me to waste. I'm too impatient for my own processes. In their complexity and exuberance I have begun to experience a Spectral Aesthetic from a polyrhythmic perspective, and it's like nothing I've known before.

REFERENCES

Lerner, Gerda. 1986. *The Creation of Patriarchy*. Vol. 1 of *Women in History*. London and New York: Oxford University Press.
Shange, Ntozake. 1977. *For Colored Girls Who Have Considered Suicide When the Rainbow is Enuf*. New York: Macmillan.
Wolfe, George. 1987. *The Colored Museum*. New York: Broadway Play Publishing.

JOAN SCHENKAR

A New Way to Pay Old Debts: The Playwright Directs Her Own

There are at least four good reasons why a woman playwright who is also a feminist might choose to chart the hazardous course of directing her own work. Here they are:

1. Good directors are very hard to find.
2. Good directors who are also feminists are *extremely* hard to find.
3. The playwright feels she's done most of the work anyway and decides to take responsibility for the rest of it.
4. The playwright feels she can do a better job than the person currently directing her work.

Reason for Directing #3 is frequently accompanied by delusions of grandeur (occasionally accurate)—as in: "I'm the *only one* who can direct my work"—and Reason for Directing #4's most common companions are competitiveness, envy, and the desire to control one's own work. In a medium that depends so heavily on physical manifestation (a very *practical* effect) for its expression, the more *practical* the reason for the playwright directing her own work, the likelier the success of that direction. Competition, envy, and control are *perfectly* practical motives; they will last longer and take the playwright farther than any inclinations toward grandeur. In short, if the playwright feels inclined to direct her own work, she should probably do so—and the darker and more durable her motives are, the likelier and the quicker the production will be illuminated by the wisdom (or folly) of her decision.

My own first attempt at directing my work was inspired by a

motive not yet accounted for here: utter ignorance of the directing process. I had just come to New York City, and Joseph Papp invited me to show him a reading of my play *Cabin Fever* (a comedy of menace with overtones of feminist revenge) at The Public Theatre. I simply assumed that, because I'd written it, I was supposed to direct it. Furthermore (see Reasons for Directing #3 and #4), a well-known actor was trying to wrest control of the play from me, and I was absolutely certain that, if he directed it, I would not see what I had written (or what I thought I had written) onstage. Of course, I didn't really understand what a staged reading was supposed to be (I had studied everything *but* theater in school). But since I had terrific actors who, the script indicated, shouldn't leave their chairs, I felt perfectly safe in directing the reading myself. I *think* I may have included an ingratiating little curtain speech explaining the play to the audience, though I sincerely hope I did not. I do know that, not having engaged a stage manager, I read aloud all the stage directions myself, including the word *finis* at the end of the script, and that I was rude to Mr. Papp when, in a paternal attempt to compliment me, he said I "wrote just like a man."

Ten years and many productions of *Cabin Fever* later I directed a kind of anniversary reading of the play at a Soho gallery with virtually the same cast. This time I didn't read the stage directions, no one told me I wrote like a man, and I enjoyed myself very much more than I had the first time around.

The Playwright-as-Director is one of the most refused and reviled positions in all of working theater. What is praised and supported in film is universally denigrated in stage work. Despite the fact that almost every experimental playwright I know has had, at one time or another, to direct her or his own work, the process is rejected by almost every one in theater. And, if it's discouraged in men, it is absolutely *denied* in women. Directing is, in any case, regarded as a category for the culturally constructed male—the culturally constructed renaissance male at that—since the director, in collaborating with so many other artists and technicians, needs to control the terms and practices of several, intersecting disciplines. The following are some of the classic remarks made to a playwright to discourage her from directing her own work. I reprint them here, painfully, for ready, future identification. All of them have been repeated to me at one time or another in my career, usually in sonata form (i.e., theme and variations):

"You need distance from a play in order to direct it."
"How can you cut your work if you're directing it?"
"What do you know about stage design?"
"What do you know about lighting?"
"What do you know about acting?"

And if the playwright works in experimental theatre:

"What do you know about fund-raising?"

Although this kind of discouragement appears to be gender blind (it's an interesting fact about theater that the level of oppression for playwrights is so great that it occasionally has the effect of degenderizing the circumstances), in fact, playwrights who are women are much more likely to be hobbled by it. It is exactly the kind of discouragement offered to women on every level of their lives and produces, when encountered in art, the effect of hideous resonance: a kind of evil, reinforcing echo.

The relationship of playwright and director in the conventional, hierarchical process of a theatrical production is a paradigm of a bad, sexist marriage—with the playwright (regardless of gender) in the role of "passive" wife and the director (regardless of gender) playing the "active" husband. And when the playwright is a woman her acculturated enfeebling is reinforced. Virtually overnight, she is moved from the role of "onlie begetter" of a work of art to the position of passive spectator of that work's second birthing. In conventional practice, she becomes someone whose smallest suggestions are not allowed to be delivered directly to cast, crew, or designers but must, weirdly, be whispered into the director's ear or tendered via note into the director's hand, so that the director can reinterpret, appropriate, or ignore them. Talk to any playwright who has suffered through a bad production—and that's *every* playwright—to see how it feels to sit on your hands as they convulse with the desire to compress the director's larynx. Talk to any playwright who has appeared like Banquo's ghost at her own rehearsals—seen and understood by only a few and those few the ones most likely to violate her intentions. Talk to any playwright who has felt frustrated and helpless at her own production, and you're talking to a playwright who is quite possibly an incipient director (see Reasons for Directing #1–4).

Of course, the best directors (for starters, those talented few who don't wish the playwright male, dead, or in another country) don't generally work within the absurdly rigid context I have just described. Nor, for that matter, do they work within the equally rigid, politically correct antithesis of that context. Creative needs and the conditions that satisfy them vary constantly in theater—and creative directors must constantly invent responses to those needs. Moreover, I have never met *anyone* whose directing work I admired who didn't, from time to time, behave like Dracula's daughter (or favorite son)—with no particular damage to either the production or the artists involved in it. More particularly, a creative director who is also a feminist—I avoid nomenclature like "feminist director" and "feminist playwright" simply because I am uncomfortable using political adjectives to modify artistic nouns—tends to make agreements with the playwright, to try to find places of empowerment in a production where the playwright can be both effective and helpful without enacting everyone's least favorite play-within-a-play: Star Wars for Playwright and Director.

Since feminism itself is a very complex and sophisticated analysis of the allocation of power and its pressures in a given structure, the director who is also a feminist is, at the very least, alert *in her behavior* to the dangers of disempowering anyone or anything involved in the production—up to and including the text. With the assistance of the better directors of my work, I have always managed to find areas of activity within the production process that, while ideally stopping short of invading directorial territory, allow me to exercise my own particular strengths. These areas of activity include working closely with designers, acting as a dramaturg, producing, mounting publicity campaigns for the play, running rehearsals from the director's notes when the director is ill or otherwise occupied, etc., etc. One of my most comfortable recent collaborations was with the director of my play *Family Pride in the 50's,* when I served as dialogue coach to the four kids in the show—an odd turning of a culturally constructed "woman's" role (minding the children) to the services of art.

I mention these possibilities for playwright-director collaboration only to suggest some of the circumstances that enable the playwright to move into an active role in the production process (crucial for any playwright who is a woman) and still not shoulder the entire burden of directing. Of course, the moment the playwright begins to assume responsibility, she has to be very careful to honor the boundaries agreed to. (Nothing is more demoralizing to a production than the sight of the director and playwright, loins girded for battle, hacking away at each other in full view of cast and crew.) When the director does not honor the boundaries—and, in the case of my work, that almost always involves controlling or neutralizing the intended effects of the work—the situation complicates itself beyond toleration.

As a writer, I think like a director. My mise-en-scènes are so elaborate and completely notated that they encompass lights, sets, sounds, movements, and even the pitch of voices. As a director, I am only a writer trying to make my work talk. I do not identify as a director (I don't want to direct anyone's work but my own—and that only occasionally). I don't feel I have any great talent for directing, don't feel badly if I'm critically attacked for my direction, don't, in short, suffer any of the puncture wounds and body blows that bad language about my writing can deliver. (Nathalie Sarraute, ninety years old and celebrated on three continents, once told me that the only reviews of her work she remembers are the bad ones.) My chief concern as the occasional director of my work is *not to limit the damage* I feel the work can and must do to the assumptions of its audience. Sometimes I fail in this endeavor, but the failure is for the most part within my control and somehow far less galling than seeing the work directed by someone who cannot realize its inherently dangerous qualities or by someone, more horribly, who deliberately neutralizes its possible effects.

The most painful example of a director limiting the damage my work could do came in a recent production of my play *The Lodger,* a vicious little comedy of menace about two Amazons stranded with the last male prisoner in the world, while the final battle between men and women rages around them. *The Lodger* is a complex and ironic play written in a mock-Attic vernacular, meant to express some complicated views about what has happened to the women's movement in the last two decades. The director of the play, unbelievably, choreographed the piece as though the two Amazons were sex kittens in a sideshow, refusing to enable the dangerous, neurotic warriors I had written, refusing to honor my notes, and, in general, comporting himself in a way I hadn't seen in years. (Working theater, like every other arm of the arts, has had, to a certain extent, to embrace the principles of working feminism; it honors, in process if rarely in product, the equality of vision of all the artists involved.) The most galling part of the whole enterprise was the excellent notices the production received. I'm still *vulcanized* at the *New York Times'* reviewer's description of the piece as "charming."

Another more insidious way that women's work can be controlled is, not surprisingly, through a process meant to enhance it: the "development" process of endless "cold" readings, "rehearsed" readings, and "staged" readings, which most women playwrights have to substitute for productions. In 1979 7% of plays produced in America were by women. In 1991 the figure was somewhere in the twentieth percentile range, which still means that most plays by women are seen and developed in the "reading" process. Time after time I have seen the initial, dangerous impulse in the work of women playwrights being "counseled" out as legions of well-meaning and ill-advised dramaturgs, literary managers, and possible directors add their suggestions to what should be the playwright's strict vis-à-vis with herself or with, at most, the chosen director of the piece.

This unnecessary process of recomposition can also attack a playwright most effectively in the last two weeks of rehearsal, when the production is usually in pieces, the actors restive, and a quick solution to everyone's discomfort appears to be an amputation of one of the limbs of the script. (In the way, say, that medieval chirurgeons, failing a cure, would open the patient's veins just to seem to be doing *something*.) This sort of cutting is sometimes very necessary, but it is important that the playwright do it where she can hear no one's voice but her own.

Whenever I'm directing my own work, I make clear to the cast from the outset the separation between "writer" and "director." This separation, which occurs naturally in a production whose director and playwright are located in different bodies, seems to be especially important when the two artistic roles are conjoined in the same person. In fact, I usually refer to the play's author (myself) in the third person as "the writer" and make certain to let everyone know that

I've left the writer at home (though she's usually sitting beside me weeping into her script). This crude but effective strategy prevents me from cutting a play during rehearsal (a bad idea since the cuts come to depend upon the actor's ability to deliver the lines at that moment). When cuts or revisions appear to be called for, I always say I'll take the play home and show it to the "writer." This imaginary splitting, conventionalized by me as a directing technique, allows me, on the one hand, to cast a colder eye on my work and cut mercilessly (but in private) when necessary and, on the other hand, it protects my work from unnecessary, on-the-spot amputations. Even when the playwright and director occupy the same body, special care must be taken to preserve the playwright's particular areas of activity.

From my own experiences as a playwright in production, and from my own struggles as a playwright/director in production with her own work, have come some hard-won principles that playwright/directors or directors working with a new play and/or playwright might find useful. One of these principles (lightly limned in the preceding paragraph) is purely practical: don't put your playwright on the spot by asking her to cut or revise hugely in response to what may be a technical problem with an actor or with a process in mid-rehearsal. If the script needs revision, cutting should be done offstage, not onstage, even if the "offstage" is during a rehearsal break. Try to begin the rehearsal process with the *playwright* (as I do with the "writer" when I direct my own work) by staging a lengthy script conference in which both playwright and director make clear contributions to revising and editing the script. This is, after all, the point at which the play is passed from the playwright's imagination to the director's imagination, and, like all rites of passage, it should have both a formal and an elegiac quality. (The celebratory part comes later—with luck and work.) It is during this initial conference, too, that the ground rules, the "boundaries" I wrote about earlier, should be firmly established and agreed to so that neither the playwright nor the director has the opportunity to feel—more than fleetingly, at least—like the other's handmaiden.

These operating rules—and any others that the director and playwright (or the playwright/director) might adduce from her/their experience—are best informed by that principle of "working" feminism that allows for the *empowerment* of every part, parcel, and person attached to the production. Of course, empowerment, like all commodities, comes in several sizes: it is not useful, for instance, to allow the light board operator the same interpretive scope as the lighting *designer* or an actor the power to change what the playwright has written, etc., etc. Empowerment as a practice is and must be hierarchical, but the model for that practice should look less like a pyramid and more like a series of odd-sized intersective spheres, with each person who contributes to the production responsible for her or his special circularity. The director who can create the sacred space on stage where this empowerment can be embodied, while still retaining firm control of the production (as well as of her *vision* of the production), is the director every playwright who is a feminist yearns to work with. It is certainly the goal toward which I turn all of my attentions when I direct my own work, though, like any category that tries to embrace the making of art, it is better thought of as process than goal, better aspired *to* than aimed *for*.

In sum, then, the playwright who directs her own work places herself in the unique position of exposing herself as a director in order to "protect" her work as a writer. It really is a double jeopardy to pick up the stitches of an entire production while attempting to honor both these positions, and it is the rare playwright who can do this regularly and with heart. But, when and if the playwright is struck by the logic of the four possible reasons for directing I began with, or when and if, as is more likely, she discovers some very good reasons of her own directing, the directing itself will, at least, provide her with a new sense of respect for the difficulties of the art, and, at most, it will enable her work to pass unimpeded, expressed, and fully realized into the world.

BIBLIOGRAPHY

Plays by Joan Schenkar

Cabin Fever. Samuel French (acting edition).
The Next Thing
Signs of Life. Samuel French (acting edition). In *Women's Project Anthology,* edited by Julia Miles.
The Lodger
Bucks and Does
Mr. Monster

The Last of Hitler. TDR: A Journal of Performance Studies (excerpts) (Summer 1991).

Between the Acts (excerpts, *Quadrille*)

Hunting Down the Sexes

Fulfilling Koch's Postulate. TDR: A Journal of Performance Studies (excerpts) (Summer 1991).

Family Pride in the 50's. Kenyon Review (theater issue) (1993).

Fire in the Future (opera)

The Universal Wolf. Kenyon Review (Spring 1991); also in *Woman on the Verge.* New York: Applause Books, 1993.

The Viennese Oyster

Plays by Joan Schenkar have been published by Samuel French, *Performing Arts Journal, TDR: A Journal of Performance Studies,* Applause Books, University of Michigan Press, and *Kenyon Review.* Published and unpublished plays are available from Joan Schenkar, P.O. Box 814, North Bennington, VT 05257.

John Lutterbie

Codirecting: A Model for Men Directing Feminist Plays

Whether or not men should direct feminist plays and, if so, under what circumstances is a complex question. It is impossible in the space allowed to address this issue adequately, but in general, if there is a woman who can direct the play, men should step aside. If, however, there is no one to give voice to the issues raised by feminism, it is better for a man sympathetic to the discourse to direct than for the issues to remain in silence.

When I directed *Dusa, Fish, Stas and Vi* by Pam Gems I found myself questioning a number of basic assumptions, not the least of which was my ability to understand the script. More important, however, were the complex and dynamic questions that arose when I began to work with the actors—the answers to which affected every aspect of the rehearsal process. I would like to pose some of those questions and, using that 1989 production, describe a model for undertaking such a project, discussing our successes and failures.

Directing, specifically in an educational framework, is the delicate and difficult task of helping young actors (often just out of high school) challenge fragile or, alternatively, overdetermined self-images in order to explore aspects of the self that may cause anxiety but are necessary to portraying the character. The situation can easily become schizophrenic. On the one hand, they will strive to "give me what *I* want" and, on the other, resist making choices that will "make them look bad." In directing a feminist play these interpersonal dynamics are complicated by the fact that it is a man encouraging them to explore and perform, intimately, what it means to be a woman and to establish relationships with other women.

The director is never innocent. Throughout rehearsals I continually had to ask myself what images of women were being created and whose values were defining what it means to be a woman. Simultaneously, I had to be aware of what I was watching and why I was watching it. What pleasure, what knowledge about women was I hoping to discover? Yet I could not divert my eyes, pretend I was not watching, pretend I was not envisioning what it means to be a woman. I too was divided. I knew the more I dominated rehearsals, the more imposing would be my definitions, while distancing myself would betray the trust the rehearsal process requires and, if anything, position me as more of a voyeur. To consider collaboration in this environment required a reexamination of the authority granted to the director and a willingness to examine the sources of gratification sought in the creative process.

For me, as a male director, trained as I was to privilege the authority of the directorial vision, surrendering any responsibility for transforming the text into performance was very unsettling. Suddenly, every aspect of the rehearsal process needed to be rethought; even those approaches to production that had become standard directing protocols had to be challenged in order to accommodate the rhythms, needs, and experiences of the women in the cast. What had worked in the past could no longer be trusted, and a search had to be initiated for new techniques that would encourage an open collaboration. While the prospect appeared daunting and immobilizing, a commitment to empowering the actors and discovering ways of privileging their voices brought a freshness and an exhilaration to the rehearsal process.

I also knew from the outset, however, that, in order to effectively break with my history and challenge my preconceptions about working with the actors, there needed to be another voice that would challenge my understanding of the play, what was happening in rehearsals, and what the actors were saying. I felt we needed another presence, a codirector, an equally authorized female voice who could establish a rapport with the women and allow them to explore areas of experience that they might hesitate to reveal to a man. That position was most capably filled by Trish Hawkins. Moreover, in diminishing my authority as a director and a male, I hoped to politicize the rehearsal process in keeping with the politics of the text. The opportunity for the actors to develop a positive working relationship with a woman in rehearsals gave the cast an experience that paralleled the discoveries of the women in the play: establishing strong connections with other women is empowering.

The codirector needed to be a woman familiar with feminist issues, who was an experienced acting teacher and director, and interested in working with a man on the project. The position was defined as a collaborator, whose authority within the production would not only be respected but also privileged—particularly in those areas requiring her ability to identify with and communicate the characters' experiences to the actors. If there is an absolute necessity when a man directs a feminist play, I believe this is it. Filling this position was imperative if the production were to have any validity. It is not an easy proposition, however, for the concept is loaded with the traps of appropriation and tokenism. And it *should* be regarded with intense suspicion because it requires the one thing men have historically been unwilling to do: relinquish power.

The approach to collaboration used in *Dusa, Fish, Stas and Vi* required that Trish be free to control the direction of rehearsals. Negotiations were sometimes tricky, especially when the reason for interrupting an exercise was not immediately apparent. It required a humbleness on my part, an openness to relinquishing the reins of the decision-making process. I knew that if this became a problem, the reasons for doing the production would need to be reevaluated because a contradiction had been encountered. The involvement of Trish as a codirector was necessary not just because of her ability to identify with the inner lives of the characters, but also to help the actors contact personal resources in ways unavailable to men. How could she communicate effectively with the performers if she was denied agency?

Implicit in this concept of collaboration is another danger: abnegation of responsibility. The surrender of authority and control, and the recognition that aspects of the text were beyond my experience, neither rendered me irrelevant nor relieved me of my obligations. To assume that privileging Trish's experience in any way lessened the intensity of my involvement with the production would have opened the way for exploitation. Distancing myself from the rehearsals would have increased the burden of responsibility on Trish unfairly, while indirectly positioning her as the scapegoat for any weaknesses in the production.

The value of a directing team in any production is the *presence* of multiple sensitivities responding to the process, enriching the process through the interplay of differing perceptions and ideologies. Active involvement within the collaboration is necessary if the experience is to be positive. Men may not be able to comprehend the exigencies that lead to choices by the actors, but they can respond to the production in terms of agreed-upon interpretations and the unfolding of the text, to character definitions and inconsistencies, and to the affective qualities of a scene. This requires the male director to be intellectually and emotionally engaged. The critical difference was in the relationship I established with the company. Although I had to take responsibility, my mode of participation needed to be nonassertive: making suggestions, asking questions, responding to what was seen and heard, offering solutions and exercises—but not expecting compliance or passing judgments.

Approaching Rehearsals

The approach taken to transforming the written word into living, physical expression occurred in three distinct stages: readings, explorations, and structuring. Each was designed to increase the actors' understanding of shifting relations between the characters and their ability to embody identifications and overcome resistances. The principle underlying every exercise was to locate in the performer the authority to make choices about the performance of the character. If the *actors* made the discoveries vital to understanding the characters, their vision of the part would deepen, giving them greater confidence. This sense of security would free them to take further risks and to resist direction that distorted or contradicted their understanding of the character's internal rhythms. This, more than any other aspect of rehearsals, required the greatest openness on my part as the male director, because it was here that the heart of the play, those aspects furthest from my experience, were to be defined.

We began the rehearsal process with discussions designed to help the actors confront their attitudes toward feminism. Although they were aware of the historical importance of the women's movement, they believed the battles had been won and that the issues raised in *Dusa, Fish, Stas and Vi* were no longer relevant. In other words, they could sympathize with the characters and their situations but had

Heather Peterson as Dusa and Suzanna Forsythe as Fish in *Dusa, Fish, Stas and Vi*. Fish: "I just sat in the rain looking out over London and wondering how many people were having their first screw." Photo by Ross Mulhausen.

trouble imagining themselves in similar circumstances. This I attributed in part to their lack of experience outside a family environment, to their class background, which cushioned them from the material struggles of the women in the play, and to their inability to recognize the imprint of dominant male ideological structures on their own values and beliefs. For instance, they all felt that it was easier to talk to men because they viewed themselves as being in competition with women, who, by definition, could not be trusted.

The issues raised in the play provided a framework for addressing these misconceptions. The actors came to recognize the importance of confronting their values and experiences if they were to perform the text with any modicum of honesty. A process of defining layers of identification and difference between themselves and the characters began. Trish and I served as facilitators in their investigations, summarizing the points of view raised and providing factual and anecdotal evidence that challenged facile interpretations. Women with expertise in other fields were also invited to talk with the cast. One such speaker discussed psychological issues related to anorexia, agoraphobia, prostitution, and suicide; another talked about the psychological and material determinants of gender. The theoretical and empirical information presented by these women forced the actors to reevaluate their interpretations of the characters and to reconceptualize their own experiences as women in a male-dominated society. The effects of these talks on the performers surfaced most clearly in informal conversations about their current relationships and in their growing commitment to the performance of the play.

While the overall effect was positive, the actors did not all become radicalized. Resistances to certain aspects of the play surfaced when the performers discovered fundamental values were being questioned. In some instances, as the actors delved more deeply into the psychic structures of their parts, the differences between themselves and the characters became exaggerated, causing them to evaluate the actions of the character negatively. Further pressure to confront these resistances would have jeopardized their ability to perform the characters sympathetically and undermined their self-confidence. To minimize the destabilizing potential, the actors were reminded of the layers of identity discovered in earlier stages of the rehearsal and were asked to contextualize the specific ideological problem within the overall trajectory of the character. The interpretive framework established to define the general movement of the play provided a positive way of conceptualizing the character, which reawakened the actor's sensitivity toward the plight of the woman.

The actors frequently addressed these resistances among themselves with minimal interference from the directors. In fact, breaks became an important opportunity for them to discuss the play. Difficulties they were having would find expression in these unstructured moments, as would discoveries about the characters and their relationships. Quite often they would be able to pierce to the heart of an acting problem more quickly and incisively than those of us "in authority," simply because they were peers. The direct and playful way in which these exchanges occurred had the additional benefit of reinforcing self-assurance among the cast and improving the ensemble. The confidence they gained from finding a solution to an obstacle among themselves seemed to increase their willingness to take risks and verbalize what they needed from one another in a specific scene. Once this level of communication was realized the need for directorial intervention was greatly reduced. Quite often our role lay in relating comments made by the actors to the evolving understanding of the text and in finding exercises that would assist the actors to the next stage of development.

These discussions, which began with the first readings of the play, continued throughout the rehearsal process. They formed a level of discourse that paralleled the exercises used to help the actors materialize their identifications with the internal lives of the characters.

From the first reading decisions concerning individual character interpretations were not encouraged in order to avoid premature emotional identification with the characters. Instead, the actors were asked to approach the text as dialogic interaction and to relate directly to the other characters. Also we emphasized developing an understanding of the action and political structures of the play. The focus on the dynamic interrelationships of the characters did not keep the performers from developing initial impressions; they were, however, encouraged to relate these images to the ways in which their character connected with the other female characters in the play. Trish and I functioned primarily as facilitators, guiding the actors into avenues that seemed particularly fruitful, while allowing them to explore other areas they found promising.

The understanding of the text gained from a week of close and careful readings provided a basis on which explorations of emotional identifications with the characters could occur. The general format for these investigations was provided by an exercise called "feeding the text."[1] A reader, ideally one reader for each character onstage, gives to the actor a short phrase without inflection. The performer undergoes a lengthy internal process that includes registering the syntax and semantic content of the phrase, relating it to the circumstances of the scene, and contacting the emotional impulse as it springs from the actor/character interaction within the exercise. Only after placing herself within this configuration and sensing the power of the moment does the performer speak the words. It was a slow, painstaking process in which our primary function was to challenge the performers if they began to approach the exercise with too much facility or without intensity.

The performers found they had the opportunity to uncover deep layers of identification with their roles, develop an understanding of the emotional content of the play, and gain a sense of the characters' rhythms. Differences between the part and the actor were also encountered and identified as aspects of the text that were most likely to be resisted. Equally significant, the actors came to grasp the internal throughline of the characters' actions—a knowledge that empowered them to trust their impulses and to recognize when they were distorting the women they were representing. Thereafter, the actors were able to take direction quickly and to detect and respond to directorial input that contradicted or distorted their understanding of the character. This authority and confidence energized their performances and enhanced their commitment to the ideas in the play, while forcing us to reconsider their assumptions about the play.

Trish frequently worked with the actors independently, particularly when they encountered a seemingly intractable obstacle in a scene or with their characters. Away from the energies of the rehearsal room and my presence as male spectator they were able to explore the problem with greater intimacy and intensity. When they returned the actors had discovered a new perspective from which to engage the difficulty, even if a solution had not been found. I was informed about what had been decided, and we would discuss its effect on the playing of the scene and the developing relationships between the characters. I avoided asking questions about the techniques used or the connections made between the codirector, the actors, and the text. To pry too deeply would have endangered the trust established between them and would have made a mockery of the political content of the play: that women need the space to develop caring relations with each other.

This period of intense exploration was succeeded by the use of more traditional techniques of staging and "polishing" in the final weeks. Blocking was set, scenes repeated with notes given at the end of each, rhythms and character relations defined in preparing the show for performance. This was not a function of choice but, rather, a response to circumstances. We had hoped to use equally undogmatic techniques throughout the rehearsal process, but unexpected contingencies required a change in method. By this time, however, the actors felt secure in their understanding of the roles and in the rehearsal process and free to question choices and suggest alternatives when a scene did not work for them. Their thorough understanding of the text, in combination with their trust in the approach taken to rehearsals, enabled them to process directorial suggestions efficiently and effectively and allowed us to spend more time on specific problems.

Rehearsals are never ideal and should not be romanticized. In the case of *Dusa, Fish, Stas and Vi* the tensions and difficulties that arose were of sufficient magnitude that a reevaluation of the process is necessary.

Evaluating the Process

The actors, in identifying differences between themselves and the characters, often located the character beyond the limits of their ideological positions, creating resistances that were intense. This raised a complex ethical issue. If we were to be "true" to the play, we needed to manipulate the actors into performances to which they could not fully commit—and, in the process, ask them to deny their experiences and values as women. Any attempt to suture over the contradictions within the performance would have placed us in an untenable political position. The alternative was to acknowledge the differences and permit the disjunctions to speak loudly. Although we continued to question the choices of the actors, in the end we accepted their interpretation, allowing them to play their parts with commitment and integrity.

This was particularly true in the case of Vi. Holly, who played Vi, rejected seeing her character as a lesbian or even as a bisexual. To press the issue would have caused the actor to withdraw from the performance of the character, effectively destabilizing the production by undercutting the power of the performances. Therefore, the decision was made to acknowledge the absence of lesbian desire within the production by indicating but leaving unresolved the sexual tension between the characters, particularly Dusa and Vi. We understood that this choice was problematic, because a segment of the audience would be excluded from seeing its experiences represented within the production. We could only hope that, by acknowledging the absence, the experiences of lesbians and others would be validated through the contradiction between what was being said but was not seen. This negative solution was never satisfactory.

This was not the only instance, however. Similarly, Heather, who played Dusa, had a difficult time identifying with the loss of the children. One audience member who had lost her child in a custody battle felt her experience had been trivialized by the onstage portrayal. In both instances we could do little to assuage the anger these women felt.

Working with Trish proved to be invaluable. The actors had a woman on whom they could count to be understanding and sympathetic in confronting problems with the play or tensions the production created in their personal lives.[2] She was able to help them contact their experiences and to use the energy they tapped in the development and performance of the characters. Her ability to listen and help them make connections gave the young women confidence in approaching the characters, the audience, and one another. Her insights into the differences and the effects of the two versions of the script and possible reasons for the changes were invaluable to understanding the play and its internal rhythms.[3] Finally, the presence of a female spectator allowed the actors to explore and express experiences and emotions, which they might have resisted doing if only a man were there.

The situation, however, was new for both of us. I had worked in close collaboration on other occasions but never in a situation in which I questioned my own authority or my understanding of the play. Moreover, my idea of the director had recently changed from the traditional "theological" concept to an open, collaborative definition, and I was in the process of seeking an equivalent practice. Trish was an experienced actor but had not developed a personal method of directing. She had worked extensively in professional theater, and her approach to actors was based on that history. The directors she had worked with were almost exclusively men, who had insisted upon directorial authority and a definition of the production that fit their vision of the text. While she was interested in exploring new approaches to rehearsal, she had difficulty adapting her way of working to this new context.

I believe, in retrospect, that my explanation of how I wished to explore the text was not sufficiently clear, particularly regarding the degree of experimentation and exploration required if the actors were to be given agency. She may also have felt that I was reneging on my obligations by making her disproportionately responsible for defining the action as well as helping the actors grapple with the complexities of the characters. If she felt the lines of authority had become ambiguous within these constructs, her uncertainty was undoubtedly aggravated by my willingness to abandon my way of working for one that was more conducive to her own. But this solution may, inadvertently, have widened rather than narrowed the distance between us.

Perhaps the problem, as I have come to understand it, can best be described through a spatial metaphor. Because we did not establish a working relationship prior to this particular project, my offer to share power was met with (historically understandable) distrust. A gap appeared between us, in the center of which was the power implicit in the authority of the director, at least as traditionally conceived. In the early stages of rehearsal Trish started to question the sincerity of the offer and began probing its limits by questioning the established approach taken to rehearsals. I hoped to reassure her by backing down on my commitment to the rehearsal strategy and demonstrating a willingness to adapt to her way of working. But she believed that I was further abdicating power and began to suspect there were no boundaries. She believed that there was no longer a willingness to share power but that the responsibility for the production was, instead, being placed on her. Given this understanding, she quite rightly pulled back. The effect of our mutual retreats was to increase the distance between us. A power vacuum threatened the rehearsal process.

We reached this impasse at the same time that the actors were prepared to move on to the next stage of development. It became patently clear that someone had to assume authority, and, as "director of record," and because of Trish's unwillingness to take control, I made that move. Although I sincerely believe that she was relieved, it nonetheless snapped whatever threads of hope there were that an equal collaboration could be woven. She continued to operate within the production, but I felt abandoned, and, I have no doubt, she felt frustrated and betrayed. The timing of these events was such that the actors were not consciously aware of the problems, and, I hope, their progress was not impaired.

As these problems indicate, the decisions a man is responsible for making when directing a feminist play are ethical. Indeed, the same question keeps returning: Whose desire is going to be given freest play? As a first and last resort, I firmly believe the male has to accede to the energies of the women in the cast. This is not a passive or an unpleasurable condition, however self-effacing it may seem, because we will find satisfaction elsewhere, perhaps in the joy of watching others work together. But, if our desire will find the means to express itself, then in those moments when we recognize its play, we must privilege what the others are saying.

There are no answers here, only questions—questions any male director must address before deciding to direct a feminist play. How can I empower the women in the cast to assume agency within the rehearsal process, to take responsibility for the creation of their characters, against the distortions of the male gaze? How can I help to create an environment that will allow the cast to examine their experiences as women and to share their discoveries with an audience? For a man to answer these questions a codirector is necessary, and this I do prescribe. To assume that I can understand the experience of being a woman, particularly in a play that questions relations between the sexes, is untenable. My desire and my seeing would, however innocently, distort the process and determine for the actors what their experience with the text should be. A codirector, however, is not a guarantee. In the instance of *Dusa, Fish, Stas and Vi* we were navigating uncharted waters, and this time it did not work: the distances and resistances were too great. It is naive to think it will be easy, but it is equally naive to think it is not necessary.

Next time I will do things differently. I will not locate a collaborator after the fact but will, instead, plan the project based on a mutual understanding of the rehearsal process. In this case too many decisions had already been made, despite my determination to remain flexible. If Trish and I had collaborated on other projects prior to *Dusa, Fish, Stas and Vi*, we would have better understood how to work with each other and would already have established, presumably, at least a modicum of trust. I hope that we would continue to explore new techniques (like feeding the text) for giving the actors agency, the authority to develop the characters out of their own experiences—whatever the limitations. If it is not a feminist rehearsal space, how can it be a feminist production? Finally, I would bring in more women to talk about the issues of feminism—if not to convert the cast, at least to give them a context for understanding the problems and recognizing the issues they will confront merely because they are women.

The one element of the process that I have not discussed is perhaps most important of all: the question of time. If time becomes a factor too early in the process, as it did in the case of *Dusa, Fish, Stas and Vi*, its pressure can only be disruptive. It takes time: for the directors to learn how to work together, for the actors to understand the characters and how they interrelate, for the actors to know and trust each other, for the issues raised by feminism to be confronted and argued out. The commercial time frame of four weeks is unacceptable because it merely reinforces traditional lines of authority. This work requires reflection, experimentation, and exploration, not only for the sake of the production but also because the trust required to share power in a way that acknowledges the subjectivity and agency of the other takes time.

And it *is* time, and there is time, for men to recognize and act on the need to empower women within theater, to privilege their voices and their issues.

NOTES

1. The exercise was first introduced by the English touring group ACTER, which had used it in preparing for their American tours. A motivating factor in choosing this mode of working was that they do not have a director.

2. Each of the actors in the play had problems with boyfriends during the rehearsal process. The central difficulty was, almost invariably, that the women

were too "self-absorbed" and did not have time for the men—a problem that rarely arises in a nonfeminist production.

3. The acting text of *Dusa, Fish, Stas and Vi*, published by Dramatists Play Service, is considerably different from the version in Michelene Wandor's *Plays by Women*, vol. 1. The latter seems to be the more recent. It uses women as examples in situations in which men were used previously; many of the more graphic sexual images involving violence to women have been deleted; and, in general, the rhythms are clearer and the action tighter. Fish's speech to the strikers in the first edition is replaced by a conference presentation in the second. We found this to be the least successful of the changes. While the speech in the second version is more overtly feminist, in the first edition the context of the speech requires a higher energy level supporting Fish's vitality early in the play.

ADDELL AUSTIN ANDERSON

Paper Dolls: Playthings That Hurt

As a child, I fondly recall playing with paper dolls. I enjoyed dressing the dolls in the latest fashions or in ornate historical costumes. I rarely questioned the fact that none of the dolls shared my darker skin color, woolly hair, broad nose, and thick lips. At the time I did not realize major companies would not make dolls that reflected my African heritage and beauty standards since they were at odds with Euro-American values. I did not realize such an attitude toward my heritage was reflected in the racial taunts of some of my white classmates. I did not realize how this denigrated my self-esteem and sense of pride toward my African roots. Paper dolls appear to be innocuous playthings; as I became older, however, I came to understand they can cut, they can hurt, they can leave scars. No wonder I was drawn to the play *Paper Dolls* by Elaine Jackson upon reading it in *Nine Plays by Black Women*.[1] The drama satirizes the stereotypes created for and perpetuated by Black women.

In 1979 Jackson completed her first draft of *Paper Dolls*. Her purpose in writing the play was to address the incongruity between Euro-American beauty standards and physical characteristics of most African-American women. Jackson also wanted to provide significant roles for Black actresses.[2] In 1982 the Women's Project of the American Place Theatre gave the script a reading. The following year *Paper Dolls* received a workshop production affiliated with New York University. Few, if any, fully staged productions of the work had been initiated before I directed it at Wayne State University in the winter of 1991.[3]

Paper Dolls concerns two former actresses in their late sixties, Margaret-Elizabeth (M-E) and Lizzie, who are in Windsor, Ontario, to judge a beauty contest, Miss International Sepia–1980. In the tradition of Laurel and Hardy, M-E plays a vain "straight man," who has little patience for Lizzie, her good-natured but slow-witted sidekick. The banter is humorous but poignant, especially when the two women are discussing their careers playing stereotypical roles. Throughout the play the two reenact brief scenes in which they have appeared. The scenes tend to depict melodramatic situations between white romantic leads and coonish or mammy stereotypes. The women also recall the demeaning methods used to change their features to more closely resemble Caucasian beauty standards. The bitter memories of the experience incite M-E to conclude that they must relive the pageant that launched their careers in order to change its outcome.

Several attempts to challenge the stereotypes set by popular media and the beauty pageant tradition end in futility. M-E, Lizzie, and two other women (Woman One and Two) create an effective strategy, however, to combat these debasing images. Dressed in the attire of minstrel showmen, Lizzie, Woman One, and Woman Two act as judges for the beauty contest, which features life-size cardboard carica-tures of popular female figures of the 1950s and 1960s: Brigitte Bardot, Gidget, Tammy, and Barbie.[4] After the judging of these contestants the women (including M-E) perform a minstrel show featuring outlan-dishly offensive racial jokes. At the end of the minstrel routine M-E takes the role of the winner of the Miss International Sepia contest and assumes the standard masculine poses of the Mr. America contest. Lizzie takes the first runner-up position as Miss America. She stands behind a cardboard cutout of a composite image suggesting the various stereotypes Blacks have depicted in popular media. Having exorcised the images, the women finally emerge victorious over the traditional standards of beauty, which so long have haunted them.

Casting

The play required six actors: three Black women (M-E, Lizzie, and Woman One); one white woman (Woman Two); one Black man (Man One); and one white man (Man Two). I held auditions for all the roles, even though I already had in mind who I wanted to cast for the two leads. Although the script does not specifically call for it, I wanted M-E and Lizzie to represent two Black female stereotypes popularized by the minstrel show and which later dominated film

Margaret-Elizabeth (played by Stacey Herring) and Lizzie (played by Angela Spencer) reliving the pageant that launched their careers in *Paper Dolls*. Photo by Patricia Clay.

during the 1930s and 1940s: the mulatto and mammy.[5] The legacy of both images can also be seen in literature, theater, and television. The mulatto has a light complexion and Caucasian features. She is beautiful by Euro-American standards and, at times, uses her looks to achieve her ambitions. The mammy is dark-skinned, fat, and seemingly asexual. Though she can be quarrelsome, she is devoted to her white masters/employers. Fortunately, our theater program had two talented students who physically fit these descriptions. The other four cast members were chosen for their ability to play the multiple roles required by the script.[6]

While I looked forward to directing the play, the conditions under which I was to perform the assignment were not ideal. For the

Woman One (played by Lona Foster) and Woman Two (played by
Mary Anne Tighe) performing a minstrel show in *Paper Dolls*. Photo
by Patricia Clay.

fifth year in a row in my academic career my show was given the
"Martin Luther King Memorial/Black History month" performance
slot, which is late January through February. I would have to audition
students in November, before Thanksgiving break; rehearse until the
final exam period in mid-December; cut Christmas break short a
week by beginning rehearsals before classes officially started; and
pray that the actors still remembered their lines and blocking. To
make matters worse, a production based on an original student script,
which I had directed the previous fall semester, had unexpectedly
been chosen for the regional American College Theatre Festival to
be performed two weeks before the opening of *Paper Dolls*. I found
myself in the unenviable position of trying to direct two plays at the

same time while performing my usual academic and personal responsibilities.

Cast Meetings and Rehearsals

One of the most important problems presented by the play concerned the relevancy of the play's references to those below the age of thirty. For a satire to be effective the audience must recognize the references that the drama seeks to ridicule. Early on in the rehearsal process and production meetings with students in their late teens and twenties, however, I learned that very few knew of Tammy,[7] Gidget,[8] Brigitte Bardot,[9] Beulah,[10] Topsy,[11] Black Beauty,[12] the traditions of minstrelsy and its legacy, and the detrimental effects of Black stereotypes. I recognized the need for the students to go outside the text not only to inform themselves of unfamiliar references but also to investigate the social and political conditions that have created racial and sexual stereotypes.

Two days after Christmas I welcomed the cast and stage manager to my apartment to discuss more fully any of the play's references or conventions unfamiliar to the cast. After performing the usual rituals of fellowship, we began our discussion of the play by talking about the subject with which I believed they would be most familiar: the beauty pageant. Everyone had watched either the Miss America or Miss USA pageant in recent years. Although most of the cast thought of these pageants as sexist, they did not see them as detrimental. Although it seemed the ethnicity of a contestant had little bearing on whether she could win a pageant, my students agreed that contestants tended not to differ greatly as far as height, body type, hairstyle, cosmetic application, and personality. Most important, they agreed that contestants had to be noncontroversial and never tire of smiling and waving. After our discussion we viewed excerpts from *Smile,* a film about a teenage beauty pageant. The movie tended to support the conclusions already drawn by the cast.

Our next topic concerned Black stereotypes. I first gave them my capsule lecture on the concept of race:

> The concept of race emerged to handle distinctions among human beings and legitimize the domination of one group of people over others. During the sixteenth to nineteenth centuries the

notion of white superiority was used to justify the enslavement of Blacks in America. Whites attempted to convince Blacks to denigrate their African heritage in order to better accept their subordinate position in a white dominated society. The Thirteenth Amendment of the U.S. Constitution freed Black slaves from their owners, but not from a belief in the superiority of Euro-American culture and values. Before the 1960s a light complexion and Caucasian facial features and hair texture represented the beauty standard for many African Americans. Consequently, African Americans' sense of self-esteem and relationships with others could be greatly affected by the color of their skin.

Predictably, the Black cast members had no problem understanding this contention; the concept, however, proved troublesome for the white actress playing Woman Two. She did not understand the meaning of her line in act 1, scene 3, when she tells M-E, "*I* was the beginning" (384). I *again* attempted to explain the concept, and the actress nodded as if she finally understood.[13] I then identified the five basic Black stereotypes found in film during the height of M-E and Lizzie's careers: the tom, mammy, tragic mulatto, coon, and brutal Black buck. We then watched excerpts from the 1959 film version of *Imitation of Life,* paying particular attention to the scenes showing Annie Johnson (a mammy figure) and her daughter, Sara Jane (a mulatto). These characters corresponded to those represented by Lizzie and M-E.

We then watched the first half hour of *Pumping Iron* starring Arnold Schwarzenegger. The documentary depicts the preparation by contestants for a bodybuilding contest, the male counterpart of a beauty pageant. The film introduced the actress playing M-E to the poses she would assume for the final scene of the play. We closed the evening by identifying other unfamiliar references and listing videos that would be helpful for further research.[14]

After the holiday break the cast was required to be off-book. Most knew their lines well enough to rarely need prompting. The actors appeared to work well together and offered suggestions and observations about one another's characterization. I promote this type of interaction as well as allowing actors to challenge my instructions to them. In this way the actors become an integral part of the creative process rather than puppets bending to the will of an authoritative director. The two male actors took most advantage of this forum. Probably because they had relatively smaller roles, the men sought ways to more fully develop their parts without taking away from the focus of each scene. During the pageant scene in act 1 the actor playing the Master of Ceremonies (M.C.) created a character close to the persona of John Davidson, the prototypical celebrity host—always smiling, never thinking. While the female contestants paraded in front of him, he used a monotone voice to sing one line over and over again: "Mammy, I love my dear old Mammy." As the other male pulled M-E in a red wagon decorated as a float, the M.C. fittingly sang, "We shall overcome."

The men appeared most effective (in act 2, scene 3) during the beauty pageant/minstrel show. As the names—Barbie, Tammy, Brigitte, and Gidget—are called, the script requires that the men parade in the pageant behind cardboard representations of the women. Through improvisation, however, the men discovered they could convincingly portray the mannerisms, posture, and walk of each woman. Wearing identical high heels and tightly fitting bicycling attire, their celebrity impressions proved to be a stinging lampoon of the ideal woman as portrayed by men.

The Production Staff

Early on, I realized that, like the cast, the production staff required sources to identify unfamiliar references. During our first production meeting I provided them with a bibliography.[15] After delving into their research each member of the technical team began to recommend creative ways to solve various production problems. The stage contained a unit set representing a hotel lobby with a staircase on either side of a platform. Stage right of the lobby featured the balcony of M-E and Lizzie's hotel room. The border detention center and café could be suggested simply by using appropriate chairs, tables, benches, and signs. A runway was built over the orchestra pit. During the pageant scenes an applause sign dropped down in front of the proscenium.

The lighting designer positioned three projectors to reflect against three surfaces on the set. The slides depicted caricatures of minstrel showmen, blackfaced entertainers,[16] Black actors in stereotypical roles,[17] and stills from films with whites in blackface.[18] Besides complementing the satire, the slides diverted the audience's attention during scene and costume changes. The device was most effective at the end of act 2, scene 1, as M-E, Lizzie, and Woman One provide narration while they view grotesque pictures of blackface entertainers.

The costume designer solved one of our most delicate problems with the cast. In act 1, scene 3, the script calls for the women to wear bathing suits over black leotards. Two of the four women expressed a great reluctance to appear onstage in such revealing attire. Instead, the designer placed each woman in a costume representing the various aspects of the competition:

1. M-E wore a swimsuit with an obviously padded bust.
2. Lizzie donned an evening gown.
3. Woman One twirled a baton in a suitable outfit.
4. Woman Two wore a tailored suit appropriate for an interview.

Music is an important aspect in all of my productions, and this one proved to be no exception. To open and close the show we, not surprisingly, chose the 1943 Mills Brothers' hit, "Paper Doll." The chorus proved to be especially relevant in its perception of the ideal woman:

> I'm goin' to buy a Paper Doll that I can call my own,
> A doll that other fellows cannot steal.
> And then the flirty, flirty guys with their flirty, flirty eyes,
> Will have to flirt with dollies that are real.
> When I come home at night she will be waiting,
> She'll be the truest doll in all this world.
> I'd rather have a Paper Doll to call my own,
> Than have a fickle-minded real live girl.
>
> (Black 1942)

For scene changes, viewing of slides, and the intermission we used other tunes by the Mills Brothers and blackface entertainers Al Jolson and Eddie Cantor.

Our choreographer staged the "stamp dance" (act 1, scene 3) and the minstrel routine (act 2, scene 3). The stamp dance was to symbolize the women's frustrations with the denigration of sexist and racial stereotyping. The dance used no music except the syncopated rhythms that flowed from the dancers' feet. The number had to remain relatively simple due to the "talents" of one of my actresses, who single-handedly proved the belief that "all Blacks have rhythm" is a myth. The minstrel routine contained uncomplicated shuffle-ball-change combinations and exaggerated postures using a hat and cane. The women performed most of the routine, while the men swayed in the background like mechanical set pieces. For the final bars of the number the men joined the women while beating tambourines.

Performance

The test of any rehearsal process is the performance. Initially, it appeared that our efforts would be well rewarded. The production opened with a benefit performance for the Black United Fund on 24 January. The predominantly Black audience of 250 persons responded enthusiastically to the show. The cast and crew were elated at the response, a response that would not be duplicated in any of the next six performances.

The audiences for the following six performances were larger (average attendance, 491 persons) and predominantly white and female. During intermission at least a dozen patrons would leave the theater. Of those who stayed until the end I could always hear a few leaving the theater sounding upset at having "wasted their time." I cannot dismiss these comments as coming solely from insensitive, close-minded whites, because some Blacks—particularly those below the age of thirty—also seemed indifferent and even hostile to the play. One reason is that the production did not invite them to enter the world of the play. The references to the past, although not so distant, appeared so foreign to them that they were not able or willing to relate the drama to their own lives. For them the satire had no meaning.

Another more prevalent reason is that the play forced the audience, especially women, to confront their blind acceptance of beauty standards, standards that belittle women's individual special qualities. Worse, these standards convince women that naturally endowed physical characteristics require the assistance of unnatural "beauty" aids. It is indeed a bitter pill to swallow that we have been duped by a multibillion-dollar "beauty" industry supported by popular media. Realizing this fact, I should not have been surprised at the defensive, antagonistic posture displayed by some audience members.

Lessons

Despite the negative responses from some audience members, I strongly believe *Paper Dolls* to be worthy of production. The roles are challenging and are within the creative range of college students. The design and technical aspects engage the artists' imaginative resources. The script requires further editing, but I found the playwright to be amenable to changes that did not compromise the play's theme.[19] Also I think that additional contemporary references can be employed to better involve younger audience members. For instance, slides of current television and music stars could be added, representing the legacy of stereotypical prototypes.[20] The names of contestants could be updated to include such current female celebrities as Madonna and Kim Basinger. Current songs could augment musical selections, such as the rap group Public Enemy's scathing indictment of movie land, "Burn, Hollywood, Burn."[21]

Most important, the play can do much more than "preach to the converted." The work can be a catalyst for discussion on such topics as the depiction of Black women in popular media and the prevailing standards of beauty and their effects on women. Some people *will* initially reject challenges to a lifelong indoctrination that allows others to dictate their own self-worth. Still, the satire can plant a seed of doubt, which may grow as people become more aware of high-profile women such as Whoopi Goldberg, Rosalind Cash, and Phyllis Stickney, who have cultivated their own individual characteristics in opposition to the Madison Avenue–inspired ideal. Eventually, the bondage of beauty standards can be broken, and women can finally take control of their own self-images. The time and money used in the futile effort to achieve the "right" look can now be spent on activities that actually uplift women. For these reasons I believe this drama can be an effective and entertaining satire depicting how Paper Dolls can hurt, yet also telling us that the source of this pain—our acceptance and obsession with artificial beauty standards—can be overcome.

NOTES

1. Playwright Elaine Jackson is a 1969 graduate of Wayne State University. As an actress and director, she has extensive theatrical credits in Michigan, California, and New York. As a dramatist, she has written *Toe Jam, Cockfight, Paper Dolls,* and *Birth Rites,* which have received productions in New York City as well as in theaters throughout the country.

2. Telephone interview with Elaine Jackson, 3 April 1991.

3. Lake Forest College also produced *Paper Dolls* the month following the close of the Wayne State University production.

4. Barbie is the most popular doll in the United States. Introduced at a New York toy fair in 1959, the Mattel catalog described her as "a new kind of doll ('She's grown up!') with fashion apparel authentic in every detail." Fashion critic Billy Boy contends, "She has the ideal that Western culture has insisted upon since the 1920s: "long legs, long arms, small waist, high round bosom, and long neck" (1987, 18, 22).

5. For a discussion of these stereotypes, see Bogle 1989.

6. For instance, Man One must play a Canadian border official, waiter, movie producer, and beauty pageant contestant.

7. A folksy, spunky, and unbelievably wise teenager, who had been raised by her grandfather on a houseboat on the Louisiana waterways. The success of the first film in 1957, *Tammy and the Bachelor,* starring Debbie Reynolds, spawned three other movies and a 1960s television series.

8. A "sun and fun-loving" but innocent teenage girl, first played by Sandra Dee in the 1959 film simply titled *Gidget.* The popularity of the character produced two other theatrical films, two made-for-television movies, and two television series.

9. A French actress who rose to fame in the 1956 film *And God Created Woman.* Film historian Leslie Halliwell calls her a "pulchritudinous French pin-up girl who, given world publicity as a sex kitten, used her small but significant talents to make some very routine movies very profitable" (1988, 50).

10. Premiering on the "Fibber McGee and Molly" radio show, Beulah was a Black mammy-type maid originally created and performed by a white man. From 1947 to 1954 this fifteen-minute radio show centered on the domestic antics of Beulah, as played by Hattie McDaniel, Louise Beavers, and Lillian Randolph.

11. A mischievous, pickaninny-type child popularized in the novel *Uncle Tom's Cabin.*

12. The title character of a fictional autobiography of a horse written by Anna Sewell in 1877.

13. When the playwright came to campus to view a performance, however, the actress asked Jackson the meaning of the line. Jackson's response agreed with mine.

14. For the mammy stereotype, see films starring Hattie McDaniel. The movie *Cabin in the Sky* includes all of the major Black stereotypes and features Butterfly McQueen. For examples of romantic white leads, see films of the 1930s

and 1940s starring Ingrid Bergman, Ronald Colman, Olivia DeHaviland, Leslie Howard, Trevor Howard, and Merle Oberon. The film *Gone with the Wind* features McDaniel, McQueen, DeHaviland, and Leslie Howard.

15. See references at the end of this chapter.

16. Eddie Cantor, Al Jolson, and Bert Williams.

17. Eddie "Rochester" Anderson, Dorothy Dandridge, Farina, Lena Horne, Hattie McDaniel, Nina Mae McKinney, Butterfly McQueen, Bill "Bojangles" Robinson, and Ethel Waters.

18. Sources for photographs: Null 1975; Bogle 1980 and 1989.

19. The playwright attended the second performance of the production. After the show Jackson told me she appreciated my cuts and the liberties taken with the prescribed technical aspects of the play.

20. The mammy: Nell Carter, Isabel Sanford. The mulatto: Jasmine Guy and the light-skinned African–American women found in the music videos of Terence Trent D'Arby, Bel Biv Devoe, and M. C. Hammer.

21. This song is from an album entitled *Fear of a Black Planet.*

REFERENCES

Bierman, James. 1987. "Crowning Miss California Again." In *Women in American Theatre,* edited by Helen Krich Chinoy and Linda Welsh Jenkins, 33–40. New York: Theatre Communications Group.

Black, John Stewart. 1942. "Paper Doll." Edward B. Marks Music Corporation.

Bogle, Donald. 1988. *Blacks in American Films and Television.* New York: Garland.

——. 1980. *Brown Sugar: Eighty Years of America's Black Female Superstars.* New York: Harmony Books.

——. 1989. *Toms, Coons, Mulattoes, Mammies, and Bucks.* New York: Continuum.

Boy, Billy. 1987. *Barbie: Her Story and the New Theatre of Fashion.* New York: Crown.

Deford, Frank. 1971. *There She Is: The Life and Times of Miss America.* New York: Viking Press.

Halliwell, Leslie. 1988. *Halliwell's Filmgoer's Companion.* 9th ed. London: Grafton Books.

Jackson, Elaine. 1986. *Paper Dolls.* In *Nine Plays by Black Women,* edited by Margaret Wilkerson, 349–423. New York: New American Library.

Kennedy, Robert. 1988. *Posing! The Art of Hardcore Physique Display.* New York: Sterling.

Nash, Jay Robert, and Stanley Ralph Ross, eds. 1987. *The Motion Picture Guide.* Chicago: Cinebooks.

Null, Gary. 1975. *Black Hollywood: The Black Performer in Motion Pictures.* Secaucus, N.J.: Citadel Press.

Toll, Robert. 1974. *Blacking Up: The Minstrel Show in Nineteenth-Century America.* New York: Oxford University Press.

Weider, Joe. 1983. *Mr. Olympia: The History of Body Building's Greatest Contest.* New York: St. Martin's Press.

Young, Mary. 1980. *A Collector's Guide to Paper Dolls.* Paducah, Ky.: Collector Books.

.

RHONDA BLAIR

"Not...but"/"Not-Not-Me": Musings on Cross-Gender Performance

One is not simply a body, but, in some very key sense, one does one's body . . .

—Judith Butler

If you would know a person, you must walk a mile in her shoes.
—Variation on a Native American proverb

We use cross-gender performance to challenge traditional representations, to illuminate gender-as-construction, and to provide actors (especially women) with access to a broader range of roles than they would otherwise have. Cross-gender casting expands a director's range in conceptualizing a production and can subvert conventional representation and realism. Crossing genders is also simply a way to increase the pleasure and fun of theatrical work.[1] This work is more complicated than just having a man play a woman or a woman play a man. A binary view of gender, which divides us or the characters we play into "Woman" and "Man" along comfortable, *normal* lines, may feel convenient because it is familiar, but it does not account for the subtle permutations that gender takes on in life or art. The oscillations of identity an actor moves through in performing the other gender is in fact a process of finding that ostensible Other in the self.

Feminist theorists have thoroughly critiqued the limitations of gender construction and the bipolarity on which cross-gender performance is often based.[2] Judith Butler, in fact, defines *gender* as the performance of an unstable identity "tenuously constituted in time . . . instituted through a *stylized repetition of acts.*" She says that gender

291

must be understood as the mundane way in which bodily gestures, movements, and enactments of various kinds constitute
the illusion of an abiding gendered self... if the ground of gender identity is the stylized repetition of acts through time, and
not a seemingly seamless identity, then the possibilities of gender
transformation are to be found in the arbitrary relation between
such acts, in the possibility of a different sort of repeating, in the
breaking or subversion of that style... gender is an "act"...
which constructs the social fiction of its own psychological interiority. (1990, 270–71, 279)

Cross-gender performance is, nonetheless, typically based on a
binary model, "crossing" Man/Woman and Woman/Man, juxtaposing the biologically and socially determined gender identity of the
performer to that of the character. It inherently carries a *Verfremdungseffekt,* a "not this, but that" message based at least as much on the
contradiction between the actor's gender and the character's gender
as it is on the performance of contradictory choices by the character
within the theatrical frame.[3] The "not... but" in cross-gender performance can reside in the contradiction between the actor's ostensibly
"real" gender and what is represented as the character's. Different
directors and actors, however, play out different motives and assumptions regarding the relationship between the performer's and the character's gender identities.[4]

Rather than trying to fix the layerings of gender identity in a
futile attempt to control them, I view cross-gender performance as
playing with "a sedimentation of gender norms... that over time has
produced a set of corporeal styles" that divide our bodies into one of
two seemingly natural binary categories (Butler 1990, 275).[5] Thus,
the director of cross-gender performance is involved in constructing
theatrical codes, developing a particular gender vocabulary and hierarchy for each piece.[6] Viewing gender as an active construction
linked to other sociocultural factors denaturalizes it and makes it possible to see it as a flow of signs, rather than an essential attribute of a
character that must be mirrored or duplicated by the performer.

In the past twelve years I have directed six productions that
crossed gender more or less consciously in various ways and with
various motives. The first was *Waiting for Godot* in 1978, which I
naively called a feminist production because I changed the characters

into women and because the company was composed entirely of women. We were looking for ourselves in Beckett's classic, which I had been taught was about a "universal" human condition. I, in fact, felt a strong identification with the characters and their situations but still could not see people like me—women (which I now see was also partly "white women of a particular class and kind")—clearly enough in the play. Frustrated because I loved the piece and because there really was no place for me in it, I wanted to claim it and say, "Women are here, too." Besides testing and celebrating Beckett, the project gave four talented actresses the opportunity to play four juicy parts, thereby addressing the chronic shortage of significant roles available to women. In transposing Beckett's characters I looked for female counterparts to the male types in the script, selectively changing elements in the theatrical code: the hobos Didi and Gogo became bag ladies; Pozzo the sadistic bully became Pozzo the sadistic, polyester-dressed club lady, complete with horn-rimmed glasses, pillbox hat, and whip; Lucky became an archetypal mother/servant/slave figure in an old cotton housedress, dingy full-length apron, and falling-down beige cotton stockings; the Boy became the Girl. We made the pronouns referring to these characters feminine but changed only one line of the script ("It would give us an erection") for obvious reasons.[7] Godot remained male; thus, the women wait for the man to arrive and "save" them, and, of course, he never does.

We wanted to approach a powerful text with a sense of authenticity and investment. We also wanted to explore the play from a woman's perspective by seeing what happened when words intended for male characters were enacted by female ones. We used many clown and vaudeville elements, but the actors were grounded in theatrical realism. Each invested in her character and remained in character throughout. Technically, our Godot was more a cross-gender "translation" than a cross-gender performance of the text, although both strategies call into question gender relations and hierarchies.

The cross-gender "translation" in my next production was sparked by a material condition in our theater community; necessity was its starting point. When I directed Pavel Kohout's Poor Murderer I had not intended to play around with gender at all. At auditions, however, there was more strength among the women than the men, and I had difficulty finding a man to play the Doctor, a key role. The Doctor, a conventional representation of a sympathetic white, male authority figure, holds the position of "objectivite" Observer in the play; onstage throughout, he watches, listens, questions. An intelligent, centered performer is required for the part. I changed the Doctor's gender and cast a woman for a number of reasons: I wanted to provide a role for one more woman who deserved it, and I wanted to cast the best actor available. This was also an opportunity for contextualizing the misogyny and madness of the central character, Kerzhentsev, more clearly from a woman's perspective. By having a strong woman therapist observing Kerzhentsev and having the power of diagnosis (i.e., *she* decides whether he is sane or insane), his actions were framed within a woman's perspective. This choice was both theatrically and politically effective.

Nonetheless, my vision was limited by the blinders of realism and compulsory heterosexuality. Though valid as far as they went, my choices for *Poor Murderer* and for *Godot* were rudimentary and rather generic; I inserted women into male texts and simply got more women onstage. While both of these missions are worthy, I took a relatively realistic approach with both pieces by matching the actor's gender to the character's. This would be less appropriate today, given the theoretical arguments of the last decade. It did not occur to me, for example, to cast a woman as the Doctor but keep the Doctor's gender male; this would have violated the "realistic" surface of the play and the relationship between actor-gender and character-gender established by the semiotic code of this production. The Doctor is not involved in any romantic situation in the play, so the characterization could stay safely within the bounds of heterosexual representation. I did not change the gender of any of the other characters, all of whom are romantically paired, and do not remember if I even considered it. But I was slowly becoming more aware of how a theater production functioned as a semiotic system and how one change in that system (e.g., casting a woman rather than a man in a role) would affect the meanings of relationships in the play as a whole. The fact is *any* configuration is possible if one can find the right code for the production.

I played with this more consciously in *The Zoo Story* in the early 1980s. The initiating impulse was again my attraction to the script. I was drawn to its urgency and danger and was intrigued by the relationships among aggression, desire, and maleness in the piece. I was curious about how the play's events are perceived because the charac-

ters are male and was thinking generally about the relationship between gender and aggression in theatrical representation. I cast two
women and two men. Under the influence of Megan Terry's *Comings
and Goings* and Spolin's theater games, the actors alternated in and
out of roles and spoke simultaneously at certain moments to punctu-
ate certain points and to provide compositional variety to the piece.
All four actors were of a similar medium build, though I do not
remember consciously looking for this in casting. In performance
they all wore jeans and plain shirts; the women pulled back their long
hair. Hair, vocal pitch, and minor variations in body shape were key
markers in distinguishing the performer's gender. We collectively
defined the physical and emotional being for each character. We
played the story straight in terms of narrative development and
changed no words in the script. The performance style was dynamic
and kinetically oriented, rather than realistic, due to both the gender
switching and the multiple/split characterizations: actors stepped in
and out of roles with great frequency and even moved directly from
one role to another.

The way we played with permutations of gender and aggression
recast the erotic and sadomasochistic elements of the script. As the
configuration of actors changed from male/male to male/female to
female/female, the audience was confronted with their own responses
to aggression, anomie, and desire; they were "reading" the surface
male/male text against the gender permutations going on beneath it.
The actors did not disappear into the characters; they showed us the
story—performing, rather than "being," the character. The foregrounding of difference between actor and character was further enhanced because the actors remained onstage throughout the performance. The actors were passionately invested in playing intentions
strongly. In short, we were playing with the semiotics of a Brechtian/
feminist *gestus,* "a gesture . . . by which, separately or in series, the
social attitudes encoded in the playtext become visible to the spectator." Because the actors did not collapse their own personae into the
characters', audience members could not "consume or reduce the
object of [their] vision" but, instead, had to confront themselves and
their own material conditions (Diamond 1988, 89, 90).

In 1985 I staged Caryl Churchill's *Cloud Nine,* which deliberately
uses cross-gender casting to illuminate gender-as-social construction;
it plays with contradictions between actor and character gender and

between the characters' mandated social roles and their desires. The cast was impressive, but their very competence gave rise to an interesting issue in relation to cross-gender performance and the critical *gestus*. This was captured by a moment from a radio interview with a reporter who saw a dress rehearsal and who knew in advance about Churchill's cross-gender role requirements:

> *Interviewer:* Why did you have Betty in act 1 played by a woman?
> *Me:* I didn't. That was a man.
>
> (Coe 1985)

Some audience members also were not aware of the actor's identity until his wig came off during the curtain call; I think this was due to a combination of the skill of his performance, failure to read the playbill, and audience assumptions regarding gender that are based on habitual reading of codes (in life and in the theater). But does cross-gender casting count if the gender of the performer is erased? I do not think it did in this case, for the discrepancy between the gender of the actor and the gender of the character is where much of the meaning of the play lies. The process by which we set up our performance code did not work for some audience members, for they did not fully understand that "Betty" was male until after the performance, i.e., they could not "read" it right. Gender-as-construction needed to be visible, highlighting the playful, contradictory oscillation between actor and character gender. At least one moment early in the performance needed to present this actor as a biological male, a "historical subject playing an actor, playing a character, who shows that women are made, not born" (Diamond 1988, 90).

In 1988 our theater program focused its faculty production on acquainting students with Brechtian performance; we selected *The Resistible Rise of Arturo Ui,* which has over fifty roles, only three of them female. I went into auditions committed to using an equal number of female and male performers, since our acting pool was configured roughly in that proportion and since Brecht's pieces easily accommodate nonrealistic approaches to performance. I knew I wanted to cast a man as the tarty gun moll Dockdaisy in order to foreground the stereotypical aspects of the role; I was open to casting all other roles with either gender. I cast twenty-four actors, half of them women and half of them men. All but a handful played multiple parts. Besides giving women an equal shot, this casting built in a *Verfremdungseffekt* that continually reminded the audience that they were watching a theatrical parable and also revealed the narrative's marginalization of women. With this production I was particularly aware of the ways cross-gender performance could liberate young performers (women in particular, since a man played only one of the female roles), expanding their confidence and expressiveness in vocal, physical, and emotional terms. This was supported by the broad performing style demanded by this piece, influenced as it was by Hitler, the Nazis, and American gangster films of the 1930s. The actors grew more than they might have precisely because they were not bound by the strictures of realism. As with the other productions, cross-gender strategies provided means for rethinking and illuminating the text and energizing the overall performance.

> There is that in me—I do not know what it is—but I know it is
>   in me. . . .
> Do I contradict myself?
> Very well then I contradict myself,
> (I am large, I contain multitudes.)
>
>   (Whitman 1975, 123)

The actor's body and the history it carries can limit imagination more than the body of an artist working in nonperformance forms; while, say, a playwright's gender affects her imagination, the interrelationship of gendered body, gender history, and imagination is not as continuously palpable as in the work of the actor.[8] Nonetheless, actors must be able to imagine themselves into a range of roles, regardless of gender. While we may derive a sense of security in daily life from society's polarization of gender (it tells us our place), this comfortable identification can inhibit the actor's ability to do cross-gender work.[9] The comfort is based on clinging to a limited sense of who-I-am and, sometimes more important, who-I-am-*not*.

Acting is typically grounded in finding some common point of identification with a character. One obvious point of identification is gender. Cross-gender work requires the actor to identify with a seeming Other, imagine what it must be like to be the Other, and break years of physical, vocal, and emotional conditioning in order to perform that Other. There is a big difference between being cognitively aware of the artificiality of the bipolar model of gender and feeling how one has been shaped by that model on deeper, precognitive levels. Conscious or not, a sense of "crossing gender" limited to a Self/Other opposition is confined to an identity based on separation and difference—a me/not-me sense of self. This does not encompass the fluidity of performance, which requires entering into the not-not-me, i.e., the imagining of oneself into a seeming Other. An actor playing the "other" gender, whatever the theatrical style, faces the same challenges as when playing any role, for any prescribed role is to some degree an Other, a not-me. Here "the director's role is mainly catalytic, [for she] assists the alchemic or mystical marriage going on as the actor crosses the limen from *not-me* to *not-not me*" (Turner 1982, 121).[10] While semiotic analysis and an alchemy of the not-not-me may seem to live in different universes, both are crucial to feminist cross-gender performance. Besides grappling conceptually with technologies of representation in a given text, the director is midwife to the relationship between the actor and the character, and this relationship's place within the overall production. Part of this is honoring the private aspects of the actor's craft and the contingent, preconscious aspects of creativity.

While gender is only one area that the director and actor have to address, the boundary between Woman/Man can feel more inviolable or impassable to a young actor than differences of age, body size, diction, accent, hair color, and even ethnicity. I sometimes encounter particular kinds of resistance when asking actors to cross a gender line, for these actors are being asked to violate a range of social taboos by imagining themselves as the "unimaginable." In cross-gender work the actor is not necessarily imagining herself as the Other in any intrinsic, biological sense; in material terms she is simply exchanging her own behaviors for those typically ascribed to someone of the opposite gender. She is also, however, embarking on performing a range of behaviors for which she could be sanctioned were they performed in earnest off the stage. Further, she probably has not internalized them in the way they would have been by someone raised to be that gender.[11] An actress may feel herself very outside of the role, caught in the impulse to stereotype. An actor may resist because she is having to perform in an unfamiliar physical and vocal range. This can be addressed at least in part through skills training. Some resistance may have to do with homophobia—a straight male actor's fear of being thought feminine, and therefore gay, a straight woman's of being thought tough or "butch."[12] Yet each of us is capable of moving beyond a socially prescribed Self in order to enact many different selves onstage and in life. (One actor whom I directed in cross-gender projects used that work in articulating his gay identity.)

Cross-gender characterizations begin to some degree with stereotyping, at least with the broad categories of Woman and Man, and we have to address stereotypes, for we construct ourselves in relation to them, whether emulating them or resisting them. They help us identify ourselves and other people, signaling who we are. Cross-gender performance can use stereotyping deliberately to emphasize the nature of character-as-construction. More often, however, a stereotype provides a starting point for the director and actor to engage a character and grapple with a psychophysical stew of identification in order to uncover the not-not-me.

Cloud Nine and *Arturo Ui* involved these issues. The actor who played Betty/Jerry in *Cloud Nine* was gifted and well-trained, yet in early rehearsals his approach to Betty was not working. He loved Betty and passionately wanted the audience to understand her oppressed position in the family. Unfortunately, this led him to play his own pain about Betty's condition, which was linked to other personal sources of anger and sorrow about women he knew whom he felt were similarly oppressed. So he initially played Betty as being extremely aware and angry about her lot; that is, he played his *response* to Betty rather than playing Betty. In this phase his characterization was tense and snappish and, hence, unfunny (which was deadly). He had sympathy for Betty, but he had unwittingly condescended toward her, feeling himself to be her intellectual and sociopolitical superior: he had the 1980s feminist picture, and she did not. What he lacked was empathy; more directly, he had difficulty imagining things from inside of *her* body, seeing things through *her* eyes, with *her* history. In particular, he could not grasp Betty's intense need to be a proper Victorian wife. She believes she *must* be a continually pleasing, self-effacing "angel in the house" if she is to be loved and accepted. She automatically, often unconsciously represses angry or sexual feelings, which are "bad" for women (because they prevent them from being "good" wives and mothers). Much of the humor and authenticity of the character resides in the contradictions between her conscious and unconscious impulses. In this phase of rehearsal the actor was projecting his own consciousness onto Betty. He had to shift his performative identification from his own awareness of the workings of social/gender hierarchies to that of someone caught within them unawares and struggling to make the best of a bad lot. *A clarification of the differences between them had to occur first* in order for him to empathize with Betty's perspective and play it with commitment and joy.

Gender was a big factor in this initial "blindness." This actor was cognitively aware that many women are taught to be self-effacing caretakers and of the taboos placed on anger, assertiveness, and sexuality for women, but he did not at first connect with the *feeling* of those experiences. He had difficulty imagining himself in those conditions because, while he understood them, he viewed them as the territory of an Other. The mere fact of gender difference prevented him initially from finding the Betty in himself. He could not see Betty's simple human emotions for seeing her as a representative of Woman's Condition. In seeing her as not-me-but-my-mother, he could not see Betty as a not-not-me, i.e., someone contained within himself. We took our solution directly from Stanislavski. We focused on specific given circumstances in the text, defined a simple, active superobjective—"I want to be liked, I want to be accepted"—and found substitutions from his own experience; rather than emphasize his personal anger about women's lot in general, he drew on his own specific desires to please others and gain approval. He then magnified the repression of anger and rebellion, complicating that impulse in a glorious celebration of reaction formations.

Other instances of resistance have been more difficult to address; in my experience this typically happens when women are being asked to play men, rather than the reverse. Certain feelings and forms of expression can be psychologically difficult and even frightening for an actor. Some young women are literally petrified of being powerful, loud, large, angry, or genuinely ominous; of taking the stage even when it is required by the role they are playing. Some women have difficulty sustaining aggressive, "nonfeminine" modes with conviction. In these cases the director must help an actor move through decades of fear-based conditioning. Not only do we run up against the reality of the body, in terms of height, mass, and vocal quality, but also we are confronted with the ways these body realities are socially shaped. Girls and boys are raised to use different codes to speak, move, and live in their bodies.

Some of this can be addressed directly by the actor through acquiring vocal/physical skills. Actors can learn new codes in a technical way while unlearning ingrained ones. Every actor does this to some degree. Technical training, however, is often not enough for women dealing with emotionally charged power issues. I encountered this in *Arturo Ui* when I cast a woman as the gangster Givola, a character based on Hitler's henchman Goebbels. We were using a broad, Brechtian style, requiring the actor to commit to a bold, theatrical presentation and to an investment in and execution of the character's *gestus*. Even in this context she did not like being aggressive, though she was physically and technically capable of performing with sufficient size *and* was an avowed, intelligent feminist. Her politics notwithstanding, she had internalized cultural and familial dictates of femininity so that she could not invest herself consistently in the physical aggressiveness and emotional cold-bloodedness of the character.[13] The major form her reluctance took was in speaking too softly: she could not find Givola's voice. While she conceptually understood "gender as an 'act' . . . which constructs the social fiction of its own psychological interiority" (Butler 1990, 279), she could not make the leap of faith necessary to play that "act." I could not find an image, or a "hook," physical or emotional, with enough specificity as a point of identification to override her fears. Though this was, finally, a respectable, honest performance, it remained stuck at the level of the cognitive.

Interestingly, other actors in the same cast threw themselves joyfully into the transgressiveness of cross-gender performance. The actor who played the floozy Dockdaisy reveled in the character-as-construction; due to a number of factors—the obvious contradiction between his gender and that of the character, a gloriously bad costume (which used his own hot-rollered and gelled hair, rather than a wig), and a fearless camp attack on the role—the audience was constantly reminded of the artificiality of the ostensibly female character. The woman who played the reporter Ragg, the investigator O'Casey, and a vegetable dealer also moved into the not-not-me with relish; her physical and vocal choices were strong—she quickly found a different spine and vocal placement for each character—and she maintained a sense of theatricality throughout (a "this isn't me, but these characters are great fun and look at what I can do with them"). She also played with a knowingness that foregrounded Brecht's points about the rise of fascism through her characters. There was no difference in the way I coached these three actors, and that, in short, was the problem: what worked for both these actors was a more physical, outside-in, Brechtian approach.

I most recently cross-gender cast a role in Charles Ludlam's *Stage Blood.* Edmund Dundreary (a role actually intended for a male) is an oily would-be leading man having an affair with a married leading lady. It is the one role whose reverse casting could reinforce (rather than undermine) the polymorphously perverse politics of Ludlam's play. My goals included teaching the actors about broad comic acting, shtick, and Shakespeare (the play includes extended scenes from *Hamlet,* some done straight, some parodied). The small cast made it easier to develop the sense of ensemble needed to make an actor feel safe taking risks. I immediately directed the actors to specific images and (stereo)types from film and theater and emphasized that our focus would not be on "telling the truth" but, rather, "perfecting the mask," to quote the play. I asked the young woman playing Edmund to look at Rudolph Valentino and Gilbert Roland and to think of Edmund as a snake. These directions were wrong for this particular actor: they were too close to her own style. Much of Valentino's and Roland's appeal was specifically their femininity. The snake image did not give the actor anywhere to go in exploring Edmund's physicality, especially the lower torso and legs. After a number of unexciting weeks we were both feeling frustrated, and she was at a dead end. Then I saw something obvious: she needed images and direction that would transform her energy into a parody of masculine sexuality. We changed the images from Valentino and Roland to John Wayne and Kevin Kline, from snake to weasel. I asked her to leave her high-heel boots at home and wear shoes and clothes approximating Edmund's to rehearsal. I nagged her mercilessly to drop her vocal pitch, drop her center, widen her stance. She found a pipe. Edmund's eyebrows became very important. Along with this we also worked on character motivation and relationship (an anarchic, ridiculous procedure with Ludlam). We emphasized spontaneity and acting on impulse within the bounds of the text and set as a goal making each other laugh. Costume and makeup—which included slicked-down hair, a penciled-on mustache, large eyebrows, chest binding, and a

A scene from Rhonda Blair's production of Brecht's *Resistible Rise of Arturo Ui*. Ui, in white, is at right. At center is Dockdaisy the floozy, played by a cross-dressed male actor. Also among Ui's henchmen, visible upstage and to the right, are actresses cross-dressed as men. Set design by Wayne Kramer; photo by Phil Wyatt.

cravat—completed the transformation. It was a parody celebrating a range of male stereotypes; she was both outside of the character and in it—a not-me/not-not-me.

Feminist cross-gender work is not a discrete performance mode inherently different from others. It is a range of performance subsets that address stylistic, cultural, and political issues about the ways our lives are shaped by constructions of gender and sexuality. In successful cross-gender work the actor interweaves a cool assessment of the politics of gender difference, an empathic identification with the character, and a solid application of craft. Once she or he enters into a production's critical framework the actor's approach to playing across gender is similar to that for any role removed from her- or himself; it demands commitment to the production and its perspective, a sensitive engagement with the text, research and requisite skill, and belief in her or his own capacity to play the role effectively. While the purpose of a cross-gender performance for an audience might be to illuminate the cultural and political implications of a *not-me*, the actor must still embrace a *not-not-me*, taking a mental and physical leap into the Other. The director's task is always somehow to help the actor find that Other, the *not-me*, in her- or himself. It is still all about the director creating an articulate, theatrically compelling production and the actor successfully making the transition into playing a *not-not-me* with conviction and panache. But feminist cross-gender performance is set apart from many other theatrical modes because it is simultaneously committed to a conscious critical perspective *and* to the contingent and highly personal nature of performance. When we do this work, besides usually having a good deal of fun, my actors and I move back and forth back and forth between these modes, swimming in a sea of gender possibilities that require us to question our assumptions about what it means to be women or men, and *always* to improvise. The analytical, the unconscious, and the imaginary are intertwined in marvelously complex ways when gender is crossed. Without any one of these our perception is limited to only a partial awareness of how gender works in our lives, and we risk replicating old habits and assumptions about what and where we think gender is. And the truth is, we all contain multitudes.

> Speech is the twin of my vision, it is unequal to measure itself,
> It provokes me forever, it says sarcastically,
> *Walt you contain enough, why don't you let it out then?*
> (Whitman 1975, 89)

NOTES

1. Historically, cross-gender casting has kept women off the stage so that men could control theatrical representation (e.g., as with Greeks, Elizabethans, and Kabuki actors). In contemporary instances women have done the reverse, playing with the possibilities of Simone de Beauvoir's statement that "one is not born, but, rather, *becomes* a woman." See Kendall's article in this volume and Case 1989.

2. For example, Janelle Reinelt: "Gender must be conceived of as a field of

experience, socially constructed, constantly changing, not a pair of bi-polar opposites inevitably fixing the subject in relation to an either/or cultural practice" (1989, 51). Barbara Freedman: Sexual (gender) identity is "a fiction which, however fostered by biology or in its service, is essentially linguistic, ideological and fetishistic" (1990, 56).

3. See Brecht 1964: " . . . besides what he actually is doing [the actor] will at all essential points discover, specify, imply what he is not doing; that is to say he will act in such a way that the alternative emerges as clearly as possible, that his acting allows the other possibilities to be inferred and only represents one out of the possible variants. . . . Whatever he doesn't do must be contained and conserved in what he does. . . . The technical term for this procedure is 'fixing the not . . . but'" (137).

4. For example, Lee Breuer directs a cross-gendered *King Lear* because "I kinda like to try to illuminate one archetype in terms of another," but Ruth Maleczech plays Lear because, "All *I* ever wanted was just the chance to say Shakespeare's words" (qtd. in Wetzsteon 1990, 39). In a similar archetypal vein Robert Wilson casts Marianne Hoppe as Lear, saying: "I knew I had found my Lear. She has Lear's face. She has Lear's voice" (*New York Times* 1990c). Socorro Valdez, who plays powerful pachuco roles for El Teatro Campesino, deliberately hides her gender, though her goal is more akin to Reinelt's "field of experience"; she says: "The roles are like an old rock, but crack that baby open and you have intricate, intricate layers of evolution. *That* is what has been my goal: it is to take these very crude images . . . and break them open so that the inside is expressed" (Gonzalez 1989, 226). Pat Carroll plays Falstaff in *The Merry Wives of Windsor* because he is older and therefore less sexual than Falstaff in the *Henry* plays. In "An Artful Falstaff Who Transcends Sex," "the critics agree, one of her accomplishments is that she makes the audience forget that the he is a she" (*New York Times* 1990a). Carroll's appeal (similar to that of drag) depends on the audience knowing that Falstaff is a woman, "not the real thing." Her gender evaporates as the performance progresses; an initial *Verfremdungseffekt* is naturalized as performer and role become undifferentiated (as in realism). Transsexual lesbian Kate Bornstein plays Tolan in a scene from Jellicoe's *The Knack,* a part she first played while still a man (see Munk 1988). In Lucas' *Prelude to a Kiss* a male actor plays first an old man and then a young woman whose soul is trapped in the old man's body; the "feeling" of being a young woman is required (*New York Times* 1990b).

5. Intertwined with other social particularities, our perceptions of theatrical uses of gender are conditioned by our perceptions of other social elements. See de Lauretis 1987 for a discussion of these interconnections and the way "the construction of gender is both the product and the process of its representation" (5).

6. Patrice Pavis (1982, 17) has a useful discussion of theater codes and taxonomies. Keith Johnstone (1979) provides a highly practical approach to character hierarchy for the director and actor-coach in his discussion of "status."

7. We did not inform the rights holder of the changes we were making; it did not seem necessary at the time. This was just prior to Olympia Dukakis's *Godot*

at the World Theatre, in which all characters but Pozzo were played as women, and long before Joanne Akalaitis's now notorious *Endgame* at the American Repertory Theatre. Beckett strongly criticized these productions for the changes they made in his scenic texts.

8. When questioned about his right to write intimately about the black condition in his country, Athol Fugard replied that he wrote from the imagination and that he had a right to imagine himself into any situation—that, in fact, it was his responsibility as a writer to do so (1990).

9. See Jane Gallop: "Difference produces great anxiety. Polarization, which is a theatrical representation of difference, tames and binds that anxiety. The classic example is sexual difference which is represented as a polar opposition (active-passive, energy-matter). All polar oppositions share the trait of taming the anxiety that specific differences evoke" (qtd. in Freedman 1990, 57).

10. "[Richard] Schechner is fond of quoting the child psychologist Winnicott's formulation, 'from *me* to *not-me* to *not-not-me*,' to express [the] process of theatrical maturation. The *me*, the biological-historical individual, the actor, encounters the role given in the script, the *not-me*; in the crucible of the rehearsal process a strange fusion or synthesis of *me* and *not-me* occurs" (qtd. in Turner 1982, 120–21).

11. See de Lauretis 1987 (esp. 12–16), for discussions of interpellation and investment.

12. I saw a male actor play Betty in *Cloud Nine* in a perverted camp style (i.e., he camped on camp) as a way of announcing his hostility both to the character and the category of women she represented (by refusing to play with a sense of investment) and to gay men (through his co-optation and distortion of camp strategies).

13. Actresses can also have this difficulty when playing female characters with these "male-identified" traits.

REFERENCES

Brecht, Bertolt. 1964. "Short Description of a New Technique of Acting Which Produces an Alienation Effect." In *Brecht on Theatre*, ed. and trans. John Willett. New York: Hill and Wang.

Butler, Judith. 1990. "Performative Acts and Gender Constitution: An Essay in Phenomenology and Feminist Theory." In *Performing Feminisms: Feminist Critical Theory and Theatre*, ed. Sue-Ellen Case. Baltimore: Johns Hopkins University Press.

Case, Sue-Ellen. 1989. "Toward a Butch-Femme Aesthetic." In *Making a Spectacle*, ed. Lynda Hart. Ann Arbor: University of Michigan Press.

Coe, Charlene. 1985, April. Interview with Rhonda Blair. WFCR-Amherst (Mass.).

de Lauretis, Teresa. 1987. *Technologies of Gender*. Bloomington: Indiana University Press.

Diamond, Elin. 1988. "Brechtian Theory/Feminist Theory: Toward a Gestic

Feminist Criticism." *TDR: A Journal of Performance Studies* 32, no. 1 (T117) (Spring).

Freedman, Barbara. 1990. "Frame-up: Feminism, Psychoanalysis, Theatre." In *Performing Feminisms: Feminist Critical Theory and Theatre,* ed. Sue-Ellen Case. Baltimore: Johns Hopkins University Press.

Fugard, Athol. 1990, June 23. Speech to the Theatre Communications Group biannual conference. Smith College, Northampton, Mass.

Gonzalez, Yolanda Broyles. 1989. "Toward a Revision of Chicano Theatre History: The Women of El Teatro Campesino." In *Making a Spectacle: Feminist Essays on Contemporary Women's Theatre,* ed. Lynda Hart. Ann Arbor: University of Michigan Press.

Johnstone, Keith. 1979. *Impro: Improvisation and the Theatre.* New York: Theatre Arts Books.

Munk, Erika. 1988. "Representation and Its Discontents." *Village Voice* (6 September).

New York Times. 1990a, 7 June, C17, C20.

———. 1990b, 15 March, C15, C18.

———. 1990c, 20 May, secs. 2, 7.

Pavis, Patrice. 1982. *Languages of the Stage: Essays in the Semiology of the Theatre.* New York: Performing Arts Journal Publications.

Reinelt, Janelle. 1989. "Feminist Theory and the Problem of Performance." *Modern Drama* 22, no. 1 (March).

Turner, Victor. 1982. *From Ritual to Theatre: The Human Seriousness of Play.* New York: Performing Arts Journal Publications.

Wetzsteon, Ross. 1990. "Queen Lear: Ruth Maleczech Gender Bends Shakespeare." *Village Voice* (30 January).

Whitman, Walt. 1975. *Walt Whitman: The Complete Poems.* Edited by Francis Murphy. New York: Penguin Books.

Len Berkman

An Interview with Amy Gonzalez: "All Ears, to Let My Ideas Transform"

I talked with Amy Gonzalez on 15 August 1990 after Amy's appointment as literary manager and resident director at the Eureka Theatre in the fall of 1989. Previously, after she received her University of Washington–Seattle M.F.A. degree in directing, Amy's work had centered in southern California—at Los Angeles Theatre Center (formerly Los Angeles Actors' Theatre), where she was artistic director of the Latino Theatre Lab and Ensemble and directed Jean-Claude van Itallie's Interview, *Ranier Hachfeld and Renier Lucker's* Banana, *and (with Bill Bushnell codirecting) John Guare's* Women and Water; *at Los Angeles's Mark Taper Forum, as a Theatre Communications Group/National Endowment for the Arts (NEA) director fellow in 1987–88; at South Coast Repertory (SCR) in Costa Mesa, where she helped develop and stage Cherríe Moraga's* Shadow of a Man *and Lynnette Serrano Bonaparte's* Broken Bough *within SCR's annual Hispanic Playwrights' Project (HPP, run by José Cruz Gonzalez); and, most recently, with Luis Valdez's Teatro Campesino, where Amy became the Teatro's first woman directing a female playwright's script.*

It was in the summer of 1988 at SCR that Amy and I first met and worked together. Like Maria Irene Fornes before me, I was project dramaturg for the six plays that would ultimately constitute the annual HPP August festival. Joining Amy and SCR's resident dramaturg, John Glore, as we developed Lynnette's Broken Bough *with playwright and cast that summer, I worked simultaneously as dramaturge with director José Luis Valenzuela in the development of* Simply Maria, *along with* Food for the Dead, *one of two plays by Josefina Lopez that Amy would direct for Teatro Campesino the following year (and which has remained in the Teatro's tour repertory). Again, in the summer of 1989, Amy, visiting dramaturg Dolores Prida, and I joined forces at SCR to develop Cherríe's* Shadow of a Man. *Further revised since HPP,* Shadow of a Man *graced Eureka Theatre's 1990–91 season, with Fornes directing.*

Among her actors Amy becomes an inventive path clearer and space shaper for their trial maneuvers. With her guidelines clear yet fluid Amy literally tiptoes among her actors to explore their performance terrain, testing out blocking with them, negotiating interpersonal options, encouraging her actors to try still other possibilities, even when "success" or "resolution" seems already in hand. By the time she arrives at her final choice neither she nor any single member of her ensemble exclusively "owns" that choice.

What follows incorporates excerpts from a 10 January 1992 interview, to update and expand upon Amy's earlier positions.

Gonzalez: Now Len, you won't ask me about feminist theory, will you? I'm not conscious of working out of theory.

Berkman: Actually, Amy, I'd love you first to share particular memories of your work on [Cherríe Moraga's] Shadow of a Man, especially since you had an all-women's group to rehearse with (except when I worked with you). Was that unique for you, working such a stretch with no male presence, no male "gaze"?

Gonzalez: I've directed other female-cast plays, like [Pam Gems's] *Dusa, Fish, Stas and Vi,* but we had a male stage manager. This was the first time everyone involved in the daily rehearsals was female. I didn't notice the difference at first, but there was a kind of comfort level. I didn't feel judgment coming from anybody. Sometimes I do feel that in other situations.

Berkman: Usually a male judgment?

Gonzalez: Not necessarily male... I'm not sure. Of course, when you worked with us we felt just as comfortable. I tend to underestimate the effect that potential judging voices have on the work: by that I mean the presence of men when it's a play about women, my mother's voice deep in my subconscious, or what I'm afraid a teacher might have thought of this work, whatever. It's been a long process to overcome these judging voices, particularly if they're male and you're female, or white and you're Latina.

Berkman: That issue of directorial authority, key to you as a feminist, fascinates me. Do you consciously, for instance, shape the circumstances of your initial contact with your production team so as to set in motion the process you want your entire production to sustain?

Gonzalez: I've been fortunate for the most part to be able to select the people, the team, I'm to work with, so my selections themselves have to do with degrees of common ground and common ways of working; or, if the others and I have a contradictory way of working, is it a productive one? If I have a question about work methods or artistic goals, I'm very straightforward about clearing it up before I decide on my team. It's not a matter of, you know, asking somebody, "Are you sexist?" It's more a matter of listening to their language, the way they respond, whether there's any condescension. It's really subtextual more than anything. But I might ask a direct question if I feel something uncomfortable or funny in that area. I'm very persistent, and eventually people see I'm not easy to push over, even though my personality makes it difficult to believe that! When I feel strongly about something I may not shout about it, but I pretty much stick to it, so the strength of my determination and commitment comes through without my having to make demands.

Berkman: Given your subtextual approach, how do you then explicitly relate the knowledge you bring to any given play to what others on your production team may differently bring?

Gonzalez: One excitement in directing is a transformation that happens when you talk with someone about a play, and they talk to you about the play, and you end up with something that's not wholly yours. Part of the fun is letting my ideas transform as they filter through different designers, actors, etc. I'm always grateful when things go beyond what I had imagined, and yet I always try to set limits so we end up with one thing, not five different things, even though that one thing differs from my original idea.

Berkman: How do you elicit this? Is there a pattern you pursue . . . of question asking? of provoking?

Gonzalez: It's different each time. I tend to talk a bit in the beginning, but there are certain things I won't divulge at first because they might constrain somebody. . . . I guess it's kind of gentle. But I get really frustrated when we travel in a direction I'm not comfortable with, and I'm very conscious of being the center point through which all must filter for the sake of unity of production. I can give you one example where I made a big mistake. When I directed *La Nona* [*The Granny* by the Italo-Argentinian playwright Roberto M. Cossa] I cast as the Granny a man who was fifty times as experienced as I and a great deal older, and I was too conscious of that. He was the nicest guy you could imagine; the problems were in my own mind. Given his experience in physical comedy, I wanted to include him in the design of his costume. The script called for a lot of places he'd have to hide food he couldn't possibly eat, so, at my meeting with the production manager, the costume designer, the actor, and myself, I let us keep suggestions he made that I didn't agree with. I thought, "Well, he knows better than I do; he's older, he's wiser." The costume was designed to his specifications, and it was a disaster! It had nothing to do with the play; it did not fit with the rest of the design; and here we were at the dress rehearsal, and all I had to do was take one look. I apologized to my costume designer because I was creating more work for her. She was a woman about my age too, and when we started discussing it honestly she admitted she herself had fallen into that trap. She'd known better, as did I, but we'd given over our own instincts. I took responsibility for the mistake with the actor too. I apologized, and he said, "Great, you know, you know best," and we moved on.

Berkman: Clearly, this wouldn't dissuade you from utilizing actors' input in subsequent productions.

Gonzalez: Absolutely not!

Berkman: Has your sense of your age in relationship to people you work with altered over the years?

Gonzalez: A little. You develop confidence through gaining experience, but I have to admit it's still there! There was a time when I overcompensated for it. I don't do that as much anymore: insist on a choice, just for the sake of flexing that kind of power. It's not very smart. But I'm still conscious of my lapses in confidence, and I'm conscious of it with regard to my ethnicity sometimes when I'm working on a play that's not a Latino play. Sometimes I feel I'm less of an authority even on an American play because I come from a different cultural milieu. I'm conscious of that, even though I've lived in this country for thirty years!

Berkman: When you describe what is necessary that a director do to assure production unity, did that change as those you worked with, and as you yourself, became more fully professional?

Gonzalez: When I was an undergraduate I yielded less. For example, though I still believe in the importance of staging and always take into consideration the set's ground plan, I don't preblock to the degree I did as a student. There's an ease of knowing what can happen in rehearsal. The more I trust myself, the more I wait to make certain decisions. Besides, with the confidence that comes with experience, you always know you can block a play in two days if you really have to.

At this point we spoke of Amy's sense of her artistic roots. She cited as contrasting directorial models the films of Elia Kazan for their behavioral and imagistic vividness and Joseph Chaikin's Open Theatre for its ensemble collaborations. Since works of the 1960s and early 1970s by the three major Open Theatre playwrights (Megan Terry, Jean-Claude van Itallie, and Susan Yankowitz) had such enduring influence on Amy, when Susan asked me to recommend a director for the 1989 New Dramatists' presentation in Los Angeles of her A Knife in the Heart *(a stunning feminist treatment of a political assassin's mother), I leapt at the prospect of matchmaking two such exceptional and kindred spirits.* A Knife in the Heart *proved a happy partnership for them.*

Gonzalez: When I found out that Susan wrote the Open Theatre's *Terminal* I realized why her name had sounded so familiar when you connected us. I was so in love with that piece. When I'd directed *Comings and Goings, Interview,* and *The Gloaming, Oh My Darling,* it was so exciting to have an immediate social and political outlet and also the freedom to invest myself in the ensemble process more than classically structured scripts ask the director to do. Yet I also felt that structurally I was grounded by the scenarios, not creating from scratch.

Berkman: At that earlier time, did you see gender consciousness in Open Theatre–inspired material, or was that not related to what had excited you about them?

Gonzalez: At that time it was not an issue. Not until graduate school in '79. The climax of that discovery was that I directed *Dusa, Fish.* Fish kills herself at the end, you know, because she can't reconcile two parts of herself, because she lives in a place that will not allow her to be a full person. I felt that was very truthful, and sad, of course, but affirming. I myself—more now at thirty-five than then at twenty—might be more aggressive about living a fulfilled life: I'd tackle that world, not surrender; but I can still understand Fish.

Berkman: Did you find other plays with similar impact?

Gonzalez: I next chose [Euripides'] *Trojan Women* but for another reason. I directed seven plays in graduate school, conscious of what I could learn differently with each. I selected plays that presented problems or challenges I wanted to encounter prior to my being turned loose on the world. For example, [Lorca's] *Blood Wedding* enabled me to collaborate on a musical score with a composer who was also a graduate student.

Berkman: Setting out as a woman to direct females and males alike did not frighten or inhibit you?

Gonzalez: At certain points, yes—never in a major way. I've been challenged as a director by both actors and actresses. Recommendation letters my professors wrote for me actually said, "Don't let her 'little voice' fool you!" So I know I have a certain demeanor that's not what some people may associate with a director. It keeps getting better, though: I have gray hair now. The stereotypical director is me during tech. The short time I worked with Joanne Akalaitis impressed me: I assisted her for two or three weeks on a revival of her *Green Card* at the Taper. She was so nonlinear and creative in ways I hadn't observed before. It seemed to be she was improvising a lot of the time, and she was physically and mentally a total part of that production. It was wonderful! She would sweat as much as anybody else; the production was very physical. She wasn't just somebody sitting in the back of the theater giving orders; she was 100 percent involved.

Increasingly, Amy made clear that she welcomed directing scripts whose focus or cultural sphere might seem exterior to her personal experience, that she did not want to be associated exclusively with any single dramatic genre, culture, or concern. If a producer sought a director for a contemporary German play, for instance (perhaps, her cherished The Conquest of the South Pole *by Manfred Karga), and preferred a director who had spent time in Germany, Amy wanted to be sure such a producer would not assume that, being Latina, she had no such geographic qualification. In no way did this deny Amy's emphatic prizing of her work with Hispanic plays and her wish to see Hispanic play production go beyond tokenism, a tokenism manifest, she pointed out, when a theater would refuse production of one Hispanic script because "we already have another just like it on our schedule." Amy expressed particular desire to stage Edit Villarreal's* My Visits with MGM (My Grandmother Marta), *another script developed (with director José*

Cruz Gonzalez, SCR's senior resident dramaturg, Jerry Patch, and me) at HPP.

Gonzalez: I feel able to direct many kinds of different plays. Anyone who directs Shakespeare won't have an immediate connection with that world. And research can be very exciting and interesting and illuminating. With plays like Cherríe's and Edit's, of course, the excitement is different; you don't have to do the groundwork; you already understand it. So you don't have to spend time figuring out certain things; they're there already. You make other discoveries. I immediately flash, too, on [Eduardo Machado's] *Once Removed,* which is so rich in subtextual patterns. I directed a reading of it with Karmin [Murcelo] that made me cry. She was so fabulous. Talk about being in your bones! That play is in my bones. Eduardo and I came over from Cuba within two months of each other, when I was six and he was about eight years old. But deep down inside I'm a structuralist. I believe beneath *any* play lies a structure and series of patterns to be discovered.

Berkman: What seems quite clear and complex is that along with your regard for women come other concerns that might in some way still excite you to direct scripts that downplay the role of women.

Gonzalez: Yes, without placing less value on exploring plays by women, without diminishing what I feel about Latina plays, theatrically I'm drawn to large issues and to all plays with theatricality and scope. Caryl Churchill is that! I can't tell you how much I want to do her *Mad Forest.*

As of this writing, administrative turnovers and dire financial crisis have suspended operations at the Eureka. Nevertheless, Amy Gonzalez receives continuing offers from theaters around the country, including her return to the 1992 Hispanic Playwrights' Festival at the South Coast Repertory. Her perseverance and vision suggest that such opportunities to direct will continue.

JOAN LIPKIN

Aftermath: Surviving the Reviews

The phone rang. I startled out of sleep, eager for the news. It was my friend with the early edition of the paper, on her way to work. "Joanie," she said, too softly. In an instant I knew. "How bad is it?" I asked.

For the feminist director, the work may be just beginning after the show opens. After identifying or creating a viable script. After locating actors who are willing to commit to potentially controversial work. After trying to interest an often reluctant press in the legitimacy of the project. The show opens, and if it has been misread by an uninformed or overtly hostile media, the hardest work of all may still be ahead. How can the feminist director counter the negativity that shapes audience expectation after a bad review? And even more important, how can she prevent her cast from internalizing those judgments in a perhaps unconscious but deeply conditioned submission to male authority?

Reviews are often wildly contradictory, so it is reasonable to question how much influence they really have. Does anybody really care what is said? I think in the case of controversial feminist work, reviews and publicity matter a great deal. They are crucial to shaping audience expectation. Reviews in particular, as printed in a newspaper or magazine (usually under a male byline), take on the familiar authoritative voice that the reader has been conditioned to accept as fact. So the experience of the play begins well before the curtain rises. The tone set by the review is often magnified at the theater as the audience arrives. If the review has been positive, there is a contagious air of excitement; if it is negative, the room feels too still. The audience then telegraphs any ambivalence it may feel to the actors, short-circuiting the dynamic exchange that constitutes the experience of live theater and undermining the leadership of the director. Unless the director actively intervenes at this point to save the production, the critics' prophecies may actually come true.

My own experience with this kind of post-opening-night crisis took place in the fall of 1990, when I co-wrote and directed *He's Having Her Baby*, a pro-choice musical comedy to be produced by That Uppity Theatre Company. The impetus for this production came directly out of current political events. Although the debate centered around Reproductive Services, Inc., a St. Louis–based abortion care provider, it was clear that the repercussions of the decision had national implications, opening the door to further restrictive legislation in every state. As I watched the theatrical spectacle of the Supreme Court decision to restrict legal access to abortion in Missouri, I decided to stage a feminist counterproduction.

I wanted to create a gender-reversal pro-choice musical comedy about a teenage *boy* who gets pregnant. My collaborator and musical director was Tom Clear, a composer and lyricist. There was no question in our minds about who would be most affected if *Roe v. Wade*, the historic decision legalizing abortion, were overturned. The answers were clear. Poor women. Teenage women. Rural women. And many women of color. But we also knew the issue of reproductive choice is so heated that humor might be a way out of the impasse. By using musical comedy and a deliberately broad acting style, we hoped to combine politics and entertainment in equal parts, and, most important, to speak beyond the circle of the like-minded, instilling a wider public empathy for women.

He's Having Her Baby is the story of Joey, a fifteen-year-old boy who is pressured into having sex and becomes pregnant on a first date with Liz, the captain of the girls' hockey team. Joey doesn't know what to do; he gets caught up in the pregnancy without enough information or support to make an informed decision. By the end of act one, he has suddenly been transformed from a teenage boy into a parent. Act two is about the difficulties of young, single, impoverished parenthood, as Joey tries to secure suitable day care, deals with sexual harassment from his female boss, and attempts to find romance. When he accidentally becomes pregnant again at the end of the show, he now makes a different decision and has an abortion.

The play moved at a furious pace to convey the urgency of the events. The actors played multiple parts, time and space were telescoped, and gender roles, government legislation, the school system, institutionalized religion, and corporate structures were examined with ferocious humor. The gender reversal even extended to the musical styles: the men sang like the Andrews Sisters while the women sang like Hank Williams.

Some of the critics, however, were not amused. I had known it would be tricky. St. Louis is one of the most bitterly divided cities in the country on the subject of abortion. The week prior to the opening of the play, a demonstration was held in St. Louis called the Chain of Life, involving over three hundred area churches; thousands of people lined the causeways as part of a nationwide protest against abortion. I assumed, probably naively, that the media would be receptive to our effort to use theater as a creative means of extending the dialogue about reproductive rights.

I was wrong. The reviews ranged between complete avoidance of what the play was trying to say ("In their next work, it would be nice to see Lipkin and Clear leave the territory of political 'statement' and venture into the truly dangerous territory—humanity"[1]) and overt hostility ("[Lipkin] rarely looks to a difficult target when a cheap shot is available"[2]). Even the positive comments felt grudging ("I found some of the show's humor pedantic, but to be fair, this may be chromosomal. My female companion laughed a lot, and remarked that she had been a victim of most of the discrimination Lipkin has on stage"[3]).

Unlike most of the critics, who fit a fairly standard profile (largely white, middle-class, middle-aged, heterosexual men), the audience included women and men of various classes, ages, races, and sexual orientations. The disparity between the critical and popular responses was sufficiently extreme to raise significant questions about the life experience and expectations that the critics brought to viewing the show. I wondered if the audiences who embraced the play were more in touch with the realities of daily life than the critics who commented upon it. I wondered how the life experience of the critics influenced their ability to assess the realities of teenage pregnancy or to be engaged with the material. Could it be that they dismissed the material as inauthentic because they found it difficult to admit that such painful inequities exist? And finally, were they unable to accept this portrait of the oppression of women as a class because it would mean confronting how they themselves were implicated?

One thing was clear. I had to do something and I had to do it fast. The reviews were beginning to take on a momentum of their own. On the night after opening, I arrived at the theater two hours before curtain to face a demoralized cast and canceled reservations. The actors were all sitting backstage. It was so quiet I could hear the tap drip. I looked at them not looking at me. Without question, the actors were depressed. Yet even with this bad review, we still had a show to do. How could we get the energy back up to where it had been at dress rehearsal and opening night? How could I make them remember what they loved about the show and how good they were and why it mattered that people see it? Not only did we have to-night's show to get through, but the run was just beginning and there was the possibility of an extension. How could I prevent them from dropping out as soon as their contracts were up?

I realized that they were probably wondering how being in the midst of this controversy was going to affect their careers. I realized that my role as director did not end when the show opened. I realized that some of the actors were scared, but that others were actually angry. I had gotten them into this and now they were looking to me for a lot more than acting notes.

I was uncertain about what to do next. There was no model for this in the directing books. To play the old dictatorial game would have suggested that my authority recognized no others; to be one of the group, however, would have suggested that I knew no more than they did. Neither style hung comfortably on my shoulders. As the director and co-writer of the show, I was obviously invested—and now, postreview, defensive.

Collective cast griping can be as cathartic as a curtain call, but I suspect that the feminist director has a great deal to lose by playing out this scenario. In the moment of crisis, adding her own anxiety will only undermine the cast's need to believe that someone calm and levelheaded is running the show. This is not to say that I didn't have those feelings, only that it was necessary to take them somewhere else.

Instead, I made a pot of coffee and sat down and talked. I talked about the reviews and why they ranged from uninformed to hostile. I talked about *Roe v. Wade,* and what was at stake. About the tragedy of seventeen-year-old Becky Bell, a high school sopho-more from Indiana who died in 1988, either from a back-alley abortion or from self-aborting. I told the actors that if the reviews closed down our show prematurely, the critics were in effect colluding with the anti-choice forces by eliminating information and debate. Most of this was groundwork that had been laid early in rehearsal, but the actors needed to hear it again, and they needed to hear it right then.

As I spoke, I could see the actors shifting, and thankfully, it wasn't just in their seats. One actor with gum stopped chewing. It was as if by focusing on the political importance of the work, they could reframe their experience of working on this show. By seeing themselves as active, collective partners in social change, rather than strictly as working professionals, the actors were able to recommit to the project. What was most important in this moment backstage was that I did not ask them to sympathize with me or to commit to me. I asked them to commit to the *issues*. Instead of trying to win them back through personal loyalty, I spoke only of the reasons why keeping this play running was literally a matter of life and death. By the time I finished, the actors were beginning to look more animated. "Hey!" one of them said. "It's half hour to curtain."

Now I had to face the audience. The night after that first bad review came out, they seemed dazed. The air felt flat without the buzz that people make when they are waiting for something they want to see. Even the guy in the front row looked miserable, as if he had been dragged there against his will. I imagined him watching the show with the review in his head, like a conductor reading the score. I looked over the crowd. It felt as if the entire audience had turned into critics.

I decided to meet the reviews head on, talking simply and openly to an audience that appeared to be as embarrassed as I was. Their initial tension gave way to a collective sigh of relief as we all realized we wouldn't have to pretend this *thing* wasn't there. When the guy in the first row relaxed enough to loosen his tie, I knew I had made the right decision. As I asked for the audience's cooperation in saving the life of the show, the battle took on its own appeal. Although it wasn't my conscious intention, this moment of fighting back to neutralize and overcome the bad review became the *counter*show and added another layer of theatricality to the evening. It wasn't easy. At the moment when I wanted to be most private, I felt compelled to perform myself in a public space. I got through it by being controlled. I made some stupid jokes. And somehow, suddenly, everything changed.

This personal appeal turned out to be much more effective than simply putting a letter or statement in the program. And I wonder if on some level my visible humanity didn't touch the audience. They had to recognize that real people were involved. The stakes were high, not just for us, but for the issues we represented. By asking the audience to invest in those issues, and to be our partners in getting the word out, we extended the experience of the play beyond the proscenium and into the streets.

Backstage, at intermission, I could see that any lingering doubts the actors might have been harboring had vanished as they realized they were not alone out there. Emboldened by my public stance, they understood that I was not asking them to do anything I wouldn't do myself. The risk was shared. We were all in this together.

My next step was to involve the actors directly in a campaign to save the show. First I actively solicited alternative views from community leaders who had liked the play. Their quotes were included in an insert in the program and in a mass leafletting and direct mail campaign we launched the weekend the reviews came out. *As a company*—the actors, the production manager, and even the running crew—we put fliers in restaurants, bars, and shopping malls. We put them on cars and in mailboxes; we handed them out to passersby. We printed postcards and asked people who had seen the show to send notes to their friends. Gradually, as word of mouth began to spread, people gave us the benefit of the doubt, and more and more came out to see the show.

I'm convinced that these immediate forms of intervention helped to save the show. I'm also convinced that having the participation of the actors was key, not only in getting the word out, but in bolstering cast morale. The actors ceased to be passive recipients of a negative critical gaze; by mobilizing physically, they were now able to look back. Ultimately, the show ran for two and a half months to modest but enthusiastic houses. The longer we kept going, the more people were able to talk about the show and the issues it raised. Eventually I came to value those bad reviews. The lengths to which some of the critics went to discredit the production only underscored how uneasy they must have felt with this kind of work and with women like me who are doing it.

Ironically, adversity creates all kinds of possibilities for connection: with people on the stage, people behind the scenes, people sitting in the house, and finally oneself. The pain of the bad reviews never fully goes away; it remains a dull reminder of what it means to challenge authority instead of accepting the usual answers. Still, there is joy in the shared struggle and small triumphs. There is a thrill in being part of a movement to create change.

The real challenge in feminist directing is to keep an open heart and an open mind. We have to learn how to filter what critics write, rather than allowing what they say, good or bad, to turn into that familiar voice of authority. Even the most hostile critic occasionally may have something useful to say to us. But we also have to learn to be our own critics, and/or to identify the people whose voices we trust.

During the run of *He's Having Her Baby*, a small group of teenage girls came up to me after the show and said, "Thank you for this play. It shows the way things really are for us. Can't you come to our high school and perform?" Another time, a woman said to me, "I'm laughing so hard I don't know why I feel like crying." And just recently, I was interviewed by a magazine writer who asked if I knew that many people were grateful for our work, that there were countless souls who didn't speak out but felt that they had an ally for reasonable thinking in the world because of our theater company. I hardly knew what to say.

Communities everywhere need theater to provide leadership and to show them what is possible. Feminist political debates enacted on a stage with real people have a different kind of power. The issues are suddenly brought home. It becomes possible to see the women sitting near us in the audience and the women on the stage with different eyes, as people whose lives are framed by laws and experience over which they still have very little control.

To be a feminist artist is necessarily to be an optimist and to believe in the possibility of social change. It isn't easy; you have to believe in your truth to make it worth the pain of telling it. But you had better know that not telling it is the greatest pain of all. Theater can make a difference. It can change how we, and the women and men who come after us, live our lives.

NOTES

1. Michael Isaacson, "'He's Having Her Baby' Doesn't Deliver," *West End Word*, 1 November 1990.

2. Joe Pollack, "'He's Having Her Baby' Is Pregnant with Flaws," *St. Louis Post-Dispatch*, 23 October 1990.

3. Isaacson, ibid.

Contributors

Addell Austin Anderson is an Assistant Professor at Wayne State University in Detroit, with the Department of Theater. She is also the Director of the Black Theater Program at Wayne State and teaches courses on dramatic literature and images of Blacks and Hispanics in film, television, and theater. Her Ph.D. is from Michigan State, for which she wrote a dissertation on pioneering Black dramas from 1924 to 1927. Her publications include an essay in *Phoebe* on Marita Bonner, a piece on the state of Black theater for the *Drama Review,* and two articles in *Contemporary Dramatists.* She currently is the editor of *The Black Theatre Directory* and serves on the Executive Council of the Black Theater Network.

Gayle Austin is an Assistant Professor in the Department of Communication at Georgia State University and has a Ph.D. from the City University of New York Graduate Center. Her background in professional theater includes some playwriting, six years as literary manager for The Women's Project in New York, and work as a dramaturg in New York and Atlanta. She has published articles in *Performing Arts Journal, Southern Quarterly, Theater Week,* and two anthologies of feminist theater criticism and is the author of *Feminist Theories for Dramatic Criticism* (University of Michigan Press, 1990).

Len Berkman holds the rank of Hesseltine Professor of Theatre at Smith College, where he has taught playwriting, theater history, and dramatic literature for twenty-two years. He is himself a playwright and has been produced both in the United States and Canada. His essays have appeared in the *Massachusetts Review, Modern Drama,* and *Parnassus,* and his plays have been discussed in such books as Helene Keyssar's *Feminist Theatre* and Ellen Schiff's *From Stereotype to Metaphor: The Stage Jew in England, France and the United States.* He also works as a playwright/dramaturg at Robert Redford's Sundance Institute and for the South Coast Repertory's Hispanic Playwrights' Festival.

Rhonda Blair is an Associate Professor at Hampshire College in Amherst, Massachusetts, where she teaches directing and acting. She is a past president of the Women in Theatre Program of the Association for Theatre in Higher Education and on the editorial board of *Theatre Topics.* She has published in *Women & Performance* and in *Theatre Topics.* She received her Ph.D. from the University of Kansas, and she periodically translates plays from the Russian into English.

Juli Thompson Burk is an Associate Professor of Theater at the University of Hawaii in Manoa. She holds a Ph.D. from the University of Washington,

Seattle, and an M.A. from Pennsylvania State. Her publications include a forth-coming book called *The Feminist Impact on Theatre and Performance* and articles in *Notable Women in the American Theatre, Theatre Journal,* and *American Theatre Companies: A Historical Encyclopedia.* She is also a director and choreographer, and her 1987 production of *Top Girls* won awards for Best Production and Best Director from the Hawaii State Theater Council.

Gay Gibson Cima is an Associate Professor in the English Department at Georgetown University in Washington, D.C., where she teaches drama and directs. She received her doctorate from Cornell in 1978. She has since published essays on modern and contemporary drama and theater history in *Theatre Journal* and *Theatre Survey.* Her book on male playwrights and female actors will be forthcoming from Cornell University Press in 1993.

Susan Clement is the Managing Director of Youth Theatre Northwest in Seat-tle, where she also directs and teaches. She is the founding member of The Works: Women's Performance Project, an organization dedicated to producing new work by women. This project, in collaboration with the Empty Space, produced two years of staged readings in a series entitled "New Voices for the Nineties." She has published in *Theater Three* and holds an M.F.A. in directing from the University of Washington in Seattle.

Glenda Dickerson is currently Full Professor and Chair of the Drama and Theater Department at Spelman College. She has also taught at Rutgers, Fordham, Howard, and the State University of New York at Stony Brook. She did her graduate work at Adelphi. Her extensive directing credits include work both on and off Broadway. She has been a resident director with the Negro Ensemble Company and has also worked with the New Federal Theatre, the Women's Interart Theatre, the Seattle Repertory Theatre, the St. Louis Black Repertory, the John F. Kennedy Center for the Performing Arts, Ford's Theatre in Washington, D.C., and the Crossroads Theatre in New Brunswick, New Jersey. She has directed for television and has created a number of original scripts, most recently *Re/Membering Aunt Jemima: an act of magic.* Her many credits and awards include an Emmy nomination for her television production of *Wine in the Wilderness* in 1972. Her article "The Cult of True Womanhood: Toward a Womanist Attitude in African-American Theatre" appeared in *Theatre Journal* in 1988.

Ellen Donkin is an Associate Professor of Theatre at Hampshire College. She has published in *Theater Three, Turn-of-the-Century Women, Theatre Journal,* and *Women & Performance* and appears in a volume of theater history essays on women called *Curtain Calls* and also in *Critical Theory and Performance.* She is an Associate Editor for *Nineteenth Century Theatre.* She received her Ph.D. in the-ater history from the University of Washington and is currently at work on a book about eighteenth-century women playwrights.

Jeanie Forte is an independent scholar, director, and dramaturg living in Palo Alto, California, who has taught drama and English at the University of Tennes-

see, De Anza College, and the University of California at Berkeley. Her publica-
tions include articles and reviews in *Theater, Modern Drama, Theatre Journal,
Women & Performance,* and *High Performance* and a book, *Women in Performance
Art: Feminism and Postmodernism,* forthcoming from Indiana University Press.
She is a contributor to several anthologies, including *Women in American Theatre,
Performing Feminisms, The Handbook of American Popular Culture,* and a critical
collection on playwright Adrienne Kennedy.

Marianne Goldberg is a writer and choreographer from New York City. She
has performed her ongoing work, THE BODY WORD SERIES, at numerous
women's festivals, including the Kentucky Women Writers' Conference, the
Women and Theatre Program, Duke University's Symposium on Women and
the Arts, and the International Conference on Women, Culture, and the Arts in
Dubrovnik, Yugoslavia. Her "performance pieces for print" have been published in *Women & Performance* and *Artforum International.* Her works include
dancing, speaking, video, and the live creation of computerized and handwritten
texts. She has served on the editorial board of *Women & Performance* and holds a
Ph.D. in Performance Studies from New York University.

Amy Gonzalez is a professional director working in Los Angeles and San
Francisco, with such companies as the Eureka Theatre Company, El Teatro
Campesino, the South Coast Repertory, the Mark Taper Forum, and the Los
Angeles Actors' Theatre. From 1989 to 1992 she served as Resident Director and
Literary Manager for the Eureka Theatre in San Francisco. She has worked
extensively in new play development, directing in-progress productions of *But-
terfly Kiss* by Phyllis Nagy and *A Knife in the Heart* by Susan Yankowitz (New
Dramatists), *Nightlight* by Keith Huff (Midwest Playlabs), *Broken Bough* by
Lynnette Serrano Bonaparte, *Shadow of a Man* by Cherríe Moraga, and *Kuba* by
Roger Schirra (the Hispanic Playwrights' Project at the South Coast Repertory).
Other productions include *New Business* by Tom Williams, *The Granny (La
Nona)* by Roberto M. Cossa (trans. by Raul Moncada), *Simply Maria* and *Food
for the Dead* by Josefina Lopez, and *Roots in Water* by Richard Nelson. Gonzalez
completed her M.F.A. in directing at the University of Washington.

Andrea Hairston is an Assistant Professor in the Theater Department of Smith
College, where she teaches African and Caribbean and African-American drama
and playwriting. Her most recent productions have been *The Colored Museum,
Golden Girls,* and *Sister No Blues.* She has directed, written, and performed
extensively in New England, through Chrysalis Theatre, Holyoke Community
College, and the Boston Women's Theatre Festival. She has received awards for
playwriting, poetry, and directing from the National Endowment for the Arts,
the Massachusetts Artists Foundation, the Seattle Women Playwrights Festival,
and the Schubert and Rockefeller foundations. She holds an M.A. in creative
writing from Brown University.

Sabrina Hamilton has worked all over the United States and Europe as a
director, lighting designer, production stage manager, and performer and is a
cofounder of Kō Theater Works. Her major credits include work with Mabou

Mines, Bloodgroup, Hesitate and Demonstrate, Leeny Sack, David Cale, and Théâtre du Grütli. She has worked in eleven different countries and in theaters and spaces ranging from the New York Shakespeare Festival and the Goodman Theatre to Estruscan ruins in Tuscany. She is a graduate of Hampshire College and has taught at Long Island University and Trinity College in Hartford and was a visiting Assistant Professor of Theater at Hampshire College for three years.

Kendall completed a Ph.D. in Drama at the University of Texas in Austin in 1986, where she was a Woodrow Wilson Fellow in Women's Studies. She has taught at Smith College and served as department chair for two years. Her articles have appeared in *Curtain Calls, Theatre Journal, Journal of Homosexuality, Women's Review of Books,* and *Contemporary Lesbian Writers of the United States.* Her book, *Love and Thunder! Plays by Women in the Age of Queen Anne,* was published in 1988, and her first feature-length video, *Dear Little Weed: Loveletters, Patterns and Projections* was completed in 1991. She is currently working in video and exploring theater for development in Lesotho.

Ann Kilkelly is an Associate Professor of Theatre and Coordinator of Women's Studies at Virginia Tech and has also taught English at Transylvania University in Lexington, Kentucky. She completed her Ph.D. in English at the University of Utah. She has published in *Women & Performance, Kentucky Review,* and *Notable Women in American Theatre.* A performer and director, she also has a long list of original scripts to her credit. She has received numerous grants and awards, including the Bingham Award for Excellence in Teaching and a Kentucky Foundation for Women Playwriting Grant.

Joan Lipkin is Artistic Director of That Uppity Theatre Company in St. Louis, Missouri. Her award-winning work has been featured on network television, National Public Radio, and in the Associated Press, as well as in academic journals and mainstream publications. In addition to *He's Having Her Baby: A Pro-Choice Musical Comedy,* her plays include *Some of My Best Friends Are . . . A Gay and Lesbian Revue for People of All Preferences* (cowritten with Tom Clear), *Will the Real Foster Parent Please Stand Up?, Love & Work & Other Four-Letter Words,* and *Small Domestic Acts,* among others. She founded the "Alternate Currents/ Direct Currents Theatre Series" and codirects After Rodney, a poetry performance group of white women and women of color. Currently, she is at work on a play about pornography and sexual construction.

John Lutterbie is the Director of Graduate Studies at the State University of New York at Stony Brook. He received his Ph.D. from the University of Washington in Seattle and has written on Samuel Beckett, Peter Handke, Franz Xavier Kroetz, and Harold Pinter. He has published in *Theatre Journal, Modern Drama, Journal of Dramatic Theory and Criticism,* and *Psychiatry and the Humanities.* He is currently at work on a book about male subjectivity.

Joan Schenkar is a well-known playwright whose works are produced at experimental theaters, festivals, and colleges throughout North America and Western Europe. She is the recipient of thirty-five grants, fellowships, and awards for playwriting and has been resident playwright for Joseph Chaikin and the Polish Laboratory Theatre. Her publishers include Samuel French, Applause Books, *TDR,* and the *Kenyon Review.* She is the subject of articles in *TDR, Theatre Journal, Performing Arts Journal, Modern Drama, Women & Performance, Michigan Quarterly Review,* the *Village Voice,* and the *Washington Post,* among others. Among her best known plays are *Cabin Fever* and *Signs of Life.*

Esther Beth Sullivan is an Assistant Professor at Ohio State University. She completed her Ph.D. at the University of Washington in Seattle and her M.A. at Washington State University. Her theoretical research is focused on a feminist analysis of the problems of narrativity in drama. She has been an Assistant Editor for *Theatre Journal* and has published in *Theatre Journal, Theatre Studies,* and *Literature in Performance.* She has had extensive dramaturgical experience and has directed, performed, and designed costumes.

Christine Sumption is a professional director whose credits include work with the Seattle Repertory Theatre, Seattle Group Theatre, Tacoma Actors Guild, the Art Institute of Chicago, the Chicago Young Playwrights Festival, the Playwrights' Center, Ensemble Studio Theatre, The Drama League of New York, and Stage Left Theatre, where she directed the American premiere of Sarah Daniels's *Masterpieces* in 1988. She has worked as a professional guest director at Bradley University, Coe College, College of Marin, and New York University's Tisch School of the Arts. Her articles have appeared in *American Theatre, Theatre Chicago, Festival Focus,* and *Views from the Bridge.* She now resides in Yokohama, Japan, where she teaches at Toin Yokohama University and serves as Resident Director of Tokyo's Theater Company Subaru.